Christian
Mummification

ALSO BY KEN JEREMIAH
*Living Buddhas: The Self-Mummified Monks
of Yamagata, Japan* (McFarland, 2010)

Christian Mummification

An Interpretative History of the Preservation of Saints, Martyrs and Others

KEN JEREMIAH

McFarland & Company, Inc., Publishers
Jefferson, North Carolina, and London

All photographs are by the author unless otherwise noted.

LIBRARY OF CONGRESS CATALOGUING-IN-PUBLICATION DATA

Jeremiah, Ken.
Christian mummification : an interpretative history of the preservation of saints, martyrs and others / by Ken Jeremiah.
p. cm.

Includes bibliographical references (p.   ) and index.

ISBN 978-0-7864-6519-4
softcover : acid free paper ∞

1. Mummies.
2. Mummies — Italy.
3. Death — Religious aspects — Catholic Church.
4. Funeral rites and ceremonies, Ancient — Italy.
5. Italy — Religious life and customs.
I. Title.
GN293.J47 2012   393'.3—dc23   2012012403

BRITISH LIBRARY CATALOGUING DATA ARE AVAILABLE

© 2012 Ken Jeremiah. All rights reserved

No part of this book may be reproduced or transmitted in any form or by any means, electronic or mechanical, including photocopying or recording, or by any information storage and retrieval system, without permission in writing from the publisher.

Front cover image: the body of St. Ranieri on display at the Duomo in Pisa, Italy (photograph by the author)

Manufactured in the United States of America

McFarland & Company, Inc., Publishers
Box 611, Jefferson, North Carolina 28640
www.mcfarlandpub.com

Table of Contents

Acknowledgments vii
Preface 1
Introduction 3

I. World Mummification

1. Mummification and Critical Thinking 9
2. The Science of Mummification 12
3. Natural Mummies 15
4. Artificial Mummies 18
5. Other Forms of Mummification 22
6. Relic-Bodies 26
7. Death and the Unknown: The Allure of Mummies 32

II. Mummies in Italy

8. Critical Thinking, Self-Reflection, and Mummy Studies 37
9. The Roman Catacombs 40
10. The Cult of the Martyrs 43
11. The Catacombs in Palermo 49
12. The Chapel of the Dead and the Skull Cathedral 53
13. Mummies of Ferentillo and San Domenico Maggiore; Papal Funerals 57
14. Polytheistic Elements of the Faith 64

III. Saints and Relics

15. The Enigmatic Catholic Saint 73
16. The History of Saint Making 78
17. Stigmata and Other Miracles 82
18. Modern Saints 88
19. Asceticism in the Catholic Faith 92
20. The Importance of Physical Remains 96
21. The Cult of the Dead 100

IV. Incorruptible Bodies

22. The Incorruptibles 107
23. Miraculous Preservation 111
24. The Preserved Bodies in Rome, Assisi and Mantova 116
25. Mummies in Florence, Naples and Sicily 122
26. Mummies in Other Parts of Italy 125
27. The Importance of the Incorruptibles 128
28. Preservation in Christianity 132

V. Influences from Other Cultures

29. Mummification in Roman Society 141
30. The Old Testament 148
31. Historical Evidence 151
32. Immaculate Conception and the Resurrection 161
33. Mithra: The Zoroastrian God of the Sun 167
34. Pythagoras and Dionysus 170
35. The Cult of Osiris 174

VI. The Egyptian Influence

36. Egyptian Influences in Italy 181
37. Alexandria and Coptic Christianity 188
38. Early Egyptian Religious Beliefs 192
39. Burial Practices 196
40. The Holy Trinity: Isis, Horus and Osiris 199
41. Religious Rituals and Practices 204
42. Integration and Assimilation 209

VII. The Reasons Behind Christian Mummification

43. The Bodily Preservation of Jesus 215
44. The Rapture 217
45. Early Concepts of the Soul 223
46. The Power Inherent in Bodily Remains 226
47. Foreign Influences 229
48. Enduring Virtuosity 233
49. Symbols of Life and Death 236

Appendix: Locations of Select Mummies or Bodily Relics in Italy 241
Chapter Notes 247
Bibliography 253
Index 261

Acknowledgments

Some of the research for this book was completed before I traveled to Italy. During my travels there, I spent time interviewing a number of individuals and taking pictures of mummies. During the first couple of weeks in Italy, I was leading a tour group in Rome and in Florence. Special thanks to the following people who helped me in this process: Dorian Duffy, Lisa Greenhalgh, Jeannie Records, Donna Ricci, and Amanda Varone. Two other friends, Kevin Rinaldi-Young and Meghan Lamarre, also assisted me by accompanying the group back to the United States while I stayed in Italy. When the group had returned to the States, I traveled to Ferentillo, Capri, Naples, Pompeii, and Palermo. Three individuals accompanied me: Dan Duffy, Dan Reiss, and James Pilkington. I am grateful for all of their help.

I need to thank Abbie Rose for suggesting some useful sources when I was initially putting this book together, and thanks to Lidia Magliari, who provided some traveling suggestions. Thanks also to Sean O'Rourke, who led me to some interesting mummies while in Florence. In addition, special thanks to the Nara National Museum, the British Museum, and the Boston Museum of Fine Arts. Special thanks to Don Rinaldo, who permitted me to take pictures of the mummies in Ferentillo, at the Chiesa di San Stefano, and to use them in this book. In addition, I would like to offer my sincere thanks to Frate Cappuccino Fracalogero Modica, who also allowed me to take some pictures for use in this text. He introduced me to Saint Bernardo da Corleone (1605–1667), and gave me a statue of the saint.

Two individuals undertook the time-consuming task of reading and editing the work: Jeannie Records and my sister, Kristen Jeremiah. I am grateful to them for their copious notes and suggestions. Thanks to Paul White and Charles Ilgenfritz for their continued support and assistance, and thanks to those other individuals who assisted me but who prefer to remain anonymous.

Preface

This book is about mummification in Christianity. The majority of the research was conducted in Italy, and most of the sources used were Christian. However, the idea for this book came from Japan. I have traveled extensively through the northern regions, researching the phenomenon of self-mummification. The information I gathered and the pictures I took were later organized in a book entitled *Living Buddhas: The Self-Mummified Monks of Yamagata, Japan* (McFarland, 2010).

There are numerous articles and books that explore the similarities between Buddhism and Christianity. At their onset, both faiths were remarkably similar, and the practice of mummification, along with the veneration of relics, was common to both traditions. It was only natural that I became interested in Christian bodily preservation, a practice that, at first glance, cannot be justified by scriptures. There are thousands of mummified bodies all over Italy, including the preserved bodies of saints and *beati* on display in churches and cathedrals. Likewise, body parts—such as the bones or the internal organs of important religious figures—are enshrined at various religious locations.

As a child, I remember visiting a cathedral in Quebec that housed the bone of a saint. The pillars of the church were lined with crutches, canes and other supports used by disabled individuals, and it was said that they had prayed in front of the bone and were cured. This interested me, and I wondered why the physical presence of the bone was necessary; maybe there was more to it than meets the eye. I also knew a bit about the unusual practice of burying some popes and saints in three different caskets, one inside the other. However, I did not know where this practice originated, and did not understand its significance. After researching the practice of mummification in Buddhism for several years, I turned my attention to the same practice in Christianity. This book is the end result of substantial research on the subject.

A number of primary and secondary sources were used in the compilation of this study. During my research, I formulated a theory about the reasons behind mummification in Italy and about early Christian practices. I then read more texts, making sure the theory still made sense. I altered it where necessary, eventually coming up with the most logical reasons for the practice of mummification in Christianity, reasons supported by abundant research.

I utilized three different versions of the Bible. One is the King James Edition, and another is the Holy Bible English Standard Version; the former is a print copy while the latter is a digital (Kindle) version. I also used an online copy of the New International Version of the Bible. Writings by Josephat and other texts outside of the Bible that mention the life of Jesus were accessed online at PACE: The Project on Ancient Cultural Engagement, retrieved from http://pace.mcmaster.ca/york/york/about-ext.htm. Other early Christian texts were accessed using the Christian Classics Ethereal Library, retrieved from http://www.ccel.org. Ancient Sumerian texts, such as the Epic of Gilgamesh, were also utilized in their digital versions. Since I am unable to translate ancient languages, I have trusted the published translations to be accurate. All translations from modern languages are my own. The original quotes are referenced, in case anyone wishes to read them in their primary languages.

Introduction

There are more than 300 preserved bodies on display in Italian churches and cathedrals. They are the mummified remains of saints, priests, bishops and other high-ranking members of the Roman Catholic Church. Some of them are well preserved, while others are only partially mummified, as the natural process of decomposition is difficult to avoid. Human beings, like all things, are eventually reduced to dust. This occurs through the breakdown of bodily tissues by internal enzymes and external bacteria, not to mention the activity of insects and other animals that accelerate the process.

Within hours after death, a body becomes cold and begins to dry out. It also changes color and stiffens while autolysis, the breakdown of bodily tissues by enzymes, begins to run its course. As if this were not enough to destroy the deceased, bodily acids also seep out and begin to devour the flesh from within. Then putrefaction sets in and the body rots, giving off a horrible stench. The body swells, eyeballs turn to liquid, blisters form and burst, and the upper layer of the skin slides away with light contact. The skin turns various shades of green and then darkens, eventually turning black. The body, possibly beautiful during life, transforms into something that many would consider hideous and revolting.

The appearance of decay seems to have been problematic to Catholic adherents, since members of its priesthood took action to prevent or to hide such decomposition. In many cases, the faces or hands were covered with wax, preserving forever the visages of important men and women. Sometimes, the bodies of holy individuals were subjected to various treatments that helped to preserve them, such as burial of the bodies without a casket in volcanic soil. Such an underground environment helps to desiccate the remains, removing all moisture, and it often results in preservation of the body. The skin on bodies that have undergone such treatment is generally darkened and hardened, taking on the texture of parchment. Many bodies with such characteristics are on display in Italy. In other cases, bodies were embalmed or even eviscerated.

St. Margaret of Cortona (1247–1297), for example, is credited with numerous miracles and it is said she was so blessed with divine grace that her body did not decay like a mere mortal. In addition, a sweet fragrance emanated from the body for many years after her death. This was also considered evidence of holiness. These phenomena, along with the events of her life, led to her canonization. Cruz (1977) wrote:

> The sacred body of the Saint lies incorrupt in a glass-sided reliquary which exposes her to view, under the main altar of the Basilica of Cortona, named in her honor. The red velvet background of the reliquary is studded with precious gems and valuable ornaments donated by grateful clients. The body is light in color and dry, but completely whole. Even the eyes

are full and all of the nails of the feet and hands are still in place — truly a miraculous preservation which has existed for almost seven hundred years [p. 94].

However, when pathologist and mummy expert Ezio Fulcheri recently examined the body, he found large incisions running across her thighs, abdomen and chest. Her viscera had been removed. She was clearly embalmed, and the body had been treated with aromatic spices and natural plant preservatives. For centuries, some individuals had simply believed that she had been naturally preserved but, in fact, she had been treated to withstand the natural processes of decay, rendering her body incorruptible. The treatment of her body was not unique. There are many other cases of intentional mummification undertaken by the Church. The most recent known case occurred in 1986, when Fulcheri was commissioned by the Church to artificially preserve the body of a cardinal (Pringle, 2001). However, they did not leave the method of embalming up to him. They wanted it done in a specific manner, following the practices of ancient Egyptians.

Truly, the preservation of certain bodies is important in Catholicism. However, the reasons have not been fully explored. According to widespread Christian beliefs, the soul of a person leaves the body immediately after death. So why would the remains of dead individuals be treated to delay or halt decomposition? In other words, if the body were insignificant, why would anyone treat it to endure? Another question that arises is why the Church wants bodies preserved in a certain manner: Why did they want the body of a cardinal treated in the same way that the ancient Egyptians preserved remains? Perhaps there is an unexplored connection between Catholicism and ancient Egyptian religious rituals. This book seeks to explore such possible relationships.

Some of the mummies on display in churches and cathedrals were initially found to be naturally preserved, and this phenomenon was thought to be evidence of the divine. Individuals whose bodies had not decayed naturally when unearthed were thought to be holy, and in many cases the Church made them saints primarily because they had not decayed. Again, this practice seems problematic. Why is the absence of decay considered holy? Nothing in the scriptures of the faith indicate that it is, and numerous individuals around the world are found to be miraculously preserved after they are unearthed. Historically, the Church has declared many individuals holy whose bodies had not naturally decayed, but all of those individuals were believers in the Catholic faith. People found to be in a similar state of preservation who were members of a different Christian sect or a different religion entirely were not considered holy, and their preserved remains were likewise not considered spiritual. The reasons lack of decay is considered spiritual for some and unimportant for others has not yet been adequately explained or explored. This book also seeks to find answers to such questions.

Various types of different mummies in Italy are described here, including those that were naturally mummified and then treated, those that have been embalmed, and those collectively known as Incorruptibles. Incorruptible remains are said to have some characteristics that other preserved bodies do not. First, the reasons behind the preservation are typically unexplainable. Second, the bodies often emit pleasing scents and the skin remains loose and pliable, as though the person were still alive. In addition, strange or unexplainable occurrences might happen in the vicinity of the remains. Sometimes, the bodies leak unusual fluids or bleed years after their deaths.

One famous example of this is the body of St. Josephat (1580–1623). A group of Orthodox Christians killed him by hacking him to death and then throwing his remains into a river. When the corpse was found it was in an incredible state of preservation, despite having been mutilated and submerged for a week. It was cleaned and then buried. Years after his burial, a politician asked the pope to canonize the individual, and the pope granted the request. In 1650, St. Josaphat's body was unearthed and moved to the Church of St. Sophia, where it would be entombed. During this process, a wound on his forehead that had been inflicted 27 years earlier began bleeding again. Certainly, there are possible scientific explanations for unusual occurrences like this, but only some of the preserved bodies have been examined by experts.

In Italy today there is a veritable cult surrounding the saints whose bodies are still in existence, and one has to wonder why individuals direct their prayers toward such corpses. According to recent surveys, the majority of Roman Catholics in Italy pray not to God or to his son, but to saints: mortals who lived and then died like all other creatures. Certainly, this cult of the dead is a major element of Italian culture and religion. In addition to answering the previously posed questions, this book attempts to shed light upon this relatively unstudied aspect of the Roman Catholic faith.

Part I: World Mummification

Jesus said, "Those who seek should not stop seeking until they find.
When they find, they will be disturbed.
When they are disturbed, they will marvel, and will reign over all."
— Gospel of St. Thomas

1

Mummification and Critical Thinking

It is difficult for people to see the truths that are right in front of them. Sometimes, they simply accept what everyone around them is saying as truth without considering it at all. Familiarity tends to promote mindless acceptance and eliminates lengthy thought. It is this mindless acceptance that blinds many people to the truths that are right in front of their eyes. For example, if you were to ask most high school and university students how many countries are in America, they would most likely answer incorrectly. The majority of them do not realize that America is two continents and not a country. (If one were to pick up a textbook about American history in Guatemala or in Argentina, for example, that textbook would not be about U.S. history but about the history of the entire North American or South American continent.)

There was a study done by a major university in which a history test was given to both high school students and some historians. Interestingly, the high school students typically scored higher on the exams than the historians. When faced with a question like "Who discovered America?" the high school students usually answered, "Columbus." Since this was the answer expected by the test creators, this was the correct answer listed on the answer sheet, and therefore the majority of high school students answered correctly. When historians responded to this question, though, their critical thinking prevented them from writing "Columbus." There were already Native Americans here, so how could anyone have discovered the continent? If anyone says that the continent still could have been discovered, then he or she should be able to respond to these similar questions: "Who discovered Italy?" and "Who discovered Japan?"

The historians also considered outsiders. Sure, there were already people in the United States, but Columbus was an outsider who arrived on the continent. Could he be considered the discoverer? Again, this did not make sense to the historians, who considered that even though he arrived here in 1492, the Chinese discovered the continent in 1421, 71 years before Columbus (Menzies, 2008). Evidence supports the possibility that a colony of Templar knights made it to the Americas years before Columbus (Sora, 2004), and there is historical evidence that Norse travelers and others may have also arrived earlier (Gordon, 1971). So how can Columbus possibly be considered to have discovered the continent? People who think critically will see that this makes no sense at all, but the majority of individuals are so caught up in their own way of thinking that they cannot see clearly. The truth might be right in front of them, but they are blind to it. In this way, the truth is literally hidden in plain sight. There is an ancient quote by Socrates that relates to this fact: "The more I learn, the more I realize how little I actually know."

Mummification is not usually associated with the process of critical thinking, but if human beings truly wish to know what makes them who they are, then mummy studies are important. Preserving the deceased is a universal trait, found in every country in the world, regardless of differing religious beliefs. The practice of mummification is innate, and it is at the core of what makes us human. What is it in the nature of humankind that forces people to preserve the bodies of the deceased? Certainly, the phenomenon can be explained in religions where the preservation was necessary due to beliefs about what happens in the afterlife, but mummification was present and important to various other cultures — cultures whose religious beliefs do not seem to encourage bodily preservation. In any religion in which the body of the deceased is deemed insignificant, for example, one would think that mummification would be non-existent. On the surface, Buddhism and Christianity are two religions that do not seem to value the bodies of the deceased, according to their holy texts.

In Buddhist traditions, all attachments are detrimental. In order to advance spiritually, a practitioner must eliminate all attachments, including the attachment to the physical body. However, the mummification of Buddhist teachers is a common practice. Likewise, in Christianity, it would seem that the body is insignificant, due to their perception of the soul. It is believed that the body is discarded at death and that the soul carries on in the afterlife. In basic Christian tradition, the soul is the true individual and the body is not important. However, in some Christian sects, the body is not discarded. It is preserved and buried in a specific manner, as part of an elaborate ceremony that is meant to help the deceased cross over from this world to the next. Bodies are embalmed and buried in caskets that will assist in their preservation. For some high-ranking members of the Church and for saints, they are traditionally buried in three distinct caskets after being embalmed. This again is to help ward off decay.

The bodies of important Christian and Buddhist people alike are not treated to stop decomposition and then left in the ground. Strangely, they are unearthed and then prominently displayed. In Buddhist cases, the bodies are sometimes gilded and then enshrined like living statues that believers can pray to. In Roman Catholic Christianity, the bodies are unearthed and then put on display in glass reliquaries in churches and in cathedrals. Most of the time, the bodies are lying down, but in some rare cases, the bodies are placed in seated positions. The function of these bodies is similar to the Buddhists'. Worshippers can view the body of a holy individual, and they can pray in front of such corpses. Viewing the body of someone whom they honor can be inspiring, and considering the life and virtues of such an individual while in a spiritual setting can help motivate worshippers to become better people by following their examples.

The Buddhist and the Christian practices of preserving the bodies of important teachers are similar, as are some of their beliefs concerning the afterlife. In early Christianity and early Buddhism, these similarities were even more pronounced, and various scholars have explored the relationship between these two faiths. Of course, Buddhism was in Judea during the first two centuries, so it is not surprising that some doctrinal similarities exist. However, some have suggested that the similarities are too pronounced to have developed from mere proximity, and they believe that there must be more to it. Certainly, nothing exists in a vacuum. Every person is a product of all that he or she has come into contact with; everything that seems important is incorporated into his or her ever-changing system of beliefs, and things that are deemed unimportant or illogical are disregarded. It is for this reason that one can determine a lot about a person by simply understanding his or her belief system.

In the same way, there is no religion that evolves completely untouched by outside faiths.[1] Each faith is influenced, to varying degrees, by the religious traditions around it, and by the beliefs and practices that preceded it. Just as the individuals who put together the doctrines and the canons are influenced by their past experiences, the body of religious ideas is also malleable and shaped by outside forces. In fact, if a new religious tradition were ever completely separated and different from the religions that preceded it, it would not likely endure. It would be rejected by others, since it would not connect to their previously held beliefs at all. In other words, if an idea is so different that it does not relate to an individual's preexisting notion of reality, it cannot be assimilated, and it will therefore be cast out. This is why the ancient Roman religion might be dismissed as nonsense by some modern Christians or Muslims. It is also why alternative versions of history are not just dismissed but not even considered by some closed-minded individuals. It is for this reason that most major religious traditions developed within the confines of one or more other traditions. Christianity developed within Judaism, for example, while Buddhism developed within the confines of Hinduism. There were certainly other traditions that also influenced them both. In this way, a respected religious tradition does not stand alone. Rather, it is the reformulation and perceived perfection of preexisting notions that have been organized into a new faith.

Therefore, when looking into the reasons behind mummification in various traditions it is often necessary to look outside the religious doctrines themselves in order to determine the true origin of their practices. On the surface, from an eschatological perspective, mummification is contrary to the teachings of both Buddhist and Christian traditions, yet for various sects within these two faiths bodily preservation is prominent. The reasons why are not readily visible. One must dig, as the true reasons for this practice are not found in the religious teachings themselves, but within the hearts of the people who follow them.

2

The Science of Mummification

Once the life essence seeps out of the body, the body begins to decay. Eventually, it returns to its original state of nothingness. When a person dies, his or her heart stops beating, and since blood is no longer pumped throughout the body, it settles. It pulls away from the top of the body and settles in the lower extremities, so if a body were in a lying position, the face and frontal portion of the body would become extremely pale, while the underside would be a dark red color, infused with blood. Cells in a living creature function both aerobically, by absorbing and transporting oxygen, and anaerobically, without oxygen. Once death occurs, the cells no longer carry oxygen, and as a result, the muscle tissues begin to create lactic acid. This creates rigor mortis, in which the body becomes extremely stiff and it typically cannot be moved. This state can set in between 15 minutes after death and several hours after death. It is affected by temperature, bodily activity before death, and other factors.

The body temperature, without blood, rapidly drops, and the body dehydrates. Eventually, without oxygen, the cells die, and the body is then no longer able to fight off bacteria. When this happens, the process of decomposition begins. This is carried out by two forces: autolysis and putrefaction. Autolysis is a process in which bodily tissues are broken down by internal chemicals and enzymes, while putrefaction is the breakdown of bodily tissues by bacteria. These two forces are designed to decimate the body. Once the bacterial organisms attack the body, carbohydrates, proteins and lipids form acids and different types of gases, which cause the body to swell.

This swelling forces remaining fluids out of the body, from the eyes, nose and mouth, as well as from other cavities. It may also cause the skin to burst. The internal chemicals also cause the skin color to change, and if maggots have access to the body, they will expedite the process. The body will begin to smell bad, and it will shrink in size. The flesh will continue to disappear until only the bones are left. This will usually occur within three years, but there are other factors that could either accelerate or halt the process. When the natural processes of decay are halted, the body is preserved.

Various factors can cause bodily preservation. Extremely dry conditions typically assist in preserving bodies, although bodies in moist surroundings can also occasionally be preserved in one manner or another. Bodies that mummify in dry conditions, such as those found in salt mines or those buried in volcanic soil, usually display some unique characteristics. For example, the skin shrivels and turns brown. It takes on the attributes of parchment. Bodies that are preserved in wet conditions typically saponify (turn to soap). A gray wax-like substance called adipocere tends to cover such bodies. It is formed by the decomposition of soft tissue, and once it forms, it hardens, preventing further decay.

Temperature variation can also cause bodies to mummify, such as bodies exposed to extreme cold. Corpses found in ice are generally remarkably well preserved, for example. Another factor that can lead to bodily preservation is the existence of certain fungi or drying compounds in the soil. Peat moss in moist locations, such as bogs, can also effect preservation. These environments can cause bodies to be mummified. There are a number of other factors that may also effect bodily preservation, including the ingestion of preservative plants and other types of foods, and even the manner of death can cause bodies to either decay more rapidly or be preserved.

In some respects, the reasons why certain bodies mummify while others do not are a mystery. In one instance, a family of five who lived in Barrow, Alaska, was killed. Huge chunks of ice were swept onto the shore by powerful winds and giant waves. The ice toppled the house where they lived, and the family perished in the wreckage (Zimmerman, 1998). They were in the exact same location, subject to the same environmental conditions, and it is likely that they all ate the same food. However, three of the bodies naturally decayed while two of them mummified. The reasons why cannot be adequately explained.

Another strange form of mummification has been dubbed incorruptibility by some, and it refers to mummification that occurs because of spiritual attainment. There is no scientific support for this idea, but bodies that are thought to be incorruptible are found in various societies. There are Buddhist monks who were (supposedly) miraculously preserved, and there were Christian saints who also were said to have been inexplicably, naturally mummified. This is not a scientifically accepted form of mummification, and new research has been uncovered to suggest that all of the so-called Incorruptibles in Italy were actually intentionally preserved.

Vreeland (1998) has proposed three distinct classes of mummification that can be used to describe just about every known type of bodily preservation. Class I preservations are also called natural preservations, and they occur due to climatic conditions. A person who falls while mountain climbing and freezes to death in ice would likely be completely preserved. This is an example of a Class I mummification. Class II mummifications are intentional, but the mummification is caused by exaggerating and exploiting natural processes. In some countries in South America, for example, Incan children were found perfectly preserved on mountaintops. In an unusual custom, the children were given maize beer to make them go to sleep and then they were placed on the mountaintops, where they would freeze to death, thus becoming, through death, gods who would protect the villages from harm. The final category, Class III mummification, is artificial preservation. This could mean evisceration, the removal of internal organs, or embalmment, treating the body with balms and herbs to effect preservation.[1]

These three classifications cover just about all of the known types of mummification, other than spiritual mummification, deemed incorruptibility, and the bizarre practice of self-mummification. The latter occurred in some East Asian countries, and there were individuals in both China and Japan who intentionally mummified themselves. This process of bodily preservation is unusual to say the least, and it therefore does not fit neatly into any of the aforementioned categories.

It is likely that the first forms of mummification in the world were all natural mummification (Class I). Individuals from various societies probably noted that some remains that they buried or disposed of in other ways had failed to decay. This might have intrigued them, and they began to wonder why such bodies had not decayed as others had. Experimentation with natural processes in order to effect decay was then probably carried out (Class II), and this simple form of mummification probably later developed into more elaborate and effective means of preservation (Class III).

Egypt is famous for its elaborate processes of intentional mummification, but it began with natural mummification in the desert sand. According to Peck (1998):

> The purpose of mummification in ancient Egypt was twofold. The body of the deceased, it was believed, had to be treated to render it incorruptible. At the same time, the physical appearance had to be maintained as nearly as possible to what it had been in life. The Egyptian conception of life after death developed early, as evidenced by the burials of predynastic (prehistoric) age. It would seem that the notion of preserving human and animal dead came about naturally in the dry climate of Egypt. Predynastic burials were simple and practical. The corpse was placed in a hole in the sand, usually in a contracted position, accompanied by such grave goods as pottery and other useful objects. No embalming process was carried out; in no way was the body prepared (mummified) for the burial, but it was often wrapped in linen, reed matting or hide. The pit was sometimes lined with matting, boards or bricks, but the cavity that received the body was more grave than tomb. A small tumulus was erected over the grave, never large enough to interfere with the warming effect of the sun. It was the hot, dry sand that served to desiccate the tissue. The result, to be observed in countless examples, is a well preserved corpse [p. 17].

It is interesting that early societies still desired to preserve the dead and this desire has not dissipated. People are often embalmed and redressed so that they may be prominently displayed at occasions like wakes. This is an unusual custom, but individuals from different societies truly wish to view the dead bodies of their loved ones. These individuals pay lots of money so that they can look at the bodies one last time before enclosing them in a crypt or burying them in a casket. The bodies are not buried directly in the ground in most cases. Instead, thousands of dollars are paid for a sturdy box that will also help to preserve the remains. If one were to ask an individual why he or she did this, an answer may not be forthcoming. There is something there, something unknown, that forces human beings to treat the deceased in this way. This desire to preserve the bodies of the dead is universal, in the sense that some group of people on every continent at one time or another engaged in mummification. The reasons why still have not yet been adequately explained. The earliest forms of mummification, based on natural processes, are a logical place to begin such inquiry.

3

Natural Mummies

Natural mummification occurs frequently in cold temperatures. Every year, the bodies of mountain climbers and explorers are found in mountainous areas. Sometimes, they fall into glacial crevasses, while other individuals are buried by avalanches (Hansen, 1998). Bodies that are found in such conditions are typically well preserved, as ice and cold temperatures halt the natural processes of decomposition. Not only are the corpses perfectly mummified, but the clothing, personal effects, and stomach contents are also frequently preserved, providing abundant information to researchers.

Sometimes, the information that is gathered by looking at frozen bodies sheds some disturbing insights into religious practices of ancient civilizations, such as the previously mentioned ancient South American practice of freezing children to death on mountaintops for religious reasons. Since they were mummified, their remains were in great shape, and a lot is now known about the early religious practices of the Inca. Some of the sacrificial children had been killed before being preserved. Examinations of the bodies revealed that some of them had been strangled or killed by blunt force trauma, while others had been drugged or poisoned before being left in the cold to die of exposure.

Cold regions that have strong winds and low humidity are beneficial to the preservation of human and animal remains. Decomposition and putrefaction generally begins right after death, but for this to occur, water has to be present. If water is frozen, bacteria cannot proliferate, and putrefaction therefore cannot occur. For this reason, many bodies that are naturally preserved are found in cold environments. Extremely cold temperatures are still used today in order to preserve bodies and body parts, and there are a number of individuals throughout the world who choose to be mummified in this way. Many people choose to be cryogenetically frozen after death, perhaps hoping for science to find a way to reanimate their corpses. It is strange that this process is carried out and points to a human desire that transcends religious and cultural traditions. Some faithful people hope that their god will reanimate them. There are many religious traditions in which a divine savior was resurrected, and believers therefore hope that they, too, will be resurrected. Other individuals, who perhaps do not have the same religious convictions, still demonstrate the same desire. They pay to be frozen after death and they hope that science will resurrect them. However it happens, there seems to be an overarching human desire to escape the unavoidable occurrence of death.

In addition to extremely cold temperatures, hot and dry conditions can also cause mummification. In 2007, the body of an individual who had died c. 540 B.C.E. was found in the Chehrabad Salt Mine in Iran. His body was so well preserved due to the drying properties of the salt that even his hair and beard were still intact. Likewise, in southern Italy it was once a common practice to bury individuals directly in volcanic soil without a casket. A Christian practice, it was done in order to preserve the remains of the deceased. The minerals in the soil caused the bodies to dehydrate and they were mummified (Quigley, 1998). Families that opted to buried their loved ones directly in the ground did so in order to desiccate the bodies. They would leave the corpses in the ground for a period of time lasting between a year and two years. Then, the bodies were unearthed and either buried formally in the ground or laid to rest in a crypt. When the bodies were unearthed, they were typically shrunken and brown, the skin dry. They were wrapped in linen, or other fabric if the family was poor, before being formally laid to rest for good.

Burial directly in volcanic soil causes preservation because of the drying properties of the earth. Sometimes, other compounds in the soil also effect preservation. One famous and unusual case of a number of mummies that were preserved due to agents found in the soil happened in Guanajuato, Mexico. In 1896, a number of corpses were unearthed because their relatives could not continue to pay the burial-plot fees for the bodies' continued care. When they were dug up, however, they did not find skeletons, but more than 100 mummies, which had been preserved in grotesque forms. It is thought that the chemical compounds of the soil caused the mummification. The bodies are remarkably well preserved, with skin, hair, fingernails, and teeth still present. Some are bodies of adults, but there are a number of children and infants who were also found preserved. Ray Bradbury (1978), referring to the mummies, wrote:

> They looked as if they had leaped, snapped upright in their graves, clutched hands over their shriveled bosoms and screamed, jaws wide, tongues out, nostrils flared. And been frozen that way. All of them had open mouths. Theirs was a perpetual screaming.... Long ago the clothes had whispered away. The fat woman's breasts were lumps of yeasty dough left in the dust. The men's loins were indrawn, withered orchids.

The mummies in Guanajuato, preserved by the unique soil conditions, are currently displayed in a museum called El Museo de las Mumias. A similar occurrence took place in San Bernardo, Colombia, which is located approximately 40 miles from Bogota. The local custom required that bodies be buried for five years before being dug up and transferred to urns. A caretaker was shocked to find that many of the bodies had not decayed naturally — that they had mummified instead. Why the bodies were preserved is unknown. It is thought that the chemical compounds of the soil interacted with some of the food eaten by the deceased, thus effecting mummification. Not knowing what to do, he moved some of the bodies to a location near the cemetery and put them on display behind glass, where they remain today. Visitors who wish to see the remains are charged a small entrance fee. In this way, the bodies of relatives and loved ones that are laid to rest with care are forced to become museum pieces, set out for the curious to gawk at. Perhaps it is for this reason that locals do not want to be preserved. Some families asked that the bodies of their relatives or even themselves be cremated if they were found mummified. Other residents are careful not to eat too many vegetables, so that their bodies will naturally decay after death. They wish to naturally decompose and then be transferred to urns after five years, as their religious customs dictate.

The natural mummifications of the bodies in both Guanajuato and San Bernardo were looked at as unfortunate occurrences. In some rural Chinese villages, the accidental preservation of bodies causes even more angst. After death, the deceased are unearthed after six or seven years, and then their bones are arranged in a pot. This is so the individual will endure. One resident explained, "The ancestors' bones will mingle with the earth unless we put them safely in a pot. There would be nothing left. Putting them in a pot ensures that the bones will still be there even 10,000 years from now" (Ahern, 1973, p. 204).

Due to this cultural practice, it is important that bones alone are found when exhumed. If the bodies had not decayed, it is thought that they had been buried in bad ground — earth that stopped a body from naturally decaying. In this event, the body is removed and reburied in another location in the hope that it will decay naturally. The body must be completely reduced to bone. All of the flesh must decay and disappear. Otherwise, the deceased would continue "just like a living man forever" (Ahern, 1973, p. 205). True death does not happen for such villagers until the body has naturally decomposed. For this reason, the preservation of bodies is an unfortunate event.

When bodies are found to have been naturally preserved in Italy, however, it is usually thought of as a fortunate occurrence, in some cases even miraculous. A small church in Ferentillo, Italy, houses the mummified bodies of a number of individuals that were also preserved due to soil conditions. A fungus in the soil stopped the natural processes of autolysis and putrefaction, and the bodies were preserved. They are now on display in a small museum underneath a church, and the bodies therein include a couple of Chinese tourists who had died of the plague, a murderer and his victim, and a few priests. It is an unusual juxtaposition of individuals from various places, holding different positions in society, and yet they are all equal in death.

Besides dry soil and soil laden with chemicals and fungi that preserve bodies, moisture can also strangely preserve the deceased. Wet conditions can sometimes speed up decomposition, but there are occasions when such conditions actually serve to preserve the remains. Damp conditions cause the development of adipocere.

> When the fatty tissues are completely transformed into adipocere, no further decomposition takes place for an indefinite period. A case of this kind caused great astonishment and became a public spectacle in London in the middle of the seventeenth century; the body of a citizen who had been buried thirty-four years in the chancel of St. Leonard's, Eastcheap, being found sound and undecayed. In this case it was noted that the fat on the body was as hard as wax and very thick; evidently adipocere" [Loomis, 1935, p. 378].

There have been cases in which saponification had been mistaken for the phenomenon of incorruptibility. It is an unusual form of mummification, and it therefore sparks interest when cases are found.

From basic cases of bodies preserved by nature, individuals in societies all over the world gradually improved the process of intentionally preserving bodies. When the majority of people think about embalming and the creation of mummies, Egypt is the place that first comes to mind. However, the first mummies in the world are probably those created by the Chinchorros in Peru. The earliest Chinchorro mummy that has been found dates to c. 5050 B.C.E. (Arriaza, Cardenas-Arroyo, Kleiss, and Verano, 1998).

4

Artificial Mummies

The Chinchorro mummies are unusual, and if one were to look at them without realizing what they are, they might not even be recognized as actual people. There were two styles of these mummies, the black and the red, and the bodies preserved were typically just children. It was possible, as Pringle (2001) suggested, that the entire process of mummification was developed in this culture only to help grieving parents deal with the deaths of their children. Mummies are typically created to preserve as much of an individual as possible after death. In other words, the majority of mummification techniques aim to make the deceased look as lifelike as possible. This is why makeup is applied to bodies in Christian wakes, and why the Chinchorros applied the physical characteristics of the deceased to their artistic mummies.

The mummies were created in different ways, although both utilized complex procedures. In the black variation, the skeletal structure of the body was reinforced with sticks and rope made from grasses, and the skin and internal organs were removed. Then, a paste from gray soil was used to re-create the approximate size and bodily features that the individual had when alive. The skin, which had been previously removed, is then put back into place, but not before being painted black with manganese pigment. A wig of human hair was also attached. The face of the individual was covered with a mask made from gray (soil) paste, which was formed to accentuate the natural facial features that the individual had in life. Other features, such as sexual organs, were also modeled.

The red style was similar to the black. In this style, the entire body was painted red using ochre, although the face was typically still painted black. They cut into the bodies in order to remove the organs and muscle tissue, and then they dried the cavities. Arriaza (2010) explained:

> They then proceeded to introduce pieces of wood lengthwise to reinforce the body. The cavities were filled with earth, feathers, and clay. Once the brain was removed, they refilled the head and adorned it with a long, black wig held by a manganese oxide skullcap and the eyes, mouth and nose were delineated, as if the person were alive. Finally, they sewed up the incisions and gave a finishing touch of paint to the body, except for the face, [which was treated] with ferric oxide, leaving the mummy with a striking red body and black face.

There was also a variation of such techniques in which the skin that had been previously removed in the mummification process was cut into strips. Then it was reapplied to the body after being tinted like pieces of papier-mâché. The resulting creation was an artistic representation of the person who once inhabited the physical body. This procedure was not reserved for the wealthy and important alone, as it is in Christian burial practices and as it was in ancient Egyptian mummification. Arriaza, Hapke, and Standen (1998) wrote:

Perhaps the most interesting aspect of Chinchorro mortuary practice was the democracy with which it was carried out. In contrast to the Egyptians, who mummified kings and nobility, the Chinchorro show no discrimination in age, sex, or social status in the mummification of their dead. The mummification of children is particularly fascinating, since in cultures throughout the world they receive little if any mortuary attention, especially those who never lived — the stillborn. The Chinchorro seemed to honor all human beings whether they contributed to society or not, paying particular attention to those who never achieved their potential. In the minds of the Chinchorro, life as a mummy may have been viewed as a second chance.

The process of preserving the dead in this Peruvian culture was most likely not for the deceased. It was for the living. Similarly, the mummification of Christians today is also more for the living than for the dead. When popes die, their bodies are embalmed and they are carried to their resting places in an elaborate ceremony, traditionally making use of three distinct caskets for each body, one inside the other. All of this is to prevent decay. The embalming solutions used to preserve popes have been changed and improved throughout the decades. The body of St. Pius X (1835–1914) for example, was embalmed using a solution that accidentally turned the skin a brownish color. Because of this mishap, his visible body, which is displayed at St. Peter's Basilica, is completely covered. A bronze mask hides his face, and his body is completely covered by elaborate robes.

The embalmment of Pope Pius XII (1876–1958) went more smoothly, using a solution that was developed by Professor Oreste Nuzzi, from Naples. He developed a new technique in which the body would be preserved for an indefinite time period, and his technique did not require incisions or injections. "It is based on the principle of osmosis, the tendency of

The body of St. Pius X (1835–1914) is on display at St. Peter's Basilica. The face is covered with a mask, which hides an embalming mistake that turned his skin a brown color (Rome, Italy).

fluid to flow from a low to high concentration of salt. During the treatment, which took three and a half hours, pungent fluids were sprinkled on the Pope's clothing and volatile resins were absorbed through the skin" (Quigley, 1998, p. 204).

The embalming process of Pope John Paul I (1912–1978) was considerably different. His death, which occurred only 33 days after he became pope, is surrounded by controversy. The Vatican issued conflicting accounts about the time and place of his death, and his autopsy was delayed an unusual amount of time (Cornwell, 1989). The official cause of the pope's death was a heart attack, but many scholars have suggested in articles and books that the pope was poisoned. "According to one account, the Signoracci brothers embalmed the pope on the night of his death to avoid the swelling and smell that had occurred with the body of Pope Paul VI and to ensure that the body could be exposed to the faithful for several days" (Quigley, 1998, p. 205). This procedure was actually against Italian law, which prohibited embalmment during the first 15 hours after death.[1]

Since the body was embalmed on the night of his death, which was unusual, it has led support to the notion that the pope's death was not accidental. Why else would the body have been treated so quickly? The embalmers injected the solution into his femoral arteries, and then made sure that the fluid was not seeping out of his nose and mouth. They stated that they did not remove any of his organs, but his organs and other parts of his body were removed in the next few days (Cornwell, 1989). This was also against Italian law. It is possible that pieces of his body were removed in order to make relics, a practice that will be discussed in further detail later, but the speed with which his internal organs and other body pieces were harvested is unusual.

The official Church-issued account, which contradicts the testimony of eyewitnesses, holds that the body was not touched until at least 19 or 20 hours after death. At that time, the body was relocated to the Hall of Preachers, where it was embalmed. In any event, the body of this pope, like most of the others, was embalmed in order to prevent decay. The preservation process was intensive, and the procedure lasted from 7:00 P.M. to 3:30 A.M. the following day (Cornwell, 1989). The body was then redressed and displayed for several days in St. Peter's Cathedral. Approximately 12,000 people paid their respects to him every hour (Quigley, 1998, p. 205). After, his body was buried in three distinct caskets. The inner coffin, closest to his body, was made out of cypress. That casket was placed into another made of lead, which was in turn placed in an even larger casket made from ebony. The body, thus encased, was placed inside a marble sarcophagus in the crypt at St. Peter's Basilica.

Mummification is not a custom of the Roman Catholic Church alone. The Orthodox Church also intentionally preserves its members. When Archbishop Sergei Ochotenko died, his body was to be mummified and then prominently displayed. They wanted his corpse to be in a seated position on a throne, with the fingers of his right hand displaying the letters V and X, which means Christ is always victorious (in the Orthodox tradition). They arranged his fingers in the manner that they wished and then stuck a Bible under his left hand, so that those who viewed the body would know that he dedicated his life to its teachings. Then, they created a suitable throne, made from gold, silver, and finely polished wood, that would be sturdy enough to hold the archbishop after his embalming had taken place.

They initially drained the blood from the jugular vein, and then they injected two pints of embalming solution into the brachial, carotid, and femoral arteries. Later that day, they added another 12 pints. The following morning, they added another 4 pints, until the fluid issued from the jugular vein. At this point, they injected cavity fluid into some of the internal organs, and then they treated his skin. His body was cleaned and redressed in expensive robes. A crown-like hat was placed on his head, and the body was positioned on the throne with a Bible in one hand and the letters V and X formed by the fingers of his other hand.

With the body thus prepared, a number of worshippers came to pay their respects to the king-like figure. They kissed his robe, laid flowers at his feet, and made religious hand-signs in front of his corpse. This truly seems like a worship of the dead. The bodies of important religious individuals in both Orthodox and Catholic Christian traditions must be preserved, and if God does not see fit to do it, the clergy take responsibility and get the job done.

The process of mummification is often carried out for the living. In Christianity, however, bodily preservation was also carried out for the deceased. It is likely that the custom of mummification was adopted from the Egyptian culture, which had a strong influence on the development of early Christian philosophy. Mummification in ancient Egypt was initially carried out through the enhancement of natural processes. Bodies were buried without a casket in the dry desert sand, where they were left to desiccate. Over time, however, elaborate procedures for preserving bodies were developed. One of the earliest descriptions of this procedure was written by Herodotus (484–425 B.C.E.):

> The mode of embalming, according to the most perfect process, is the following: they take a crooked piece of iron, and with it draw out the brain through the nostrils, thus getting rid of a portion, while the skull is cleared of the rest by rinsing with drugs; next they make a cut along the flank with a sharp Ethiopian stone, and take out the whole contents of the abdomen, which they then cleanse, washing it thoroughly with palm-wine, and again frequently with an infusion of pounded aromatics. After this, they fill the cavity with the purest bruised myrrh, with cassia, and every other sort of spicery except frankincense, and sew up the opening. Then the body is placed in natrum for seventy days, and covered entirely over. After the expiration of that space of time, which must not be exceeded, the body is washed, and wrapped round, from head to foot, with bandages of fine linen cloth, smeared over with gum, which is used generally by the Egyptians in place of glue, and in this state is given back to the relations, who enclose it in a wooden case which they have made for the purpose, shaped into the figure of a man. Then fastening the case, they place it in a sepulchral chamber, upright against the wall [Herodotus, 1920, p. 86].

The embalming process carried out by the ancient Egyptians was done primarily for the benefit of the deceased. Bodily preservation was necessary in order to perpetuate the existence of the individual in the afterlife. In other words, if the body were not preserved, it would mean the true death of the individual. This is an interesting phenomenon that can be observed in innumerable cultures and religions — that death is not easily defined. Sure, there is the definition of clinical death: We can precisely pinpoint bodily death, but such scientific concepts do not relate to religious and cultural perceptions of death. There is no clear-cut boundary between life and death in most traditions, and for this reason the process of mummification becomes valued and important to various societies.

5

Other Forms of Mummification

Although the majority of mummification cases can be categorized using Vreeland's three classifications, there are some unusual types of mummification that do not fit neatly into such categories. One of these is the phenomenon of self-mummification, in which individuals take action to actually preserve their own bodies, and the other is the phenomenon of spiritual mummification, called incorruptibility.

Incorruptibility is said to be mummification that occurs miraculously due to divine intervention. Thiofried of Echternach (d. 1110) said, "Decay stems from nature, its absence ... from merit and divine grace."[1] This phenomenon is thought to be common in Catholic and Orthodox traditions. When bodies are found in this state of unexplainable preservation, followers may travel long distances to see and to touch the body. The body of Jacinta Marto (1910–1920), one of the children who claimed to have seen the Virgin Mary in Fatima, Portugal, is said to be a miraculous preservation. When she was seven years old, she and two other children experienced three visions that centered on the Virgin Mary. The first time, Mary asked the children to come back to the same spot on the same day for the next six months. She asked them to establish a religious order, provided an image of hell to them, and then gave them other information. She had asked the children not to reveal the content of her speeches to anyone, but one of the children, Lucia, decided to tell people anyway later on in life. This is why the information that the children (supposedly) gained is now known worldwide. There was allegedly a third secret that they did not publish, as the Virgin Mary had requested.

Jacinta was the youngest witness, and she died three years later of influenza, when she was only ten years old. Years later, the Church declared her blessed (*beata*), an official recognition that can only be bested by the title of saint. After her death, it was said that a beautiful fragrance emanated from her remains, not unlike the smell of flowers. Her body was dressed in a Communion dress and placed in a wooden coffin in the Church of the Holy Angels. Dr. Lisboa, who had treated the body after death, set the coffin up on some wooden stools so that patrons could come in and view her remains.

Many people came in and touched her body, making contact with their hands or religious items like rosaries and statues, which (according to their belief system) would have become charged with spiritual energy. The number of people making contact with her small body worried the attending priest. He did not think that the body had been preserved in any way and he did not want anyone to get sick, so he moved the body to a locked room in the church and left her under the care of the undertakers. They allowed small groups of Catholic believers to continue to visit the remains and watched as individuals kissed the hands and face of the corpse for several days (Rengers, 1986).

After four days, her body was sealed in a lead coffin and entombed in a sepulcher. Fifteen years later, her casket was opened to check on her condition. This is still a standard Christian process: Bodies are unearthed and viewed before being moved to another location. This is done primarily for identification purposes, but the condition of the bodies was also checked, as through the twentieth century a preserved body could have been the impetus needed for the Church to name the unearthed individual a saint. When Jacinta's casket was opened, her face was found to have been perfectly preserved. It was still rosy in color. They wondered if the rest of her body was likewise preserved, but no one wished to remove her clothing or look under it. People who were there touched religious objects to the corpse again and wiped handkerchiefs on her face, later taking them home as religious relics.

The preservation of her body is thought to have been miraculous, and for this reason she is called an Incorruptible. This phenomenon, along with her vision, allowed the pope to give her the title of Venerable in 1986 and then the more esteemed title of Blessed in 2000. It is unknown whether or not she will ever become a saint.

This type of alleged miraculous preservation is also common in some forms of Buddhism. One such example is the body of Dashi Dorzho Itigilou (1852–1927), who was the Khambo Lama in Siberia. As many Buddhist monks do, he predicted the exact date of his death, and he left instructions regarding the burial of his body after death. He sat in meditation when he felt that death was near, and he continued meditating until the life slipped out of his body. His followers, having seen him die, buried his body in a wooden coffin and then dug it up again after a few years, as he had requested. The body was perfectly preserved.

It was not treated in any way, but it was reburied. The remains were later unearthed another few times, in 1955, in 1973, and then finally in 2002, when the body was exhumed for the last time and enshrined at Ivolginsky Datsan, located in East Siberia near Lake Baikal. At this location, doctors, monks, and scientists examined the body, and they determined that he appeared as though he had died only 36 hours earlier. There was no sign of decay, and the internal organs were intact and preserved. Twenty-seven years after his death, the body was still perfectly preserved, even though it had not been embalmed or intentionally preserved using other methods (Sacred Destinations, 2005). Amazingly, the body even bleeds if the skin is punctured.

This idea of incorruptibility, common in Christian and Buddhist traditions, has not been adequately researched, so it is unknown if the bodies had been intentionally yet secretly preserved or if there are other natural explanations for the mummifications. Until such investigations take place, the means of mummification will remain technically unknown. Therefore, it cannot be easily placed into the existing categories of mummification. Self-mummification is another concept that does not fit neatly into the available categories either. It can technically be catalogued as Class II mummification, but the enhancement of natural processes is typically carried out in order to mummify someone else. In other words, people do not usually try to preserve their own bodies. Sometimes, people pay to be mummified after death by others, but auto-mummification is unusual.

There are a number of these self-mummified individuals on display in northern Japan, but it is likely that the idea originated in either China or Tibet.[2] The process of self-mummification takes almost a decade to complete, during which time they regulate their diets and train in ascetic practices. Initially, they abstain from cereals, and they supplement their diet with unusual substances that help to preserve their physical bodies. These substances include pine bark, resin, and pine needles. They also include butterburs and other less palatable items like small river stones (Matsumoto, 2002). Some of the self-mummified individuals drank from a water source that had high levels of arsenic as well. Over time, they continued to decrease the amount of food they ingested. Their aim was to preserve themselves by means of their dietary change, but they intended to kill themselves by starvation. Over the course of ten years, they continued to decrease the amount of food eaten until they felt that death was near. Once they were ready, they sought out a suitable place to be buried, and a hole was dug for them.

They sat in wooden coffins in meditative positions, which were then nailed shut, leaving only a small (bamboo) tube through which they could breathe. The coffins were then buried under the earth, and those within rang a bell and prayed until they finally died. When followers could no longer hear the bells ringing, they assumed that the individuals had died. They removed the breathing tubes and sealed the holes. The bodies remained buried in this state for three years. After three years, they were unearthed to see if they had mummified. Successful preservation was indicative of high spiritual progress. If they had not been mummified, the bodies were simply reburied, but if they had been preserved, they were redressed in religious robes and then enshrined in local temples.

The interesting thing about these individuals is not necessarily their unusual method of suicide and auto-mummification, but the reasons behind the act. They believed that there was not a single indivisible soul, but two spiritual essences that were connected to the physical bodies. These essences were called *kon* and *haku*. The kon aspect of the spirit is what animates the physical body. It is the equivalent of a life force. Once it leaves the body, death occurs, and after death, it returns to heavenly realms. The haku element, however, remains with the physical body and slowly seeps out into the earth. This spiritual essence does not perpetuate the existence of a person after death, but it has power that, (according to their belief system), can be used for various purposes. Such purposes include miraculous healing and the granting of other types of spiritual assistance to others. Since there are two spiritual essences and only one passes on into the realm of the afterlife, true death occurs slowly. It is not complete until the haku element completely leaves the body. Therefore, an individual who has recently died is not completely dead. He or she is in a transitory state between existences. Hoffman (1986) wrote: "The deceased does not pass over immediately to a world from which no return is possible. One belief is that the spirit of the dead person remains near the world of the living for forty-nine days; another is that the spirit hovers on the borders of the world of the living for some decades and only then, if all goes well, does it merge with the greater order of the cosmos" (p. 30).

The composite view of the soul shared by the individuals in northern Japan who mummified themselves is similar to the indigenous Chinese idea of the soul. They also thought that there were two spiritual essences. Theirs were known as *hun* and *po*. They believed that there were three hun souls and seven po souls and after death the essences separated. The hun souls traveled into the sky and the po souls seeped into the soil. However, the po souls lasted longer. They remained with the body for a long period of time, and as the body decayed they seeped out. Since the essences separated, the individual could not continue to exist (as a whole) in the realm of the afterlife. The only way to maintain the existence of the individual was to preserve the body, and thereby halt the dissipation of the po souls.

Since the process of mummification kept these spirits in the body longer, the remains could also continue to be a source of miracles. It was this spiritual essence that made miracles possible. If this helpful spiritual essence was to remain, the body had to be preserved. Many Buddhist monks were preserved after death and then enshrined in temples, where they functioned as living statues — objects of devotion and inspiration.

The early Christian tradition shared similarities with both the Chinese and Japanese beliefs in the composite nature of the soul and in the practice of mummification, which continues today. Plutarch (46–c. 120), referring to the concept of the soul, stated that it was not a singular and indivisible essence, but that it consisted of various layers. If part of it remained with the body, like it did in some Japanese and Chinese traditions, then mummification in Christianity might have been utilized for a similar purpose — to help perpetuate the existence of the individual into the afterlife, and to keep the spiritual essence within the remains longer, so that it could be of assistance to the living. The reasons behind Christian mummification are not as clear-cut as this explanation alone, but this is one of seven major reasons behind the practice of mummification in Christianity. The early Christian concept of the soul was not influenced by the ideas of either China or Japan. It is likely, however, that the Egyptian concept of the spirit was influential in the development of the Christian idea instead.

In the ancient Egyptian beliefs, the spirit of the deceased remains with the physical body for 40 days. This concept can also be found in Christianity. Ascension day, which celebrates the rising of Jesus into heaven, takes place 40 days after his resurrection (Gadalla, 2008). The Egyptian concept is complex, considering the existence of various spiritual essences. In early Egyptian religious beliefs, there were approximately eight spiritual essences that survived death. Along with the physical body, the combination of these essences formed each individual person. Little is still known about all of these essences, and most texts that refer to the Egyptian concept of the spirit only mention three or four of them, including the *Ba*, the *Ka*, and the *ren*, but there are others, such as the *khu*, the *khaibit*, the *sahu*, the *sekhem*, and the *ib*. In order for all of these spiritual essences to continue to perpetuate the existence of the deceased, the physical body had to be preserved. This is one of the reasons why mummification was common in ancient Egyptian traditions. The preservation of bodies in all of these faiths results in relics — human remains that serve as objects of veneration.

6

Relic-Bodies

In many religious traditions worldwide, in the present as in the past, statues are used as objects of meditation and veneration. It is easier to contemplate the attributes of a valued person or deity while looking at his or her likeness. It is simpler to meditate upon his or her sacrifices or divine qualities when a representation is available. For this reason, statues show up in religious traditions found in nearly every country. In some traditions, however, the actual physical bodies of the individuals in question are used, taking the place of statues made in their image. These true-body statues are called whole-body relics.

The worship of relics is common to both Catholic Christianity and Buddhism. The veneration of body parts is an unusual custom that can only be explained and understood by looking at the corresponding beliefs of the spiritual essence as held by traditions that have this custom. In the Christian tradition, the religious ideas that justify the veneration of body parts are bound to the idea of bodily resurrection, and it will be explained more fully later. Early Christians had no doubt that the bodies (or body parts) of martyrs and other saints were the saints themselves. The saints were actually present in the bodily remains. However, simultaneously, they were in heaven (Bynum, 1995). Similar to the Egyptian and the Buddhist ideas of multiple aspects of the spirit, the soul was layered, with various aspects, and although part of the essence traveled to heaven to be close to God, part of it remained with the body. In early Chinese religious ideas, it was likewise thought that the souls within the body passed away slowly. They remained with the body for a lengthy period of time. For this reason, relics are valued in various religious traditions. In Catholicism, when a saint or high-ranking member of the Church dies the body is preserved. Then pieces of it, or at least pieces of the clothing that he or she is wearing (or other objects that touched the body), are sent to various other locations. The former (the body parts themselves) are called primary relics, and the latter (things that touched the body) are known as secondary relics. These objects are thought to possess the spiritual essence of the person who once inhabited the body, and they are therefore venerated. When an entire body is preserved, its value is even more pronounced.

The existence of an entire relic-body was beneficial for a number of reasons. Any church or temple that housed one became an important site for pilgrimages, and it therefore made more money (Sharf, 1992). The bodies were also thought of as reservoirs of divine energy, so the presence of such remains was thought to be spiritually beneficial in Buddhist tradition, and was said to keep away the devil in Christian faith. Believers in both religions thought that the bodies could also effect miracles. It is for this reason that relics were often stolen during the Middle Ages. Priests would steal relics from one church, only to relocate

A secondary relic being carried through the streets toward the cathedral at the festival of St. Paolo (Rome, Italy).

them to their own (Geary, 1991). This was considered necessary by Catholics who relied on the miraculous powers of the body parts for protection and guidance. From a Buddhist perspective, such bodies were infused with divine energy gained from their practices of austerities that is called merit. The bodies were thus treated as "reservoirs of spiritual power" (Sharf, 1992, p. 6).

In the Buddhist and Catholic perspectives, the bodies of the deceased also functioned as a reminder of the transitory nature of life. Followers could meditate in front of the remains, pondering the true significance of life and death. So, there are four major reasons why whole-body relics are common in such faiths: They make money for the temples and churches where they are displayed, they can cause miracles, they serve as living statues honoring the deceased, and they are reminders in-the-flesh of the inevitability of death.

Whole-body relics were important, and it did not matter how they were created. Some of the bodies were found to have been naturally preserved, while others were intentionally mummified. For example, the bodies of Buddhist monks in China, Taiwan, and Tibet were often preserved and then gilded after death. Many of these monks were naturally preserved, and then further steps were taken in order to make the remains endure forever. One example is Shi Cihang (1895–1954), whose body is now located in Taiwan. Like other Buddhist monks, he predicted the exact date of his death, and he also predicted that his remains would not decay after death. He left instructions to his followers for the exact treatment of his body.

Once he died, his body was placed in an egg-shaped jar, where it would remain for three years. He asked that his body be exposed and then treated after this significant period of time.[1] However, it was not. They disregarded the instructions that he had left regarding the proper treatment of his body because a suitable place to enshrine it had not yet been built. Once it was completed, two years later, his body was unearthed and found to be well preserved. It was thin, but his nose, lips, and teeth were still intact (Demieville, 1965). The skin was flexible and it had retained its elasticity, and his hair and beard had grown substantially.

The treatment of his remains took several months. First the body was wrapped in silk, and then it was covered with red lacquer. After this, there was another layer of silk, and another layer of lacquer. This process was repeated one final time, and then artificial eyes were put into place, so that he would appear alive again. The gilding process came next. The body was wrapped in 28,000 gold foils, which effectively turned the corpse into a statue (Travagnin, 2006). After this, the body was redressed and enshrined. In a sense, he is a living statue, like the others in Taiwan. There are five other famous bodies that were preserved, gilded, and enshrined in like manner, and there are many more in parts of China and in Thailand. There are variations of such relic bodies found in Tibet and in Japan as well. Some of them were found to have been naturally mummified and then lacquered and enshrined. Others were dried with incense smoke and candle fires before enshrinement.

Relic bodies are common in Catholic Christianity as well, and among the thousands of bodies on display in Italy are several hundred that qualify as whole-body relics. These are primarily the bodies of saints, beati, and venerables that have been preserved, redressed, and then enshrined in churches, monasteries, cathedrals, or even catacombs, where they are prominently displayed. Similarly, there are many bodies that are enshrined and displayed

This is the relic body of the martyr St. Tarcisius, located at the Basilica of San Domenico Maggiore (Naples, Italy). Only his bones remain. They are housed in a mannequin designed to resemble him.

in other European countries. These bodies, called Incorruptibles, are relic bodies, and they are an important aspect of Catholicism.

Like the Buddhist mummies, many of these bodies were found to have been naturally preserved, and then they were later treated in order to endure. Saint Bernadette Soubirous (1844–1879) for example, is currently on display in a chapel named after her in Nevers, France. She claimed to have witnessed an apparition of the Virgin Mary 14 different times. There were some who did not believe Bernadette; they thought that she was mentally ill. However, the Church decided that her visions were real. After a papal investigation, the Church stated that the "visions of the Virgin Mary really did occur at the Grotto of Lourdes" (Pettinger, 2007). Although this does not mean anything to historians, it does mean something to believers, who think that the pope cannot err. Since he cannot make errors, Catholics believed that the young girl had really been visited multiple times by the mother of Jesus and therefore sought to canonize Bernadette after her death.

The body was first exhumed on September 22, 1909, 30 years after her death. It had been buried in two caskets, one wood and the other lead, in order to effect preservation. The wooden coffin was unscrewed and the lead coffin was cut open to reveal the body. Cruz (1977) wrote: "On opening the lid, they discerned no odor and the virginal body lay exposed, completely victorious over the laws of nature" (p. 288). Two doctors who examined the body created the following report:

> The coffin was opened in the presence of the Bishop of Nevers, the mayor of the town, his principal deputy, several canons and ourselves. We noticed no smell. The body was clothed in the habit of Bernadette's order. The habit was damp. Only the face, hands and forearms were uncovered. The head was tilted to the left. The face was dull white. The skin clung to the muscles and the muscles adhered to the bones. The sockets of the eyes were covered by the eyelids. The brows were flat on the skin and stuck to the arches above the eyes. The lashes of the right eyelid were stuck to the skin. The nose was dilated and shrunken. The mouth was open slightly and it could be seen that the teeth were still in place. The hands, which were crossed on her breast, were perfectly preserved, as were the nails. The hands still held a rusting rosary. The veins on the forearms stood out.
>
> Like the hands, the feet were wizened and the toenails were still intact (one of them was torn off when the corpse was washed). When the habits had been removed and the veil lifted from the head, the whole of the shriveled body could be seen, rigid and taut in every limb. It was found that the hair, which had been cut short, was stuck to the head and still attached to the skull — that the ears were in a state of perfect preservation — that the left side of the body was slightly higher than the right from the hip up. The stomach had caved in and was taut like the rest of the body. It sounded like cardboard when struck. The left knee was not as large as the right. The ribs protruded, as did the muscles in the limbs. So rigid was the body that it could be rolled over and back for washing. The lower parts of the body had turned slightly black. This seems to have been the result of the carbon of which quite large quantities were found in the coffin [Comte, 1919].

Although Bernadette was affected by the natural processes of autolysis and putrefaction, the caskets and the carbon in the coffin halted decay and the body was relatively well preserved. As soon as it was freed from the two caskets, however, the body began to turn black due to the introduction of fresh air. Action was then taken to make sure that the body did not decay further and to make it look lifelike again. They washed and treated her body, likely with an embalming solution, and they also covered her remains with a saline solution to effect preservation. Then they put her into another two coffins. The first coffin, again made from wood into which her body was placed, was lined with zinc, which often functions as a preservative of human remains. It was nailed shut and then placed into an outer lead casket, which was soldered shut and ceremoniously sealed in seven locations.

In 1919, the cause for her canonization was approved. She was given the title of Venerable, and the body was unearthed. Dr. Comte (1919), the attending physician, wrote: "The body is practically mummified, covered with patches of mildew and quite a notable layer of salts which appear to be calcium salts. The skeleton is complete, and it was possible to carry the body to a table without any trouble. The skin has disappeared in some places, but it is still present on most parts of the body. Some of the veins are still visible."

The body was treated again, only this time it was also covered with wax in order to preserve her facial features and to continue to delay decomposition. It was then reburied later that evening. Six years later, she was going to be given the title Blessed, so the body had to be viewed again. Pieces of it also had to be cut off. This Catholic practice requires that pieces of the bodies of important individuals be removed. This task fell to Dr. Comte. He wrote:

> At the request of the Bishop of Nevers I detached and removed the rear section of the fifth and sixth right ribs as relics; I noted that there was a resistant, hard mass in the thorax, which was the liver covered by the diaphragm. I also took a piece of the diaphragm and the liver beneath it as relics, and can affirm that this organ was in a remarkable state of preservation. I also removed the two patella bones to which the skin clung and which were covered with more clinging calcium matter. Finally, I removed the muscle fragments right and left from the outsides of the thighs. These muscles were also in a very good state of preservation and did not seem to have putrefied at all. From this examination, I conclude that the body of the Venerable Bernadette is intact, the skeleton is complete, the muscles have atrophied, but are well preserved; only the skin, which has shriveled, seems to have suffered from the effects of the damp in the coffin. It has taken on a grayish tinge and is covered with patches of mildew and quite a large number of crystals and calcium salts; but the body does not seem to have putrefied, nor has any decomposition of the cadaver set in, although this would be expected and normal after such a long period in a vault hollowed out of the earth [Comte, 1928].

The body was eviscerated and embalmed, and then it was placed into an elaborately decorated coffin. It was made from gold and glass, so that all could look at her body. She was redressed, and her facial features were touched up, making her look as though she were still alive. The body was then placed on display in her gold reliquary in a chapel named in her honor in Nevers, France.

The treatment of her body was not unique, and there were many individuals who were buried and treated in a similar manner. When the bodies were unearthed and found preserved, they were considered miraculous. Some of the individuals were vaulted into sainthood because of the condition of their remains, and the majority of them were displayed in churches as whole-body relics. Such bodies were thought to be infused with spiritual powers, and their mere presence was thought to have been responsible for various miracles and other favors. It is for this reason that pieces of the remains were cut off and sent away, so that other people could likewise make use of their magical powers.

Mummies in various cultures were thought to have possessed such powers, and certain individuals went through some serious trouble just to get their hands on a dead body that had been preserved. In Buddhism, the bodies were covered with gold and then enshrined as living relics. In Christianity, the bodies were preserved, pieces of them were sent out, and then they were enshrined in gold reliquaries and placed on display in churches and cathedrals. In Egypt, bodies were likewise preserved, covered with gold, and then entombed in religious temples and other locations. All three of these traditions held that the bodies were a source of magical powers — that the corpses were infused with spiritual power that could be used to assist the living. In this way, the living were influenced not only by the spirits of the deceased but also by their physical bodies.

7

Death and the Unknown: The Allure of Mummies

In some respects, dead bodies were historically despised. They were a source of disease. They were symbols of the inevitability of death—a constant reminder that life is short and will soon come to an end. However, in other respects the bodies of dead people were revered and sought after. In medieval Europe and during the Renaissance, for example, many individuals started to pay big money to get their hands on a new wonder drug: mummy.

Egyptian culture had a strong influence on European civilization. The great pharaohs and kings of Egypt were admired, as were their riches and religious sites. Some of their religious customs and practices were integrated into new emerging faiths, and the practice of mummification was well known. The stories passed down from Egyptian religious traditions were believed by some, and the bodies of the ancient Egyptians were thought to be infused with spiritual powers. For these reasons, the bodies themselves, which were blessed with supernatural powers, were used to cure the living of ailments and disease.

The drug called mummy was made from the bodies of ancient Egyptians. The mummified flesh and bones of a mummy were ground up into the form of a powder, mixed with liquids, and then drunk. Pharmacists in Europe claimed that it could cure a myriad of ailments, including poisoning, contusions, vertigo, bug bites, ulcers, concussions, headaches, and incontinence. As evidence of the power of the human mind, many individuals who used this drug remarked about its miraculous effects. Many individuals took the drug and were amazed with its results. The Medici family, in particular, was a strong supporter of its efficacy. The French king Francis I carried a small pouch of mummy with him at all times, just in case there was a medical emergency, and his daughter-in-law, Catherine de Medici, sent some individuals in her employment all the way to Egypt in order to procure more of the drug (Pringle, 2001).

The taking of mummified bodies from Egypt was illegal though, so the supply of mummy was scarce. There were many individuals out to make a profit who risked arrest and stole various bodies from Egyptian cemeteries. In 1586, for example, Sir John Sanderson headed to Egypt and located a tomb that housed the mummified remains of many individuals. After bribing local officials, he took 600 pounds of these bodies back to Europe to grind into powder and then sell (Pringle, 2001). Since the supply was scarce, people paid a lot of money for mummy. Therefore, many individuals wanted to continue selling the drug, even when no more was available. To accomplish this end, they made counterfeit mummy. They treated the bodies of the recently deceased in Europe and then passed them off as Egyptian mummies, which could be ground into the highly sought-after drug. Other naturally mummified bodies from other countries were also sold as mummy, including bog bodies — the bodies of individuals who were preserved due to the composition of bogs. Fischer (1998) explained how bogs preserve such bodies:

> The flora of raised bogs is scanty in species and, naturally, dominated by peat moss (Sphagnum), the leaves of which are of special construction. Only a small proportion of the leaf cells contain chlorophyll granules and are therefore able to carry out the process of photosynthesis. The rest of the cells, which lie among those containing chlorophyll, are dead, empty structures of cellulose with an extraordinary ability to absorb water. They do not absorb subsoil water but rather imbibe surface rainwater, and the underlying peat retains it. The nutritive salts that the peat moss requires, i.e., Ca, Mg, Na and K, come from atomized seawater carried into the atmosphere; the amount of nutritive salts increases the closer one gets to the sea. Measurements have shown that the annual growth of raised bogs is some 15mm, but pressure from the upper layers reduces the true annual growth to about 6.4 mm. This compression prevents oxygen from coming into contact with the underlying layers, thus oxygen dependent bacteria cannot destroy the peat and the organisms contained in it. Bog moss (Sphagnum) has a substance known as sphagnan in its cells. When the moss dies, the sphagnan is slowly released, dissolved into the bog water, and converted into humic acid. Sphagnan, the intermediate compounds, and the humic acid all produce two results: the bacterial growth is stopped, and the skin, hair and nails of the body are tanned [p. 238].

Bog bodies were miraculously well preserved, and the color of the remains also approximated the intentionally mummified bodies of the ancient Egyptians. Therefore, they made perfect substitutes for counterfeiters. In time though, even these bodies became rare and counterfeiters, still eager to make a profit, substituted the mummified bodies of animals, which they ground up and then sold as the drug.

The drug mummy was thought to have been extremely effective; so much so that people continued to pay a great deal of money for the ground-up bodies right up until the beginning of the twentieth century. According to a German pharmaceutical text published in 1905, mummy was still available and common. The text cautioned people, however, that the mummy that was normally encountered was not true mummy, from Egypt, but imitation mummy. It suggested that everyone check his or her mummy powder to make sure that it was genuine. After this publication, many began testing their mummy for arsenic content, and soon the practice of using mummified bodies as a drug ceased. However, its use by some individuals in various religious ceremonies has continued. It costs more than $40 per ounce, and it is sold in specialized pharmacies in many countries, including the United States (Harris and Weeks, 1973).

The mummified bodies of the deceased were also used to make different-colored paints. Artists were always seeking new substances with which to make different specialized colors. "To render the traditional blue robes of the Virgin Mary during the Renaissance, they bought an expensive gem, lapis lazuli, and ground it into powder. And in later times, they sought out ever more exotic sources. To obtain a beautiful golden yellow known today as Indian yellow, they purchased soil from India that was drenched in the urine of cows fed a special fodder — mango leaves" (Pringle, 2001, p. 202). Human remains were used to make various dark colors, and artists used such substances not only for the purposes of coloration but also for adding special attributes to their paintings. Using a human body to create a portrait was thought by some individuals to have infused the painting with human characteristics. In this way, the power that mummies are thought to have is not confined to religion and superstition alone. The bodies are considered to retain the attributes of the spirits that once inhabited them. It is perhaps for this reason that mummies continue to invoke fascination and awe.

The bodies of the deceased, on display in temples or smeared across a canvas, are a constant reminder of the inevitability of death. They occupy a position in the transient realm between life and death. It is for this reason that many look at mummies as a way out — a means of escaping death itself. A feature of Christianity, Buddhism, and ancient Egyptian faith is the resurrection of the body and the infinite nature of the soul.[1] Mummification was often carried out in order to allow the soul to continue and to permit the individual to attain victory over death. Many people still opt to be mummified after they die. They pay to be cryogenically frozen or preserved like ancient Egyptians. They loathe to give up this existence, and they hang on to anything they can. They cling especially to the physical body, since they were so close to it for such a long period of time. Some people who are nearing death cannot help but look back. They do not look forward, and they cannot let go of the past. Mummification makes the transition seem less extreme.

II. Mummies in Italy

Jesus said, "Know what is in front of your face, and what is hidden from you will be disclosed to you. For there is nothing hidden that will not be revealed." — Gospel of St. Thomas

8

Critical Thinking, Self-Reflection and Mummy Studies

Mummification, as previously explained, is known to nearly every society. The techniques utilized to achieve such preservation are often recorded in books and articles in modern times, as they were recorded on papyri, scrolls and tablets by ancient civilizations. The preservation of the deceased is one practice that has endured throughout the ages, and as such, it can serve to link human beings of the present with those of the past. Modern individuals who are alive today might believe that they are unique, that they have surpassed the civilizations of the past, and that they have more knowledge than people who lived hundreds or thousands of years ago. However, new research is continually pointing to the fact that ancient civilizations must have had access to superior knowledge in order to have accomplished what they did, knowledge that we are just now beginning to understand.[1] Some believe that civilizations of the past had greater (spiritual) knowledge, and that somehow that knowledge was forgotten or lost as time progressed. There is a famous parable that illustrates this fact:

> The Baal Shem Tov went into the forest and sang the songs and said the prayers, and found the Holy Spirit, Blessed Be His Name. His student lost the way to the forest, but he remembered the songs and said the prayers, and it was enough. His student's student forgot the songs but remembered the prayers and it was enough. We no longer know our way to the forest and we have forgotten the songs, and when we say our prayers, we no longer remember the exact words, but it is still enough.[2]

In order to understand what the ancients understood, people must first open their minds to alternative viewpoints and theories. They must rid themselves of preconceived ideas and study the teachings of ancient times with open minds in order to rekindle such lost information. They must question how things are today and make comparisons to how they were in the past. It is ignorant to simply assume that those living in the present are wiser than those who were living in the past. People are people, and there are things that they know and there are things that they do not understand. It has been said that an intelligent man knows what he knows, while a wise man has a thorough understanding of what he does not know. However, it is difficult for some people to truly know what they do not understand, and to accept that there are some things that are outside of their ken.

It is human nature for people to try to fill in the gaps, to try to explain a phenomenon based upon the limited knowledge and experience that they may have. In simpler terms, it is common for people, from every era of history and from every location in the world, to think that their beliefs are accurate and that their knowledge is extensive. Consider the accepted version of history as it is presented in schools: For the most part, there are no gaps and there are no questions left unanswered. Any element of history that does not neatly fit into the preexisting record is either ignored or trivialized. If a serious question ever arises about it, we simply state that we have not yet figured out where it fits into the accepted version of history.[3] It never occurs to some people that their version of history could be either incomplete or inaccurate. It never occurs to them that they should revise their theories based upon contradictory discoveries. Instead, they dismiss those discoveries as nonsense because they contradict the existing theory.[4] This is editing history and scientific finds to fit a theory, and not altering a theory to support truths uncovered. Truly, humankind causes its own ignorance. It is far better to acknowledge that there are some things that are not completely understood — that there are some things that we are unable to explain fully. Such a mind-set is more open to new ideas and less apprehensive about contrary beliefs, and it can serve to promote progress. To put it simply, if humans admit that their knowledge about history and science is incomplete, they will be more open to the truths of existence that may be right in front of them.

Not only is knowledge about history, science and other subjects deficient, but humans know very little about themselves. Many do not know why they do the things that they do and why they believe the things that they believe. This ability is considered to be a component of critical thinking, a buzzword in pedagogy today, and ever since the publication of *A Nation at Risk* in 1983 by the U.S. Department of Education it has been a goal of curricula developers and educators to develop such skills in students. However, just about all of the research that has been done in the area suggests not only that students are unable to think critically but also that the majority of teachers cannot think critically either (Willingham, 2007). Some are unable to engage in higher-order thinking, and most of them are incapable of metacognition: They are unable to rationalize why they believe what they believe (Hufford, 2008).

For example, if one were to ask 100 individuals how many faiths that they researched before settling upon the religious beliefs that they currently hold, many of them would likely respond that they did not research any. They would likely say that they simply accepted what their parents or people around them told them to be truth and, after time, they became either unable or unwilling to question it. This is not unusual. It is difficult for people to truly see themselves. However, they can see others more easily. For this reason, anthropological and historical studies serve not just to inform others about different belief systems or different cultural practices but also to lead to self-reflection and a better understanding of who they are as human beings. The study of mummification, a practice that has endured throughout time in just about every society on the planet, even those that developed independently of other cultures, is therefore important. It can assist people to understand others and to understand themselves. Since mummification deals with the transition between life and death as well, such study can help people to better understand the change and to clarify their beliefs about the metamorphosis. For these reasons, it is useful to study the practices of preserving and displaying the dead in detail.

Some people today view mummification as a mere curiosity, and they may wonder why ancient civilizations went to such trouble to preserve the bodies of the deceased. However, it must be noted that bodies continue to be preserved in cultures all over the world today. There are those who pay to be cryogenically frozen or embalmed after their deaths, and there are others who are preserved by loved ones, so that their remains present a lifelike appearance at occasions like wakes. Truly, mummification is not a thing of the past but a continuing part of human civilization. However, if you were to ask why, most people would be unable to formulate a response based on fact.

It is easy to explain why certain civilizations mummified their dead, as their religious beliefs encouraged or even necessitated the practice. For example, the ancient Egyptians needed their bodies prepared so the two parts of the soul, the ba and the ka, could reunite in the afterlife. Likewise, the Buddhist monks in northern Japan who mummified themselves needed the body preserved so that the merit accrued during their lives could be of assistance to humankind, even though their spirits did not remain. There are other traditions in which the preservation of the body is deemed necessary or desirable, so mummification practices can be easily justified. However, mummification is not so easily explained in religious traditions in which the human body is considered insignificant after death. The embalming (or preservation by other means) of Christians, for example, cannot be easily explained by studying their religious texts or spiritual practices. Therefore, a study of the importance of bodily preservation to members of this faith (and others like it) can provide illuminating insights into the nature of not only their belief systems but also the very nature of humankind.

Although mummies can be found in just about every country in museums or in caskets, they are found everywhere in Italy. One of the most famous mummies in modern history is actually located in Italy. In 1991, a body was found partially frozen yet nearly perfectly preserved in a glacier at an altitude of 3,210 meters on Mount Hauslabjoch, located in the Otzal Alps between Italy and Austria. At first, police thought that it might have been the body of a university professor who had disappeared in the mountains in 1938. It took several days to get the body down from the mountain, and the police used compressor drilling to remove the body from the ice. It was slightly damaged during the removal, and an archaeologist names Konrad Spindler (d. 2005) was consulted the following day. He believed that the body was at least 4,000 years old, but radiocarbon dating was performed later that revealed that the body was approximately 5,200 years old. It was nicknamed the Ice Man, and it is alternately known as Otzi, a word formed by combining "Otzal" and "yeti" (Hansen, 1998). Today, the body is located at the South Tyrol Museum of Archaeology in Bolzano, Italy, and tourists who visit the site are greeted by a life-size hologram of the man who met his untimely death in the mountains. The man's clothing is displayed in various cases, and there is a life-size replica of him. The man himself is visible, although only through a small window. He had been refrozen in an attempt to keep him well preserved. However, he shows signs of decay, and it is unfortunately only a matter of time before the decay consumes him.

Besides the Ice Man, there are literally thousands of mummies and other corpses on display all over Italy that anyone can visit. Many of these bodies are the preserved remains of martyrs or other saints, and the bodies themselves, along with the reverence shown toward them, provide insights into Italian religious beliefs and customs. Many people know that such bodies are on display, although they might not completely understand the reasons behind the custom. When people think about the existence of corpses in Italy, the catacombs in Rome is often the locale that first comes to mind.[5] Aurelius Prudentius Clemens (348– c. 413) once exclaimed, "How full Rome is with buried saints and how rich the city's soil with sacred graves!"

9

The Roman Catacombs

The Roman catacombs are basically a labyrinth of underground tunnels that were used as a place of burial for individuals of various religious affiliations. The early Roman religion did not advocate the need for burying the dead. Instead, people were cremated after their decease.[1] Individuals who wished to bury their family members or other loved ones after death often buried them on their own property. However, this was only possible for wealthy landowners, and poorer people, if they wanted their loved ones buried, were out of luck. For this reason, necropolises were created. "Necropolis" literally means "city of the dead." They were large underground burial sites, like the catacombs that can still be visited in Rome and in other cities. The first large catacombs were created in the second century C.E. outside of Rome, as no bodies were allowed to be buried within the city walls. Later, once Catholicism began to infiltrate Roman life, there were catacombs built within the city as well.

There are 60 known underground burial areas in Rome, but there are possibly more, as some passageways were built on top of older passageways. Forming a complex underground maze, the catacombs consist of *arcosolia*, burial chambers large enough to have accommodated the dead members of entire families, and *cubicula*, other large burial chambers that were decorated with frescoes of biblical scenes. Within such rooms are sarcophagi, elaborate coffins made primarily of stone or marble. Joining such chambers together is a labyrinthine set of passageways headed in various directions that are lined from top to bottom with niches in the walls called *loculi*, into which bodies (typically wrapped in linen) were placed.

In such passageways are various Christian symbols carved into walls, symbols such as the fish, which was an early symbol for Jesus. In Latin, the words "Christ" and "fish" have similar anagrams. Since Christianity was illegal for some time, the symbol of the fish came to be representative of Jesus, its true meaning only known by Christians. It also reminded them of one of his teachings, since Jesus asked followers to be fishers of men. One example of this is found in the Gospel of St. Matthew: "And Jesus, walking by the sea of Galilee, saw two brethren, Simon called Peter and Andrew his brother, casting a net into the sea, for they were fishers. And he saith unto them, follow me, and I will make you fishers of men" (4:18–19). The same story is repeated in the Gospel of St. Mark.

Other signs found in the catacombs include the anchor, a Christian symbol for hope, and the dove, which is representative of true believers: those who are saved. Also within the complex are crypts, which are small underground churches that were decorated with religious paintings, statues, or other symbols. Many of them were originally also adorned with relics of saints or Christian martyrs, and some of them had tombs dug into the floors called *formae* that housed the remains of martyrs, saints, or other important Christians.

Five of the catacombs in Rome are considered especially important by the Catholic Church. These are the catacombs of St. Callixtus, St. Sebastian, St. Domitilla, St. Priscilla and St. Agnes, all of which can be visited by tourists and religious pilgrims alike. Pope John Paul II (1996), speaking to the Pontifical Commission for Sacred Archaeology, stated, "From the very beginning of Christianity, my predecessors have cared for the catacombs. Pope St. Zephyrinus was the first to create one on the Appian Way for the Roman community, entrusting it to the care of the deacon Callixtus, who, when he became Pope, linked his name to what became the largest network of the catacombs in Rome."

St. Callixtus succeeded St. Zephyrinus as Bishop of Rome c. 218 and was the head of the Church for five years. He founded the Church of Saint Maria in Trastevere and was involved with the burials of martyrs. He was also given the title of martyr by the Church, although he was not killed because of his faith. The Church decided to call him a martyr because there were many anti-Christians in important positions while he was pope (Hoever, 1955). Being named a martyr meant that he was awarded posthumously with his own feast day. It also meant that other Christians would pray to him. He died c. 223.

The catacombs of St. Callixtus were created during the second century. The total size of the catacombs is approximately 90 acres and it stretches about 12 miles long in four distinct levels, reaching a depth of 20 meters. There is an open area underground that has two basilicas; the eastern one once contained the remains of the pope Zephyrinus and the martyr Tarcisius. The rest of the complex includes various open areas designed for burials, including the Crypts of Lucina, the area of the popes and the area named after St. Cecilia. These were built during the second century. During the third century, three other crypts were built and named after St. Miltiades, St. Eusebius and St. Gaius. A hundred years later, two other areas were added: the Western area and the Liberian area. These two are especially important to Catholics because they were the official burial place of nine popes, including the popes Sixtus II, Fabian, Antherus, Pontianus, Eutichian and Lucius.

Nearby is the crypt of St. Cecilia, the patron saint of music. She was honored for nearly 500 years at this location, but in the year 821 her remains were transferred to Trastevere, where they were enshrined in a basilica constructed in her honor. There were also remains of martyrs and monuments celebrating their lives in the catacombs, including a poem inscribed on a marble slab written by the pope Damasus in the fourth century. There are other mosaics and paintings of martyrs such as Quirinus, Polycamus and Sebastian. St. Sebastian (d. 288) was born in Gaul but educated in Milan, where his parents lived. At some point, he became Christian, but he managed to hide his faith from the authorities. Eventually he was accused of being a Christian and was ordered to appear before Emperor Diocletian. Refusing to renounce his faith, he was condemned to death by arrows.

The sentence being carried out, he was left for dead. An old woman found his body, realized that he was still alive, and nursed him back to life. Perhaps he did not consider the ramifications of his actions, but once he had recovered, he returned to the emperor and reproached him for his previous harsh treatment. One must wonder what ran through the emperor's mind before passing down another death sentence. He ordered that Sebastian be beaten to death with clubs. This time, his killers were successful. Once they were sure he was dead, they threw his body into a sewer. Someone found it, however, and relocated it.

They buried it in the catacombs of St. Callixtus. Artistic representations of St. Sebastian and other martyrs found in the catacombs demonstrate the important position they held in early Christianity and the respect that believers felt toward them.

A veritable cult sprung up around the martyrs and their relics, and this relic cult has not dissipated. It remains today, and the relics of saints, venerables and beati are still praised by Christians in Italy (and abroad). In the past, believers would hold special memorial ceremonies underground in the catacombs, some of which continue today. When such ceremonies were first conducted, they were secretive in nature, but after Christianity became the official religion of the Roman Empire in 381 the catacombs became an important site for Christian pilgrims. They would travel (sometimes very long distances) to visit the bodies of the dead and to pray before their corpses. Why the dead bodies were of such importance to members of the sect will be discussed in more detail later in this book, but for now it will suffice to say that the Christians had a fascination with the bodies of holy individuals. Their bones and decaying flesh were considered to be infused with spiritual and supernatural powers.

Within the next couple of hundred years, however, there was a change in burial practices. The bodies of saints were no longer laid to rest in underground tombs and chambers within the catacombs, but they were kept in churches (or in church cemeteries). Sometimes, they were displayed in glass coffins like mannequins in storefront windows. Otherwise, they were laid to rest in sarcophagi in church basements, in special rooms in religious buildings, or even under altars. Once this practice became commonplace, the catacombs were then typically used for the memorial services of martyrs alone. Such underground observances became less and less common throughout the years, and by the tenth century the catacombs were just about completely forgotten. That is, until they were rediscovered in 1578. Antonio Bosio (c. 1576–1629) spent many years of his life researching the catacombs and excavating the burial sites. He excavated 30 of the 60 known sites, and he wrote a book about the subject entitled *Roma Sotteranea* (Underground Rome), which was not published until 1632, three years after his untimely death. Bosio is known as the "Columbus of the Catacombs" because of his discoveries, and he is considered the father of Christian archaeology. He found the underground burial sites extremely interesting and he dedicated a great portion of his life to their study. Not surprisingly, he was also very interested in the study of the martyrs and their popular cult.

10

The Cult of the Martyrs

The Christian martyr is not easy to explain, as the connotations of the term have changed over time. Martyrdom, therefore, is difficult to define. Kelley (1972) wrote: "A legal concept, a value judgment, a psychological condition, a social role, a weapon of propaganda — again it was all these, and more. The idea, if not the terminology, long antedated Christianity. As early as the fifth century B.C.E., for example, Athenians killed in war were assured of deification; and this notion of dying in battle for a just cause has always been associated with that of martyrdom" (p. 1328). It is evident that the Christian idea of martyrdom did not originate independently. It was not a unique idea. Rather, the concept was taken from earlier religions and adopted to fit the changing structure of Christianity as directed by the politically inspired Church. The term "martyr" comes from the Greek term *martus* and it originally referred to an eyewitness who testified.[1] In other words, he or she personally witnessed an event, acquiring knowledge firsthand, and then provided an account of the event for others. However, in time the term came to have a different connotation. A martyr was one who testified to a fact, but there was always a grave risk involved — that testimony could lead to severe punishment or even death. The meaning of the term continued to evolve, and today a martyr is considered one who believes in something so much that he or she would prefer to suffer death than to deny its existence. (The change here is that previously a person had to be an eyewitness to an event. Over time, a so-called martyr did not have to actually witness an event, but belief alone could suffice.)

St. Stephen is thought to have been the first martyr after Jesus of Nazareth. Stephen was one of the leaders of the early Church, responsible for handing out alms to the poor. According to biblical accounts, he was also credited with numerous miracles: "And Stephen, full of faith and power, did great wonders and miracles among the people" (Acts 6:8). The display of such magical powers alarmed the authorities, and he was taken into custody and brought before the Jewish Court (the Sanhedrin). Witnesses claimed that he had committed many acts of blasphemy, which was illegal under Jewish law. They said, "For we have heard him say that this Jesus of Nazareth shall destroy this place, and shall change the customs which Moses delivered us" (Acts 6:14). He was stoned in the streets as punishment for this crime. According to the Acts of the Apostles: "They stoned Stephen, calling upon God and saying, Lord Jesus, receive my spirit. And he kneeled down and cried with a loud voice, Lord, lay not their sin to charge. And when he had said this, he fell asleep" (6:59–60).

This account of his martyrdom is significant because it demonstrates what was expected of an early martyr for the faith. The individual had to have been a devout believer in the Christian faith, he must have adamantly clung to that faith when arrested and charged by authorities, and he must have forgiven those who ordered his punishment. In other words, the early idea of a martyr was applied to those individuals who were arrested, charged, and killed in a manner just like Jesus. All martyrs were also considered saints, and therefore, becoming a saint in early Christianity was simple. One only needed to die for the faith. Over time, however, the meaning of the term "saint" changed and it became increasingly more difficult to be named a saint by the Church.

For the most part, when Catholics refer to martyrs they only mean those individuals who had died or who were severely punished for their belief in the Catholic faith; people who had the same mind-set about a different religion were not considered martyrs. In fact, according to the Church, members of the Orthodox sect, although Christians, were not able to become martyrs. It was the Catholic Church that determined martyrdom, and only its members were eligible.

However, individuals from many different religions are considered martyrs to other people outside of the Catholic faith. Although non–Catholic martyrs are not recognized by the Church as martyrs, to be a martyr one does not have to be Catholic. In fact, many individuals who are considered martyrs were actually killed by the Church, ordered to death by the pope or by other religious officials. Although the Roman Church did not consider the people whom they killed martyrs, such individuals are considered martyrs by others because they died for their own faiths, like the early Christians who refused to say that they did not believe. Although the actions of these individuals, both Catholic and non-Catholic alike, were the same, they were not viewed as being the same by the Church. It only honored its own members with the title martyr.

John Foxe (1517–1587) was born in a tumultuous time, in which Martin Luther began the Protestant Reformation, thus challenging the authority of the Catholic Church. Among other ideological differences, Luther did not think that the intercession of the Church was necessary for a person to get into heaven. That could be accomplished, rather, by a person's own conduct and actions in life. Luther also did not support the wealth accrued by the clergy and the evil practices perpetrated by the Church.

Protestantism became popular in England, until Queen Mary instituted a Catholic reformation, undoing the work that her father and brother had done before her. She ordered non–Catholics to repent and become Catholic. Those who refused to do so were executed. The individuals who were killed were recorded by John Foxe in his book *The History of the Acts and Monuments of the Church*, which is popularly known as the *Book of Martyrs*, originally published in 1554. It was first translated into English in 1563. Also displaying a prominent place in his book are important figures in Christianity, such as William Tyndale, John Calvin, and John Bunyan. Their lives are recorded as examples of persecution and martyrdom.

The first chapter of Foxe's book provides the names of individuals who were killed under the first persecution of Nero; chapter two covers those individuals martyred in what he refers to as the ten primitive persecutions. Other chapters cover persecutions in Scotland, England, the Netherlands, Persia and Bohemia, as well as the Inquisition, in which Pope Innocent III made a number of individuals Inquisitors. It was their job to locate individuals whose beliefs did not correspond exactly to those of the Church. Called heresy, this charge was brought against anyone who spoke out against the Church's wealth or evil actions, or against anyone whose religious beliefs did not conform exactly to the beliefs that the Roman Church ordered.

If people were judged to be heretics, non-believers in the Roman Catholic tradition, they were punished by torture and imprisonment, or they were sentenced to death. In any case, all of their possessions would be confiscated by the Church. The following is an account of a mass execution sanctioned by the Roman Catholic Church that took place in Madrid:

> The officers of the Inquisition, preceded by trumpets, kettledrums, and their banner, marched on the thirtieth of May, in cavalcade, to the palace of the great square, where they declared by proclamation, that, on the thirtieth of June, the sentence of the prisoners would be put in execution.
>
> Of these prisoners, twenty men and women, with one renegade Mahometan, were ordered to be burned; fifty Jews and Jewesses, having never before been imprisoned, and repenting of their crimes, were sentenced to a long confinement, and to wear a yellow cap. The whole court of Spain was present on this occasion. The grand inquisitor's chair was placed in a sort of tribunal far above that of the king.
>
> Among those who were to suffer was a young Jewess of exquisite beauty, and but seventeen years of age. Being on the same side of the scaffold where the queen was seated, she addressed her, in hopes of obtaining a pardon, in the following pathetic speech: "Great queen, will not your royal presence be of some service to me in my miserable condition? Have regard to my youth; and, oh! consider that I am about to die for professing a religion imbibed from my earliest infancy!" Her majesty seemed greatly to pity her distress, but turned away her eyes, as she did not dare to speak a word in behalf of a person who had been declared a heretic. Now Mass began, in the midst of which the priest came from the altar, placed himself near the scaffold, and seated himself in a chair prepared for that purpose. The chief inquisitor then descended from the amphitheater, dressed in his cope, and having a miter on his head. After having bowed to the altar, he advanced towards the king's balcony, and went up to it, attended by some of his officers, carrying a cross and the Gospels, with a book containing the oath by which the kings of Spain oblige themselves to protect the Catholic faith, to extirpate heretics, and to support with all their power and force the prosecutions and decrees of the Inquisition: a like oath was administered to the counselors and whole assembly. The Mass was begun about twelve at noon, and did not end until nine in the evening, being protracted by a proclamation of the sentence of the several criminals, which were already separately rehearsed aloud one after the other. After this followed the burnings of the twenty-one men and women, whose intrepidity in suffering that horrid death was truly astonishing. The king's near situation to the criminals rendered their dying groans very audible to him; he could not, however, be absent from this dreadful scene, as it is esteemed a religious one; and his coronation oath obliged him to give a sanction by his presence to all the acts of the tribunal [Foxe, 1563, chapter V].

Typically, those who were judged as heretics were burned by the Church. This was thought to be a purification of the body through fire. Besides burning non-believers to death, the Church utilized other methods of execution, including beheadings, tying the condemned to a wheel and then beating them to death, and ripping their bodies apart (Chandler, 1813). Sometimes, individuals were strangled, or their throats were cut with a knife and the condemned choked to death on their own blood. Individuals who met their ends in such ways are called martyrs.

Although people killed by the Church are considered martyrs to Protestants and members of other distinct religions, the Church itself only honored Catholics who met their ends as a result of their faiths. The title of martyr was reserved only for its own, and the bones and relics of martyrs are still revered by followers today. An example of the awe and respect still shown to martyrs and their physical remains is the so-called Cathedral of Skulls in Otranto, Italy. In 1480, Ottoman soldiers attacked the town and demanded that its inhabitants renounce the Christian God and convert to Islam. Eight hundred individuals refused and were therefore beheaded. The hill where the massacre occurred was renamed the Hill of Martyrs, and skulls and bones of all of the individuals were piled together and arranged artistically in the town cathedral, where they remain today.

Among the martyrs honored by the Church and its followers, the earliest Christians were considered especially important. In ancient Rome, citizens were expected to worship the gods in accordance with the national religion. Christians denied the existence of these gods and were therefore breaking the law. For this reason they were persecuted. (Jews also did not worship the gods of the Roman pantheon, but they had a legal right to worship their deity, Jehovah, and were therefore not persecuted.) Many Christians were sent to death as atheists. Some denied that they were Christians in order to escape with their lives. Others, when rounded up and questioned, claimed that they were no longer Christians. If ex-Christians repented and made sacrifices to the gods, they were pardoned. Those who refused to make such concessions were sentenced to death. Such individuals were known as martyrs. In the second century, when individuals refused to renounce the Christian God and they were imprisoned or tortured rather than killed, they were not considered martyrs. Instead, they were given the lesser title of confessor. Although their convictions and actions may have been the same, the distinction between confessors and martyrs was in their punishment. To become a martyr, one had to die.

It was, according to Kelley (1972), the "most exalted and yet in some ways the simplest form of sainthood" (p. 1324). If Catholics wanted to guarantee their spot in a heavenly realm, all they had to do was state their belief in the Christian God and die for their convictions. It did not matter what they had done previously in their lives. As if this were not simple enough, by the third century becoming a martyr was made even easier. Death became unnecessary, and the title of martyr was given to some individuals while they were still alive. St. Cyprian (d. 258), for example, gave the title to bishops and priests who were condemned to penal servitude in mines. In the fourth century, the term "martyr" was given to some individuals who had simply endured some hardships because of their loyalty to Christianity.

The definition of a martyr has changed throughout the years, but all of these individuals were respected and honored by Catholics either during their lives or after their martyrdom. This was in part because Catholics thought that martyrs could assist them in the afterlife. All martyrs became saints, and according to Roman Catholic belief, they reside in heaven beside God because this title had been bestowed upon them by the Church. In this sense, the Church decides who will be admitted into heaven and who will be prayed to by others. Since martyrs were with God, they could function as intermediaries and assist others to get into paradise after their bodily deaths. Augustine stated that "men who had shown themselves, as martyrs, to be true servants of God could bind their fellow men closer to God than could the angels."[2] It was for this reason that many believers wished to be buried in close proximity to the bodies of martyrs or other saints. That is, until Augustine declared that one did not have to be buried next to such intermediaries in order to be saved. He said that no matter where people were buried, provided that they were pure of heart and faith they would find salvation. However, he may have been skeptical about his own claim. "Maybe martyrs did remain close by, foraging for souls and assisting the afflicted at their tombs. Augustine could not disprove it, but tales of phantom figures, extraordinary visions,

This crucifix, located at the Church of St. Ignacio de Loyola, is surrounded by skulls and other bones: the relics of saints and other holy individuals (Florence, Italy).

and sudden cures could not tempt him into the camp of the credulous" (Kaufman, 1994, p. 7).

The actual number of martyrs is unknown. There were hundreds, if not thousands, of individuals who were put to death because of their religious beliefs. Often they were killed in gruesome ways. Some were ripped apart and eaten by animals, while others were crucified, stoned, or dragged to death (Kaufman, 1994). In addition, some of them were thrown from bridges. Many were tied to stakes and burned, and sometimes the burning occurred in large groups rather than individually. There was one occasion in which approximately 84 Christians were all burned at once on a ship (Carrothers, 1999).

One famous martyr is St. Mark, to whom the Gospel of Mark is credited. He was dragged to death in the streets. Parts of his body, his relics, were initially kept in Alexandria, but they were stolen in the ninth century and taken to Venice, where they were housed in a basilica specifically built for the purpose. Over a thousand years later, one relic was given to Pope Cyril VI of Alexandria (1902–1971) at his request. It was a small piece of bone. The presentation of this relic was done in a ceremonial fashion, attesting to its importance to Catholics. A delegation of bishops and other clergy received the relic from Pope Paul VI (1897–1978) in Rome, who had previously received the bone from Giovanni Urbani (1900–1969), a cardinal in Venice.

After martyrs were killed and their bodies mutilated, relatives were often permitted to gather the remains for interment. These remains were called relics, and they held special significance to members of the Catholic sect who considered such items more valuable than silver, gold, or any precious gemstone.[3] The bodies of martyrs or relics of their bodies were

Close-up of the human remains that surround the crucifix. Note the skull in the center (Florence, Italy).

often interred in underground crypts and chapels. Sometimes they were buried under the altars in chapels, thus consecrating the altars themselves.

Pope John Paul II (1998) stated, "The catacombs also preserve the tombs of the first martyrs, witnesses of a clear and most steadfast faith, which led them as athletes of God to triumph over the supreme trial. Many tombs of the martyrs are still preserved within the catacombs and generations of the faithful have paused in prayer before them." The faithful traveled to such underground locations to honor the martyrs. They also venerated the relics of saints and other holy individuals that were interred within. The underground cities of the dead were especially important to Christians in Italy, but they did not just contain the relics and the bodies of saints and martyrs. In some locations, there are hundreds or even thousands of other bodies, some that naturally decayed and others that were intentionally or naturally preserved. The Capuchins' catacombs in Palermo, for example, contain thousands of mummified bodies.

11

The Catacombs in Palermo

There are more than 8,000 dead bodies on display in Palermo, Sicily. They are located at the Catacombs of the Capuchins, next to their monastery. Originally, there was just a cemetery, but the monks started to excavate and build crypts beneath it, until it became a huge underground burial site — one that was reported to have some unusual preserving qualities. Many of the bodies that were placed in the catacombs resisted decay and naturally mummified. This was first learned in 1599, when the monks were moving some corpses from old coffins into new resting places. According to available records, "In 1599, bodies were relocated from old graves to new ones. Upon opening the tomb in order to collect the bones, there was no bad odor, [and] 45 bodies of friars were found intact and whole to the point of being recognized. Some in particular had hair and beards, and looking at them, it seemed that they were sleeping rather than having been dead for such a long time."[1]

After this occurrence, news about the miraculous preservations spread, and many people in Sicily (other than friars) opted to be buried in the catacombs after their deaths for this reason. The first nobles who received permission to be buried in the catacombs were Don Carlo Firmatura in July of 1634 and Don Carlo Agliata, his wife, Giuseppina, and their son Don Bernardino in June of 1636. In November of that same year, Don Scipione Cottone also received permission to be buried within. After these individuals were buried in the sanctuary, the floodgates were opened and many other individuals came to be buried and preserved in the catacombs as well. The Capuchins worked with the poor and the sick. They worked in hospitals and comforted the homeless. The care that the Capuchins provided did not cease with the deaths of the poor and unfortunate. Such individuals were cared for both during life and after death by the Capuchin friars.

For this reason, over the course of more than 300 years the catacombs continued to be filled with the bodies of Capuchin brethren, priests, men, women, children, and babies. The rich and the poor alike were laid to rest within. Some were well-known individuals. Others were not. Death is the great equalizer, and no matter who they were in life, no matter their vicissitudes, they were laid to rest in underground crypts as equals. The Capuchins cared for them all, preserving many of the bodies artificially so that they would endure. It seems that many wish to avoid the natural processes of death by any means necessary. Although some of the bodies on display at the Capuchins' catacombs had naturally mummified, many of them were actually embalmed. In 1599, possibly after some bodies were found to be naturally preserved, the monks intentionally mummified one of their brethren, Silvestro of Gubbio, using an arsenic-based embalming solution.[2] Artificial mummification was an accepted and relatively common practice of Christian monks and other members of the Christian Church, so this mummification was not unusual.

After this intentional mummification, many of the other bodies placed within the catacombs for interment were also similarly preserved. From the 1500s through the 1920s, thousands of bodies were intentionally mummified and placed on display in the underground caverns. The caverns and the hallways connecting them are lined with shelves that have bodies positioned horizontally on their backs or sides. Some are in glass cases and others are displayed in standing positions. Some are even positioned in elaborate lifelike postures, dressed as though they were still alive. The friars are all dressed in the robes that they wore in life, and some of them have ropes around their necks that they had worn as a type of penance.

The bodies are separated into different sections and labeled. There are distinct sections for men, women, children, virgins, priests, monks, and teachers. The bodies are in varied states of preservation. Some look lifelike, with seemingly flexible skin covering their bodies, and are in positions that suggest that these mummies are interacting with similarly dressed mummies to their sides. For example, there is one section that has a few mummified children seated at a table together. Other individuals are only partially mummified, and their dark skin is dry and stretched out, exposing the skulls and skeletal structures beneath. Still others are but skeletons alone, with only small patches of skin adhering to their brittle bones.

The friars utilized various methods to preserve the inhabitants of their catacombs. Some of the bodies were embalmed and injected with preserving fluids. Others were dipped

A number of the skeletons and mummies found at the Capuchins' catacombs in Palermo, Sicily. There are thousands of bodies found at this location, including many mummified children. Among them is Rosalia Lombardo, whose cheeks still appear rosy. She looks like she is alive, even though she died almost 100 years ago (Palermo, Sicily).

into lime or arsenic. Arsenic baths were used exclusively in periods of epidemics in order to preserve corpses. Such treatments resulted in the dead displaying a rosy glow to their skin tone: a lifelike, reddish complexion. There are other liquids used to preserve bodies that also tend to turn the skin a reddish color. One famous body that is found at the catacombs displaying this skin complexion is a young girl named Rosalia Lombardo, who died December 6, 1920. Rosalia died when she was only two years of age, and her parents hired a noted embalmer, Dr. Alfredo Salafia, to preserve her body forever. He acquiesced and preserved her, using a technique that was lost for many years. Eventually, the formula was found in his notes. He did not remove her organs and X-ray analysis reveals that they are still remarkably intact, but he drained her blood and replaced it with a preserving fluid that was a mixture of formalin, alcohol, glycerin, salicylic acids, and zinc. According to Karen Lange (2009):

> Formalin, now widely used by embalmers, is a mixture of formaldehyde and water that kills bacteria. Salafia was one of the first to use this for embalming bodies. Alcohol, along with the arid conditions in the catacombs, would have dried Rosalia's body and allowed it to mummify. Glycerin would have kept her body from drying out too much, and salicylic acid would have prevented the growth of fungi. But it was the zinc salts, according to Melissa Johnson Williams, executive director of the American Society of Embalmers, that were most responsible for Rosalia's amazing state of preservation. Zinc, which is no longer used by embalmers in the United States, petrified Rosalia's body.

Her body is currently kept on a marble pedestal in a glass coffin, and she can be seen by visitors to the catacombs today. Johnson, Johnson, and Williams (1993) described the condition of her remains: "Appearance and color of the face and head would lead one to believe she had been dead at most a few days" (p. 54). It is a miraculous preservation that continues to endure.

The most common method that the Capuchin friars used to preserve bodies corresponds to Vreeland's second category of mummies: enhancing natural processes in order to effect preservation. The underground crypts became famous because some bodies placed within had naturally mummified. In dry, volcanic soil such preservation is quite common. In order to facilitate this, many of the bodies were left in special rooms in the catacombs in cells, which resembled barbeque pits and facilitated the drainage of cadaveric sewage. The cells contained grates that the bodies rested upon that were made of terra-cotta. The doors of the rooms were hermetically sealed and the bodies naturally drained and dried out over a period of 8 to 12 months. At the end of this time, the bodies would have been dry and the skin would have darkened substantially. Once this occurred, they were bathed in a solution of water and vinegar, redressed as though they were alive, and then displayed in niches, cases, and wooden coffins or placed in other rooms in lifelike positions.

Besides the Catacombs of the Capuchins in Palermo, there are other locations in Italy where the remains of Capuchin friars are located. The order is called the order of the Capuchins because of the clothing that they wear. They wear *cappucci*, or hoods, on their religious habits and over time have taken on the name that references their outfits. One other famous location where the remains of the Capuchins have been artistically arranged and displayed is the Crypt of the Capuchins in Rome, located at the Church of the Immaculate Conception on Via Veneto.

In 1631, the Capuchins left their old monastery and moved to this one in Rome, and

The Church of the Immaculate Conception, in Rome, Italy. In the crypt beneath this church are approximately 6,000 skeletons and mummified bodies that have been artistically arranged. Their presence is a reminder that life is short. There is even a sign that reads, "What you are, we once were. What we are, you will become."

they took the bodies of their deceased brethren with them. For the next 200 years, the Capuchins continued to arrange the bones and bodies artistically, and today it has become a popular tourist destination, separated into six separate areas. The only area free of bones is the mass chapel, which is used as an area for religious services and quiet contemplation. The other areas are called the Crypt of the Resurrection, the Crypt of the Skulls, the Crypt of the Pelvises, the Crypt of the Leg Bones and Thigh Bones, and the Crypt of the Three Skeletons. Before this location became a tourist destination, it was arranged in this unusual way for spiritual purposes. According to literature provided at the crypt, it was done in order to inform people of one fact: "Death closes the gates of time, and opens those of eternity." There is another interesting statement on a sign in the last room of the crypt. It is a message for visitors, written as though the dead themselves were speaking. It reads:

> What you are, we once were.
> What we are, you will become.

12

The Chapel of the Dead and the Skull Cathedral

Otranto, located near Lecce in southern Italy, is a small seaside town with many beaches found in the heel of the boot-shaped country. The ocean is crystal clear, and the narrow, winding streets of the town are a reminder of old Italy. Most known for its famed Otranto Castle, the town has had a storied and bloody history. An incident occurred here more than 500 years ago that changed the course of Italian history, and quite possibly the history of Christianity and the Western world as we know it. It was here that 800 people were decapitated, one after the other, atop a hill that was called the Hill of Minerva.

In 1453, the capital of the Byzantine Empire, Constantinople, was overrun by an army of 250,000 Ottoman troops who were under the command of Sultan Mehmet II, later called el-Fatih (the Conqueror) because of his military exploits. Having seized this Christian city, he used it as a launching point for military strikes against various other nations, intending to expand his domains and to spread Islam. His progress was not without setbacks. He met with several defeats, including being pushed out of Belgrade by Hungarians and being halted by Stephen the Great of Moldavia in 1475 at the Battle of Vaslui, but even these setbacks did not halt Mehmet's progress. Even through defeat, he managed to move his conquering army into increasingly advantageous positions from which to strike out at other forces. After losing the battle to Stephen the Great, he fortified his position, strengthened his army, and then launched another attack a year later, which he easily won.

He then decided to push his way through the Wallachian mountains but was stopped by a merciless prince who has since become the subject of historical documentaries, bloody legends and horror stories: an individual known as Vlad the Impaler, or Vlad Tepes (1431–1476), better known as Vlad Dracul, who became the protagonist of Bram Stoker's famous novel, *Dracula* (1897). This in turn led to a veritable vampire craze throughout the world, with other novels, movies and even television shows about vampires. Vlad was feared because of his treatment of defeated armies. He is known to have enjoyed torturing individuals, and there are historical stories that depict him as skinning, boiling, and even eating his victims or feeding their flesh to his victims' friends and relatives. When the offense was not so severe as to require death, he meted out other forms of grotesque torture. For example, he would skin people's feet, cover them with salt, and then permit goats to lick off the salt. He also put the heads of defeated soldiers on pikes, and he impaled a number of individuals. This practice eventually led to him being called the Impaler. Figures of the number of his victims stretch from 40,000 to 100,000 total and no one knows how many people for sure that he killed, but it will suffice to say that he was known as and continues to be spoken about today as a ruthless and evil person who left a trail of bloody victims in his wake.

In 1462, Vlad disguised himself as a Turkish soldier and infiltrated the camps of the Ottoman forces. He killed countless people and even wrote about the massacre in a letter to Corvinus:

> I have killed men and women, old and young, who lived at Oblucitza and Novoselo, where the Danube flows into the sea, up to Rahova, which is located near Chilia, from the lower Danube up to such places as Samovit and Ghighen. We killed 23,884 Turks and Bulgars without counting those whom we burned in homes or whose heads were not cut by our soldiers.... Thus your highness must know that I have broken the peace with him [Tepes, 1462].

This attack spurred the hatred of Mehmet, who raised a force approximately two times the size of Vlad's own forces and then advanced upon Wallachia. They overpowered the Wallachian forces and occupied the city of Targoviste. Vlad continually launched small attacks, including the infamous "night attack," in which 15,000 Ottoman troops were killed. Eventually, Mehmet and his armies were pushed completely out of the Balkans and el-Fatih ruminated over the defeat. He set his sights on a new prize: Rome. He wished to convert the reigning pope and bishops to Islam, thus marking the end of Christianity in Europe. He planned to use St. Peter's basilica as a stable for the Ottoman cavalry (Bunson, n.d.).

Led by the general Pasha Ahmed, a force of 90 galleys, 15 galleasses and 48 galliots, carrying in total more than 18,000 warriors, headed toward the port city of Brindisi, in Puglia. The weather changed, however, and they landed 50 miles south, in Otranto instead, where there were only about 400 soldiers garrisoned to protect the city. Once the fleet was spotted, messengers were sent north to warn others and to request backup, and the town, lacking any real means of defense, awaited the decision of their attackers.

At the time this attack took place, the treatment of defeated citizens was harsh. Women and children could expect to be slaughtered or taken as slaves. However, the Ottoman troops at Otranto were especially generous. Provided that the town surrendered, everyone would be spared and allowed to live. The town itself would be taken. The inhabitants of Otranto likely shocked the Ottoman troops when they refused to surrender and then barricaded themselves behind city walls. The 18,000 troops laid siege, and it took them almost two full weeks before the walls were brought down. They killed resisting defenders and made their way to the town cathedral, where many people were praying for assistance, along with the archbishop Stephen Pendinelli. Unfortunately, no one heard their prayers. The attackers commanded the archbishop to rid himself of Christian symbols and to embrace Islam. He refused and was beheaded.

Having made the Ottoman forces work for two weeks to bring down the city walls, the citizens were forced to pay the price for their refusal to surrender. All men over the age of 50 were killed, and women and children under the age of 15 were taken away as slaves. The general Pasha Ahmed ordered that all of the other men of the town be brought before him. There he stated that if they renounced the Christian God and converted to Islam, they would be saved and permitted to live. But if they refused, they would be killed.

A tailor named Antonio Primaldi[1] spoke to the crowd: "My brothers, until today we have fought in defense of our country, to save our lives, and for our lords. Now it is time that we fight to save our souls for our Lord, so that having died on the cross for us, it is good that we should die for him, standing firm and constant in the faith, and with this earthly deed we shall win eternal life and the glory of martyrs" (Quoted in Bunson, n.d.). He stirred up the crowd with this impassioned speech, and Pasha Ahmed pronounced their sentence: death. The next day the men were all bound together and led up to the top of the Hill of Minerva. Starting with the tailor Antonio Primaldi, who is thought of as a hero in modern Italy, they were one-by-one asked to convert to Islam. All that refused were beheaded,[2] and all of them, one at a time, refused to convert, believing with all their heart that a martyr's death would make them saints — that it would take them to God.

At the end of the day, all 800 of them having been beheaded, the attacking troops turned their attention north, toward Rome. However, the two weeks in which the Otranto citizens held out was enough time for a large force to be amassed with which to drive out the Ottoman armies. After various battles, the Ottoman troops were defeated and killed. Without the bravery displayed by the citizens of Otranto, it is unlikely that Pasha Ahmed and his soldiers would have been defeated. The citizens of Otranto were thought of as heroes, and the martyrs who met their ends on the Hill of Minerva would be forever remembered and honored. Their remains were gathered together, placed in reliquaries and put in a chapel next to the cathedral. The hill was renamed the Hill of Martyrs. Some of the relics were sent to other churches and cathedrals, and today in Otranto the skulls are arranged artistically behind glass along the interior walls of the cathedral.

Pope John Paul II visited Otranto in 1980, 500 years after the beheadings, and he declared that they were indeed killed out of "hatred of the faith." This declaration officially made them martyrs and, hence, saints. (Before this statement was made, they were not official martyrs as sanctioned by the Church. It took 500 years for them to be officially recognized.) He stated: "Many confessors and disciples of Christ have passed through this test in the course of history. The martyrs of Otranto passed through it 500 years ago. The martyrs of this century have passed and are passing through it today, martyrs who are unappreciated, otherwise little known and who are found in places far away from us" (Bunson, n.d.).

The aptly named Chapel of the Dead is located at the Church of Santa Maria della Grazia in Comiso, Sicily. Erected in 1693, it contains the mummified remains of 50 individuals. All of the bodies are located in niches above the entrance and in the walls of the church, and they are all positioned so that they are peering inward. Their faces are all pointed toward the center of the church. All of the bodies are male, and they are all affiliated with the Capuchin friars. Some of them were clerics, while others were laymen. Twenty of them have labels that tell visitors who they were and when they died. All of the bodies on display that have labels died between 1742 and 1838. It is probable that the unlabeled mummies are much older, some of them having likely died as early as 1693, when the church was first built (Ascenzi, 1998). All of the mummies are dressed as they would have been dressed in life, and all of them, save one, are dressed in monastic garb. The one odd body is dressed in common 18th-century clothing. The bodies were redressed after they had been preserved. To facilitate this process, the monks' robes were all cut along the back. Although they were redressed after having been mummified, it is unknown if any deliberate action was taken in order to facilitate the preservation of the bodies.

Ascenzi, Bianco, Fornaciari and Rodriguez Martin (1998) wrote: "Examination of the bodies revealed that the mummies were natural, in the sense that none had been submitted to any type of treatment, neither evisceration nor craniotomy. Natural mummification of the bodies was probably made possible by the hot, dry climate of Comiso, which is at the same latitude as Tunis" (p. 270).

This type of natural mummification is very common in Italy, and there are many bodies that are on display not just in underground crypts, catacombs, and tombs but also in aboveground churches that display the characteristics that accompany this type of mummification. Occurring frequently in environments that are extremely dry and either hot or cold (temperatures that both discourage the growth of bacteria), bodies become extremely rigid. The skin turns brown in color and takes on a texture like parchment. The bodies of many saints that have been translated to coffins in churches display such characteristics.

13

Mummies of Ferentillo and San Domenico Maggiore; Papal Funerals

Ferentillo is a small town in Umbria located approximately 19 miles southwest of Spoleto and 11 miles northeast of Terni. It is known for its many hiking trails and for being located near the largest waterfall in Europe, the Cascata delle Marmore. There are also castle ruins nearby. Ferentillo is virtually unknown to tourists, but it has an interesting yet unusual display of mummified bodies. Throughout most of the country, the mummies on display in churches and cathedrals, and the mummies found in underground crypts and catacombs, are the remains of religious individuals — either high-ranking members of the Roman Catholic Church or the preserved bodies of martyrs or other saints. Ferentillo has a number of bodies, however, that do not fit this general profile.

Some of the naturally mummified bodies on display in Italy were only discovered after the Napoleonic Edict of Saint-Cloud, enacted in 1804, which disallowed burials in churches and in populated areas for health reasons. After this edict was put into place, some previously buried bodies were unearthed in order to be reinterred elsewhere. Excavators were shocked

The mountainous town of Ferentillo, in southern Umbria, Italy. The ruins of several castles can be seen on the mountaintops.

to discover that many bodies, in various locales, had mummified. They expected to unearth bones alone, but instead, they exposed bodies that were covered with skin — bodies that still had hair, fingernails and even eyelashes in some cases. In some parts of Italy, the bodies were preserved as a result of burial without a casket in volcanic soil. In other cases, though, the presence of certain types of bacteria and fungi actually assisted in preserving the remains. These fungi halted decay and preserved the bodies.

There is a church in Ferentillo called La Chiesa di San Stefano (the Church of Saint Stephen) that was built in the 16th century over the ruins of an earlier church. The lower ruins were used as makeshift catacombs; bodies were placed there below the upper church. When the edict was passed down that forbade such burials, however, the bodies were unearthed. When they were exposed, it was found that they had all been strangely preserved. After a number of scientific tests, it was determined that a fungus in the soil halted decay and led to mummification. Today, the bodies are behind glass at the same location and it has been turned into a museum of sorts.

Visitors can go beneath the upper church and see the original church that was first built in the 13th century. There are even some frescoes on the walls. The bodies that are located behind glass in this church, however, are unlike the bodies found in most churches and cathedrals in Italy, as they are not the remains of religious personages alone. There are some priests whose bodies are on display, but with the priests are a number of outsiders, including some older people who likely died of natural causes. Along with them are the mummified bodies of some children and the preserved remains of a mother and her child. But there are even stranger things on display in this church.

Tourists travel to Ferentillo in order to see the strangely preserved bodies, located at the Church of St. Stephen.

In the sixteenth century, the Church of St. Stephen was built over the ruins of an earlier church. The original frescoes, dating to the thirteenth century, are still visible in the crypt (Ferentillo, Italy).

In one case are the preserved bodies of two Chinese tourists, their skin like parchment. They were husband and wife, and the husband had died of the plague while the two of them were on vacation. The wife took his dead body to the entrance of the church, and there she died while praying beside his remains. Besides the Chinese couple is a man who was killed while in a church belltower. Apparently, the bell began ringing and he was struck and killed by it. There is clearly damage caused by the bell that can still be seen on his remains today. Visitors will see two men next to this individual. One of them was a lawyer who was murdered and then buried beneath the church. Right next to his mummified remains is the body of his murderer, who was likewise buried at the same location in order to ease his transition to heavenly realms in the afterlife.

Many individuals wished to be buried in locations that had been deemed holy and spiritual. It was thought that saints and priests who might have been buried nearby would linger between this realm and the next in order to assist newly departed souls in finding their way to heaven. One must wonder, however, how the murderer's victim would feel about his body remaining for centuries next to the person who killed him. It is an unusual display of human remains that indicates that there is a fascination with death and (the absence of) decay throughout all of Italy.

The Basilica of San Domenico Maggiore, built in the 14th century, is located in Naples. It contains a number of mummies that were embalmed, including ten Aragonese princes and other nobles who died in the 15th and 16th centuries. Among the embalmed individuals located within are King Alfonso I (d. 1458), King Ferrante I (d. 1494), King Ferrante II (d. 1496), and Queen Giovanna IV (d. 1518). It also contains the preserved bodies of other

Some of the mummies that are found at the Church of St. Stephen, in Ferentillo.

This wall of skulls is also found in Ferentillo, Italy, at the Church of St. Stephen. Some of them are just bone, while others have been strangely preserved.

famous individuals, including Ferdinando d'Avalos (1489–1525), a general in the Spanish army who participated in the Great Italian Wars, also known as the Habsburg-Valois Wars. All of the corpses have been mummified and they are all generally well preserved. As an example of the type of treatment performed on the bodies, the body of Pietro of Aragon, who died in the 16th century, is found in a large sarcophagus. His remains were treated, redressed in rich clothing that he would have worn in life, and then placed within a wooden coffin that was lowered into the sarcophagus. Plants like boxwood, laurel and rosemary covered the body, and under his body was a layer of small limestones. This layer was to assist in the drainage of cadaveric fluids.

Of the bodies located at the church, almost half of them have been embalmed. Only 12 have not been treated in any obvious way. Fornaciari (1998) wrote: "The majority of them had been embalmed, which is certainly not surprising, considering the high social class of the individuals in San Domenico" (p. 272). Mummification was a common practice among the wealthy and important, including members of the Church, as high-ranking members were often embalmed prior to burial.

The preservation of the body is a practice that has not dissipated throughout the years, and it is important to Catholics today. The bodies of commoners are often preserved for Christian ceremonies like wakes, and the bodies of important personages in the Church are preserved more fully for other lavish celebrations. When popes die, for example, the bodies are preserved and prepared so that they can be viewed by a multitude of believers who look upon popes as something more than men, as vicars of Christ perhaps. They are dressed in crimson papal robes and the faces are covered with miters, the tall hats that are worn by bishops. Traditionally, popes are buried in three distinct caskets. First, they are dressed in papal robes and placed in cypress coffins along with bags of copper, silver and gold that correspond to the number of years that they served as popes. Then, the inner coffins are tied with silk ribbons and placed into lead caskets. These caskets are engraved with the names and dates of the popes and then soldered shut. Finally, the lead caskets are placed into larger caskets made of elm, a rare and expensive wood in Rome, and then nailed shut with golden nails.

The use of three distinct caskets, in conjunction with preparing the bodies to lie in state (on display) for many days after their decease, suggests that the preservation of the bodies is an objective of the Church. In addition, the elaborate ceremony and the expensive metals used in papal burials are traditions that cannot be attributed to the known teachings of Jesus. However, they can be compared to the elaborate burial rituals of kings and queens in some ancient societies, such as royal burials in ancient Egypt.

Although modern popes are laid to rest in the Vatican underground tombs of St. Peter's, a church called Santa Maria Maggiore in Rome also houses the remains of a number of popes, including Pope Clement VIII, Pope Clement IX, Pope Nicholas IV, Pope Pius V, and Pope Sixtus V. The church also contains the relics of Saint Jerome (c. 347–420), who is recognized by the Church as the patron saint of librarians, writers and translators. He wrote a number of texts that are considered extremely important in Catholicism today, and interestingly, while he was in Rome, he spent a great amount of time in the catacombs honoring the martyrs whose relics were therein enshrined. He wrote:

> Often I would find myself entering those crypts, deep dug in the earth, with their walls on either side lined with the bodies of the dead, where everything was so dark that almost it

The exterior of San Domenico Maggiore. There are many bodies buried in this church, although none of them are viewable (Naples, Italy).

seemed as though the Psalmist's words were fulfilled: Let them go down quick into Hell. Here and there the light, not entering in through windows, but filtering down from above through shafts, relieved the horror of the darkness. But again, as soon as you found yourself cautiously moving forward, the black night closed around and there came to my mind the line of Vergil, "Horror ubique animos, simul ipsa silentia terrent" [Horror on every side, and even the silence is terrible]. [Commentarius in Ezzechielem 40:5].

The importance of the martyrs, their bodies and their relics cannot be overestimated. They were a source of inspiration to many Christians throughout the years. Today, the cult of the martyrs has been overtaken by the still extant cult of the saints. The preserved bodies of many individuals who were named saints are on display in various churches and cathedrals throughout Italy, and bone fragments and other body parts that received relic status from the Church are similarly displayed.[1]

14

Polytheistic Elements of the Faith

There are many bodies on display at holy locations throughout the world. In Italy, at least one is found in just about every church and cathedral. These are not just any bodies, however, but the bodies of saints, beati, or venerables. It is not permitted for just any person deemed holy to be enshrined in a church or represented by statues or paintings. The Church has to approve such people. They must be given a title of either saint or Blessed in order to be venerated. César Augusto dos Santos, a Brazilian Jesuit from São Paulo, began the cause for canonization for José Anchieta (1553–1597). When asked why he had been putting so much effort and money into the cause for the past several years, he responded, "The canonization is part of a broader work of evangelisation. I'm not only spreading Anchieta's life and teachings, but also the values of our Christian faith" (Society of Jesus, n.d.). In this sense, since the purpose of canonization has to do with spreading the faith, the process is both political and spiritual. Anchieta was declared a Blessed by Pope John Paul II in 1980, but that is not sufficient for Santos. He explained the difference between a saint and a Blessed: "The difference between a blessed and a saint is that the first can only be honored only [sic] in certain regions, while the latter is allowed to be venerated all over the world" (Society of Jesus, n.d.).

If the Church declares someone a saint, it is okay for people everywhere to venerate him or her. The title Blessed only permits people to venerate the holy figure locally. If the person is not given such titles, however, he or she cannot be venerated at all. The Church does not extend permission to its members to venerate unapproved people. In this way, the Church regulates who is honored by the populace. Once it declares certain individuals saints, then congregations are able to put up statues or other artwork representing these saints. They are also encouraged to procure pieces of the saints' bodies or secondary relics in order to bless the churches in which they are enshrined. Having pieces of the bodies in holy locations is important for Catholics. Even more valuable is having entire bodies there on display. This practice might seem morbid to outsiders, who might wonder why Christians have such an obsession with corpses. Some might say that it is not an obsession with the dead but with the saints who once inhabited the bodies. However, dead bodies are on display everywhere in Italy, the birthplace of the Roman Catholic faith.

It is undeniable that there is at least a fascination with the dead in Italian culture, which has been heavily infiltrated by the Roman Catholic faith. Historically, there were many who converted to Christianity for safety reasons, as non-believers were attacked or even killed by Christians at different time periods. Once Christianity took hold and was accepted by the governing parties, however, the faith grew to dominate Italian culture.

Beliefs were promulgated to force allegiance. For example, the Church told its followers that a person could not get to heaven without its intervention. In other words, the intercession of the Church was necessary for a person to be close to God. Such claims were not taken lightly by credulous followers, and so they did what the Church told them to do. The influence of the Church upon Italian culture and society has been pervasive, and it has lasted for so long that it is difficult for some Catholics to even consider the existence of their faith without the Church. Although the Church is an organization of politically inspired men, many Catholics believe what they have been told for years: that these men know the will of God and through their intercession sins will be forgiven. In an interview, one Catholic was asked: "Would your religious beliefs change if the Church ceased to exist?" His response was, "I don't know."[1]

This answer points to an underlying phenomenon that must be considered herein, that the Church has told its followers what to do for so long that they would not know what to do if the Church was eliminated. For those who believe that intercession by the Church is necessary in order to go to heaven, too, the thought of the Church's absence must be terrifying. Since the Church has influenced the Italian culture and its followers in other parts of the world so much, it is difficult for some people to step back and critically analyze the Church's beliefs, practices, and teachings. It is also difficult for people to critically consider from where the teachings of the Church originated. It is probable that the burial practice of popes, for example, did not originate in the teachings of Jesus as recorded in historical documents. If not, from where did it originate? In addition, the practice of mummification is commonplace in Christianity, and members of the clergy are still embalmed today. However, there is nothing in historical Christian literature that would support or encourage the custom the way it is performed today. So where did the practice come from?

Ascenzi and Bianco (1998) wrote that "mummification was never a Roman custom" (p. 263). Mummification is a Christian custom. Although the procedures and reasons behind it were likely adopted from earlier religious or cultural traditions, mummification is definitely a Christian custom (Mojsov, 2005). In order to explore this idea, it is important to take a look at the mummies of saints, beati and venerables that are on display in churches and cathedrals, bodies that continue to be revered by Catholics in Italy and abroad. They visit the remains of such individuals and pray before their corpses. This fascination with the dead, when considering the preserved bodies of saints becomes something more. It becomes a worship of the dead and in this respect, Catholicism no longer seems like an exclusively monotheistic faith.

Old religions that had multiple deities were thought of as polytheistic faiths. Looking at the pantheon of Greek and Roman gods, there were a multitude of different deities, and followers prayed to many of them for diverse reasons. They prayed to Hera, Athena, Poseidon, Apollo, Artemis, Aphrodite, Hephaestus, Demeter, Hestia, Ares, Hades, and Dionysus, among other deities, but above and beyond all of these deities was Zeus, the King of Men and Gods, whose counterparts in Greek and Etruscan faiths were Jupiter and Tinia, respectively. Various gods were worshipped more frequently in diverse locales, so the chief deity differed from city to city and from town to town. However, a number of philosophical schools emerged that questioned the nature of the gods and their relationship to each other and to mortals. Different schools of thought posited that there was a singular entity that embraced all: an all-pervasive deity that could be found in all things. The ancient Egyptians, for example, "did not perceive a discrepancy between the great god who was seemingly one and the myriad of gods. Ultimately, all gods were reflections of the same godly essence that was non-definable and mystical" (Mojsov, 2005, p. 33). In Catholicism, it is thought that each saint has divine attributes that are imitations of the virtues and perfections of the Godman, Jesus Christ (Hoever, 1955).

These polytheistic examples sound like Catholicism, if you disregard the labels used to describe the deities. For example, if the gods under Zeus were called saints and not gods, the Greek and Roman religion would be very similar to Catholicism today. This is because the majority of Catholics pray not to Jesus, but to tutelary deities: saints, who all serve God in heaven. Each town in Italy, in most of Europe in fact, has its own tutelary deity as well, so different locales tend to pray to different saints for intervention. In Catholicism, these particular deities are known as patron saints. A famous one is St. Patrick, the patron saint of Ireland, but many towns and cities in Europe also have patron saints. Italy, in particular, is loaded with different patron saints, all of whom are called upon to protect various towns or regions.

Other than the Greek and Roman traditions, there are other so-called polytheistic religions that are worth taking a look at before moving ahead. Shinto, the indigenous religion of Japan, is a religion that has a multitude of deities, possibly millions. This is in part due to its nature as an animistic faith, in which followers recognize the presence of spirits in all things. They recognize that all things in nature have a spiritual essence, including trees,

Although Shinto, the native religion of Japan, is very different from Catholicism, there are some similarities. This gate, or torii, is what marks a sacred space (Miyajima, Japan).

grasses, and even certain rocks and stones. All is part of creation. Everything was created by God, so everything has this divine nature in one form or another. Among the Shinto deities described in mythological accounts of the beginning of creation, two deities, Izanagi (the male) and Izanami (the female), brought all things into being. They formed the world as we know it from the floating bridge of heaven, and it was through their intercourse, the mingling of opposites, that all living things were created. They also created all of the gods, and even in Shinto there is a chief deity: Amaterasu, the sun goddess.

The Shinto pantheon is not unique, but it is interesting to consider the general outline of the faith when considering unrelated religions like Catholic Christianity. There is still an all-pervasive spiritual essence that joins all things, and it was the interplay of opposites that spurred creation. Many deities were created, followed by a variety of other creatures and human beings. Everything stemmed from the same source. There are spirits found in everything, and yet there is still a chief deity, Amaterasu. Even she was created by a supreme pair of gods, though. This again is not distant from a general notion found in Christianity in Italy. Jesus was not God, although he is perceived as having the same essence of God by followers. He was the son of God, and God is the father. Even more interesting considerations are brought to light when we add the Holy Spirit to this mix, forming what is known as the Holy Trinity. There is God the father, Jesus the son, and a spiritual essence that joins them together and pervades all things.

If names and titles are stripped away, even seemingly dissimilar religions like Shinto and Catholicism are similar in their core structure. Noah Levine (2004) quoted his father in the preface to his book *Dharma Punx*: "That which is true is found in all spiritual and religious traditions. No one has the corner on the Truth." All religious traditions aim to explain and to understand things that by nature cannot be completely understood or explained. There are other religions, too, that have the same outline: They are often considered polytheistic religions, but there is a supreme deity that pervades all things, just like in Catholicism. Such religions include Hinduism, which has a multitude of different deities but has something greater: "Vishnu is the all-pervader in whom abide all creatures" (Kim, 1973, p. 7). The structure of Mahayana Buddhism is also similar to the previously discussed traditions, and there is another figure that is introduced in this faith: the Bodhisattva. In order to more easily understand the true nature of Catholic faith, it is useful to take a look at the structure of Mahayanist religious beliefs, as it is by looking at the culture of others that we can more accurately view our own.

There are many Buddhas, enlightened ones, but among the Buddhas there is one known (in Sanskrit) as Mahavairochana Buddha, also known as the Cosmic Buddha. His nature is thought to pervade all things and to encompass all of the other Buddhas. This is the divine essence that can be found everywhere. Beneath Mahavairochana and the other Buddhas are creatures known as Bodhisattvas, universal saviors. They were humans, on the path to Buddhahood, complete awakening, but they decided to postpone their complete enlightenment in order to assist other creatures. In order to become a Buddha, one must extinguish all desires. He or she must sever all attachments, so that a complete awakening is possible. This includes any attachment that one might feel toward others and the potential sadness that one might feel when he or she sees someone else suffering. The Bodhisattva wishes to help ease the suffering of others, so he or she delays becoming a Buddha. This concept is similar to the idea of the Catholic saint.

There are distinct differences between all of the religious beliefs herein presented, but they have been mentioned in order to put the true nature of Catholic Christianity into the correct perspective. The idea of the Bodhisattva is particularly interesting when we delve into the histories of both faiths. At their onset, Buddhism and Christianity were very similar. Over time they grew apart, but at the beginning they were alike. Some concepts that many would describe as being Buddhist are actually found in Christian gospels, most notably the Gospel of St. Thomas. Even more interesting is the fact that this particular text is one of the few that were actually written in Aramaic, the language that the historical Jesus would have spoken.[2]

An important connection for this particular study is that found between Christian and Egyptian religious traditions. At the beginning, there were many gods and goddesses who were worshipped by people. Ra, the sun god, was considered the chief deity, but different gods began to be more and more popular in different towns and cities. Eventually, Osiris emerged as a supreme deity, and when this happened the Egyptian religion became a monotheistic faith (Mojsov, 2005). There are many parallels between the cult of Osiris and Christian traditions that will be explored more fully later, but for now it should be considered that even the Egyptian religion, which was one of the world's earliest monotheistic religions, has its roots in polytheistic ideas.

Linguistic conventions notwithstanding, the Roman Catholic faith cannot be viewed as a purely monotheistic religion.[3] The existence of the cult of the saints, in particular, makes the religion polytheistic (Brown, 1981). There is a supreme deity, God, who is thought to be the creator of all things. Then there is Jesus, his son, who has divine attributes but is not actually God. Then there are archangels: generals on the battlefield of heaven who will eventually direct angels during the great battle that will (allegedly) ensue at the end of time. Following the angels are saints, holy individuals who are thought to function as intermediaries between Jesus, God and humankind.[4] When something goes wrong in the lives of believers, they do not necessarily rush to the top in order to pray to God or to Jesus. In fact, the majority of Catholics do not pray to God. This is likely because his true nature is unknown and believers therefore cannot easily relate to him. Rather than pray to God, some of them pray to his son. However, the majority of Italian Catholics do not pray directly to Jesus either. Instead, they pray to saints.

Paolo Rossi, postulator general of the Capuchins, said that at the second Vatican Council "they recognized that devotion to the saints had taken the place of devotion to Christ, the central mystery to our faith. Even now, in Italy, you notice that when people go to church they no longer go to the Blessed Sacrament and genuflect, but kneel in front of a statue of a saint. You see this and you realize that we are losing the concept of who is who" (Woodward, 1996, p. 189).

Catholic Christianity today is different from early Christianity, and followers generally adhere to the teachings of the Church in Rome instead of the teachings of Jesus of Nazareth, meaning that if one teaching contradicted the other, Catholics would generally follow the Church. There are many practices that the Church demands that definitely cannot be found within the historical teachings of Jesus. One individual was interviewed about his religious beliefs and about how some of the elements of his faith contradicted the historical evidence and the recorded teachings of Jesus. His reply was, "Why would I care about early Christianity?" He meant that the early faith was not directly relevent to him today since he lived in a different era. Some outsiders would think that Christians generally choose to follow the teachings of Jesus, but this is not necessarily the case. Roman Catholics follow first and foremost the instructions of the extremely wealthy religious organization the Roman Catholic Church. Therefore, those who truly follow the teachings of Jesus as recorded in historical documents could have a much different faith than those who follow the teachings of the Church. Religious beliefs and rituals change over time as well, despite how they were historically. Modern Catholicism is not a monotheistic faith in which believers worship God alone. They have a multitude of lesser deities — saints, martyrs, angels and archangels who can perform miracles and grant favors to believers.

They also think that their belief alone can be enough to save them from everlasting torment, as there is a rather dangerous element of the faith that states that all believers can access heaven, but non-believers cannot. According to Roman Catholic belief (at the time this is being written), people who are not Christian, no matter what they might do in life, cannot go to heaven. According to this belief, the kindest person in the world cannot get to heaven without the intervention of the Church, so if a person grew up in the wilderness and did nothing but kind things, he or she still could not go to heaven because there was no intervention by the Church.

This teaching is convenient for an organization that desires wealth and political aggrandizement, but it cannot be found in the historical documentation of Jesus. It is a teaching perpetrated by the Church that was quite possibly put into place for political reasons. This is dangerous because unquestioning followers might think about the teachings of the Church as a whole and realize that any non-believer is actually going to hell. Eventually, when the end of time arises, the non-believers will be combatants in the great battle between heaven and hell, fighting on the side of Satan. Uneducated Christians who believe this teaching 100 percent could potentially do immoral things to such people because of this belief. Modern Roman Catholics follow the teachings of Jesus only through the Church. They do not interpret the teachings of Jesus for themselves. They embrace the teachings of the Church, as influenced by the teachings of Jesus. This is a major difference, and it must be understood.

Even the Church, though, cannot completely control its flock. The Vatican has recognized the problems inherent with the worship of holy people by its followers, and this is quite possibly why the saint-making process was put into place. The Church specifically told people that no one was to be worshipped as a saint unless he or she was specifically approved by the organization.[5] In this way, the Church could control who the general public honored and could therefore curb potential cults before they got out of hand. Some individuals who normally would have been deemed saints were denied sainthood only because their following was too large (Woodward, 1996). In this way, the Church regulates devotion and is more able to control its flock.

The saint is an enigmatic figure in a semi-monotheistic religion like Catholicism. Sainthood is not unique to Christianity. There are other similar figures in various religious traditions, such as the Buddhist Bodhisattva, which has already been briefly discussed. In addition, there are similar figures in Judaism, and it can be argued that the cult of saints has origins in this tradition, where admiration for holy individuals and martyrs extended far into death (Geary, 1978). The equivalent of the Catholic saint can also be found in Islam, which honors the *awliyā' Allāh*, who are considered to be individuals close to God, like the Catholic saints (Brown, 1981). However, the Catholic saint is unique in that it is the Church, and not the people, that determines who is and who is not a saint and the faithful rarely question the decision. In order to properly examine the practice of preserving saints and displaying them in churches and in cathedrals, it is necessary to first determine what it means to be a Christian saint and what differentiates a saint from beati and venerables.

III. Saints and Relics

Any relic of the dead is precious, if they were valued living. — Emily Brontë, *Wuthering Heights*

15

The Enigmatic Catholic Saint

The Catholic saint is one of the most enigmatic and puzzling of figures, and although the saint is revered by Catholics, many of them do not know what the term means.[1] There are some who might think that a saint is simply defined as a holy and pious individual, but this is not the case.

Consider Mother Teresa (1910–1997), for example, possibly one of the most respected and kindest people to have ever lived. Her given name was Agnes Gonxha Bojaxhiu, and she was born in Skpoje, Macedonia, of Albanian descent. She felt a calling to the spiritual life at the age of 12 and decided at an early age to devote her life to the teachings of Jesus. When she was 18 years of age she left her parents' home and joined a convent called the Sisters of Loreto, which often did charitable work in India. It was in India, in 1931, that she took her initial vows as a nun. For the next 17 years she taught at a school there, but the sight of poor and unfortunate people on the streets in Calcutta consumed her, and she decided to devote her life to caring for them.

She did not desire the wealth and luxurious lifestyle that many Catholic priests enjoyed. Instead, she wished to live with the poorest of the poor in India and to devote all of her time and energy to making them as comfortable as possible. In the opinion of many, she is one of the holiest people to have ever lived. Many would call her a true saint. However, from a Roman Catholic perspective, they would be wrong. Mother Teresa is not a saint. Nor (at the time this is being written) is she eligible to become a saint, because the title of sainthood is not bestowed upon individuals for their piety and kind deeds alone. In fact, kindness is not necessarily a requirement for canonization, and there have been individuals canonized in the past who have been described as arrogant and even downright mean.

Saint-making is an elaborate and expensive process that lasts for years and has many requirements. There are lengthy, specialized documents that have to be created about the life of the candidate. Then these documents have to be studied. After this stage, testimony must be heard and the candidate also has to be credited with a specific number of miracles in order for canonization to occur. Mother Teresa does not have the required number of miracles to be made a saint.

Sometimes, individuals are declared saints who were not kind. When this occurs it often spurs controversy. One of the most controversial processes is likely the canonization of Opus Dei founder Josemaria Escrivá de Balaguer. After the reforms put into place regarding the saint-making process by Vatican Council II, which began in 1962, a *positio* must be prepared for any individual who is to be considered for canonization. A positio is a lengthy biography of the candidate, often more than 1,000 pages in length. It is also very expensive to print, as the Vatican only uses one specific printing company for all of its documents. "It can cost $20,000 or more to print a positio of 1,500 pages, and thus they are seldom printed in runs of more than 150 copies" (Woodward, 1996, p. 221). This positio is given to a number of individuals involved in the saint-making process who read the extensive biography of the individual and then decide whether or not the candidate is a model that other Catholics should follow.

The positio of Josemaria Escrivá de Balaguer was an enormous volume of 6,000 pages, but according to people who knew him and worked with him, it did not paint an accurate picture. It was as though anything bad or questionable that the individual may have done in his life had been edited out, revealing only the biography of a likely saint. Besides the positio, every cause also includes testimony from individuals who knew the candidate. However, the Church can decide from whom they wish to hear testimony. In Escrivá's case, only one individual was allowed to testify on his behalf. Testimonies from numerous other individuals who worked closely with him, testimonies that abounded with examples of vanity and anger, were not permitted. "The examples they gave of vanity, venality, temper tantrums, harshness toward subordinates, and criticism of popes and other churchmen were hardly the characteristics one expects to find in a Christian saint. But their testimony was not allowed to be heard" (Woodward, 1996, pp. 10–11).

In Escrivá's canonization process, two of nine judges dissented, but their votes were ignored. For what many individuals believe were political motives alone, Pope John Paul II declared Escrivá a Blessed in 1992, and he was made a saint in 2002. The pope's statement puzzled some and sparked outcry in others, but the new leaders of Opus Dei used one of the core beliefs of Roman Catholicism to silence complainers — papal infallibility. Catholics believe that the pope cannot make errors. Before he is pope, he is able to err, but once the title of pope is bestowed upon him, he is no longer capable of making errors — he is infallible. (Interestingly, in order to "maintain the impression that Popes cannot err, Popes deceive — as if distorting the truth in the present were not a worse thing than mistaking it in the past" (Wills, 2001, p. 14). The idea that the pope cannot make errors has been propagated for centuries, and it still continues to be maintained.) Since it was the pope himself who declared Escrivá a saint, he has to be a saint (according to Catholic beliefs). This left many Catholics confused and torn between beliefs: that of papal infallibility and that of the unworthiness of Escrivá. However, such confusion can be understood, because the entire process of saint making itself is confusing.

The process of saint making is one of the most puzzling of religious practices, as the process is elaborate, more political than spiritual, and exceedingly expensive. Sometimes, it can cost as much as $500,000 to make a saint. Considering that this money could be used to care for the poor and needy, it makes sense that most kind and humble individuals would probably not want to be saints; they would likely prefer that the money be used for more noble purposes, such as providing food, clothing, or housing to the less fortunate.

There have been some individuals who had specifically asked not to be canonized after their deaths for this reason. However, in some cases their requests were ignored by the Church, which collected money and began the process of canonization anyway, against the wishes of the potential saints. Dorothy Day (1897–1980) was one such example. From Brooklyn, New York, her family moved to the South Side of Chicago when she was just nine years old. This was an extremely poor area, and the sight of the homeless and poor made a strong impression on her. It was there that she became attracted to Catholicism. While she was a university student, she did not spend much time on her studies, preferring to read radical literature instead. After a couple of years she dropped out of school and moved to New York, where she worked as a reporter for *The Call*, a socialist newspaper. Later she wrote for *The Masses*. The editors and writers of this magazine opposed killing, and they therefore opposed the involvement of the United States in World War I. She worked to educate people about the evil inherent in war and to rectify other societal issues that she felt needed attention. She was arrested and imprisoned in 1917 for protesting for women's rights in front of the White House, after which she was taken to a workhouse with the other involved women. Later, they were all freed by presidential order after they had engaged in a hunger strike.

After her release, she worked as a writer for various socialist publications. At this time, she married a reporter and became pregnant. However, she did not have the child. She had an abortion instead. This event saddened her, and it was the subject of her novel *The Eleventh Virgin*. She later wrote about the sadness and loneliness that she felt after the abortion in her autobiography, *The Long Loneliness*. This sadness may have influenced her decision to become increasingly more religiously oriented. She also knew that there were many social injustices in the United States, and she knew how difficult it was to change the existing structures through protesting, writing, and educating the masses. Perhaps this difficulty also provided the impetus for her to turn to religion.

She started attending church in New York, and when she moved around to places like Chicago and then New Orleans she continued going to services. In 1924, she moved back to New York, where she met and married a man named Forster Batterham. She became pregnant and gave birth to a daughter named Tamar Theresa Day on March 3, 1927. Dorothy did not want her daughter to follow in her own footsteps, so she decided to have her baptized as a Catholic. She wrote, "I did not want my daughter to flounder as I had often floundered. I wanted to believe, and I wanted my child to believe, and if belonging to a Church would give her so inestimable a grace as faith in God, and the companionable love of the saints, then the thing to do was to have her baptized a Catholic" (Forest, n.d.). It seems that Dorothy turned to Catholicism only because that was what was around and if she had been surrounded by a different faith she likely would have turned to that one just as easily. She liked the hint of the spiritual but did not necessarily like the practices of the Church. In fact, she angered some members of the Church because of her writings, as she openly questioned some of their immoral practices.

"Day felt a deep ambivalence toward the Church she was entering. 'The scandal of businesslike priests, of collective wealth, the lack of a sense of responsibility toward the poor, the worker, the Negro, the Mexican, the Filipino' distressed her" (Woodward, 1996, p. 30). In her writings she expressed dissatisfaction with the Church. She loved the teachings of Jesus but did not love the Church. A priest named Romano Guardini told her that Jesus could not be separated from the Church, however, so she would have to deal with the imperfect organization (Woodward, 1990). Why she thought that Guardini was correct — that she could not follow the teachings of Jesus outside of the Church — is unknown, but she apparently believed him and she embraced the faith.

Trying to merge her humanistic ideas with the ideas and practices of the Church was not easy, but she eventually succeeded, using Christ's Sermon on the Mount as a basis for ethical behavior in life. This famous sermon was recorded in the Gospel of St. Matthew and begins with this statement by Jesus:

> Blessed are the poor in spirit, for theirs is the kingdom of heaven. Blessed are they that mourn, for they shall be comforted. Blessed are the meek, for they shall inherit the earth. Blessed are they which do hunger and thirst after righteousness, for they shall be filled. Blessed are the merciful, for they shall obtain mercy. Blessed are the pure in heart, for they shall see God. Blessed are the peacemakers, for they shall be called the children of God. Blessed are they who are persecuted for righteousness's sake, for theirs is the kingdom of heaven. Blessed are ye, when men shall revile you, and persecute you, and shall say all manner of evil against you falsely, for my sake. Rejoice, and be exceedingly glad, for great is your reward in heaven, for so persecuted they the prophets who were before you [5:1–11].

One of the important points that she took from this gospel was that service to the needy was an important part in the life of a true Christian. She started a newspaper called the *Catholic Worker*, and the movement that took the same name continues to this day. She also started a number of homeless shelters called Houses of Hospitality. She devoted the rest of her life to serving the poor and unfortunate, and primarily for this reason she won the hearts of many people and was considered an especially holy person.

A second important teaching that she took from the Sermon on the Mount was the idea of pacifism. She did not think that killing was acceptable, and she therefore protested U.S. involvement in World War II and Vietnam, and she protested against other indiscriminate attacks on civilians by the United States. Her stance against killing was contrary to the stance and the practices of the Church, which blessed armies and sanctified death for a number of centuries (Forest, n.d.). Also contrary to the practices of the Church — the richest religious organization in the world — she took vows of poverty and chastity.

Her practices made her an especially important individuals for Catholics in New York and throughout the United States, and after her death many people considered that she was a perfect candidate for canonization. Archbishop O'Connor announced that he intended to seek the canonization of a high-ranking member of the Church: Cardinal Cooke, and many people asked him to consider Dorothy Day instead. He began some preliminary research and announced his intention to suggest Dorothy for canonization. Pope John Paul II gave him permission to open her cause in 2000, which made her an official "servant of God." This was done despite her wishes to the contrary.

Before her death, Dorothy Day knew that some might attempt to canonize her and she specifically asked that this not be done. Rather than wasting such a great amount of money on the bestowal of an empty title, she wanted the money donated to the poor instead. She wanted the money given to one of her homeless shelters: one of the Catholic Worker houses. Since Day was against canonization, members of the Catholic Workers were also against her canonization. They felt that the Church should respect her wishes. One of Dorothy's granddaughters wrote a letter attempting to halt the cause:

> Dear Folks,
> I am one of Dorothy's granddaughters and I wanted to let you know how sick your canonization movement is. You have completely missed her beliefs and what she lived for if you are trying to stick her on a pedestal. She was a humble person, living as she felt the best way to improve on the world's ills. Take all of your monies and energies that are being put into her canonization and give it to the poor. That is how you would show your love and respect to her [Woodward, 1996, p. 32].

However, the appeals of many individuals to halt the process were largely ignored.

Although Dorothy Day is admired by many, people apparently do not admire her enough to follow her wishes. She did not wish to be canonized, yet her wishes and requests seem to have been ignored and the cause to make her a saint is still open. When considering the process of saint making, thinking about both Dorothy Day and Mother Teresa, and their respective causes, is enlightening. The saint-making process is confusing, and it has changed substantially over the years. Based on today's requirements for canonization, many saints who were canonized in the past would not have been made saints if they had to go through the difficult and lengthy process that is currently utilized. Today's saints must go through a strict and formal process before sainthood is conferred.

16

The History of Saint Making

The term "saint" is unusual, as it is nothing more than a title provided by an organization.[1] It does not necessarily refer to a kind or holy person. It only refers to those who have fulfilled certain requirements imposed by the Church — the verification of which costs hundreds of thousands of dollars. Still, those individuals who have been named saints are important to Roman Catholics in Italy. The reasons why are multifaceted, and they vary from person to person. Hugo Hoever (1955), who wrote the *Lives of the Saints*, stated in his preface: "Each saint is an imitation, in some degree, of all the virtues and perfection of the God-Man, Jesus Christ.[2] At the same time each imitates more fully and depicts more vividly one perfection of our Lord. Thus, the diligent and prayerful reader is confronted with an overall, brilliant picture of the numberless perfections of Christ" (p. 4). By this definition, and by similar definitions of what it means to be a saint, one would think that it is solely a holy individual who is deemed worthy of imitation, but the truth is much stranger. The process of becoming a saint is elaborate, and although it started off much more simply, today there are numerous requirements that have to be fulfilled in order for a person to be nominated a saint by the Church, not the least of which is a great deal of money. To properly understand what it means to be a saint today, it is necessary to understand the history of saint making.

Christianity began as a cult — a dissident faction within Judaism — and the Christians were therefore a threat to the established social order (much like some modern cults today). They were deeply moved by the crucifixion of Jesus of Nazareth, and after his martyrdom they even took the symbol of the cross as a symbol of their own faith. It then served as a constant reminder of the martyrdom that attracted many individuals to the religious movement. It is likely for this reason that other martyrs — other individuals who had died in a similar way or for a similar purpose — were likewise honored and respected. In early Christianity, martyrs were considered saints. They were individuals who had died like Jesus. At the onset of Christianity, all believers were in mortal danger, because the cult was still illegal. Once it became accepted, however, and it was made legal, there was no longer a grave risk involved with being Christian. It was at this time that magical powers began to be praised.

Individuals who cured others inexplicably or worked other miracles were then thought of as saints, because again, they were following in the footsteps of Jesus. There are many examples of miracles performed by Jesus in the New Testament. Here is one:

> Jesus stepped into a boat, crossed over and came to his own town. Some men brought to him a paralyzed man, lying on a mat. When Jesus saw their faith, he said to the man, "Take heart, son; your sins are forgiven."
>
> At this, some of the teachers of the law said to themselves, "This fellow is blaspheming!"
> Knowing their thoughts, Jesus said, "Why do you entertain evil thoughts in your hearts?

Which is easier: to say, 'Your sins are forgiven,' or to say, 'Get up and walk'? But I want you to know that the Son of Man has authority on earth to forgive sins." So he said to the paralyzed man, "Get up, take your mat and go home." Then the man got up and went home. When the crowd saw this, they were filled with awe, and they praised God, who had given such authority to man [Matthew 9:1–8].

Most of the miracles that Jesus is reported to have accomplished in the New Testament were medical miracles: curing people of incurable diseases or curing crippled people so that they could walk. Once martyrs became scarce, the Church began looking at miracles as evidence of divine powers and as evidence of potential sainthood. In other words, if men were able to duplicate (or at least approximate) the miracles performed by Jesus in the flesh, it would demonstrate that they were in fact following in his footsteps. Such miracles included acts like curing diseases, appearing simultaneously in different places, and even raising people from the dead. Martyrs were canonized because they imitated Jesus in death. Those who performed miracles were canonized because they followed Jesus in life. The value of miraculous occurrences cannot be overemphasized with regard to the cult of the saints. Those who performed miracles not only were following Jesus, but the powers demonstrated to either cure or assist in other ways were considered to be evidence of the divine and, therefore, evidence of the sanctity of the individuals who performed the feats. Fascination with miraculous feats has not dissipated, and even today, for a person to be considered for sainthood, he or she generally has to be credited with a specific number of miracles.

The term "miracle," in a sense, is problematic. It refers to something unexplainable, something that quite possibly demonstrates evidence of divinity. The word is derived from the Latin term *miraculum*, "object of wonder," from *mirari*, the verb "to wonder," and the related term *mirus*, which means "wonderful." According to the *Longman Dictionary of American English*, it is "an action or event that is impossible according to the ordinary laws of nature, and that some people believe was done by God." The term is comparable to "magic," but the definition of magic as found in the same dictionary is "a secret power used to control events or to do impossible things, by saying special words or performing special actions." In other words, the unexplainable phenomena do not necessarily come from God. Both of these phenomena, magic[3] and miracles alike, can be found within the Catholic faith, but another (seemingly) inherent problem exists with miracles. Often, saints are credited with performing various miracles. Since a miracle by definition is something influenced by God, the saint actually functions as an intermediary. So although some individuals pray to saints, asking them for help, if assistance is granted in the form of a miracle, it is not the saint working alone. It is Jesus working through the saint.

There is a dogmatical issue here that is not easily understood. In the granting of miracles and the like, people might pray to saints, but Jesus is always there. It is Jesus who actually performs the miracle through the saint. The power that the saint has is not exactly his or hers; in a sense, it is borrowed. It is divine power that works through the saint. The potential problem (in the saint-making process) is this: If a person prays to both Jesus and a saint, the miracle can be credited to the saint for the purposes of canonization, since Jesus is always involved anyway. However, if a person prays to a number of different saints, as well as to Jesus, and the miracle is granted, it is not attributed to any of the saints, because it cannot be attributed to any particular person with any assurance. It is the saint-making committee that attempts to sort through such information to determine the sanctity of a candidate.

This is an important understanding, and it is one of the reasons that there is a veritable cult of the saints in Italy, a reason that will be more fully explored in subsequent chapters.

Christian miracles were more common in the past. As scientific knowledge and medical understanding have increased, there are fewer and fewer events that are unexplainable; there are fewer events that can be deemed miraculous. For example, early in the history of saint making one common miracle that was recorded in multiple accounts was raising a person from the dead. It is likely that extremely sick individuals who were not dead were simply thought to be dead and when they recovered after herbal (or other medical) treatments it appeared as though they literally had returned from the dead. However, as medical knowledge increased, the frequency of raising people from the dead continually decreased, and today there are no cases of raising people from the dead. It is not done. Today, there are fewer unexplainable phenomena that can be considered miraculous. Therefore, the modern guidelines for making a saint have been changed.

Today, only two miracles are required for non-martyrs to become saints. Starting in the fifth century, there were a number of elements (in the life and death of a potential saint) that were explored in the process of canonization. It was the presence or absence of these elements that helped the Church to decide whether or not to bestow the title upon potential candidates. These included their reputations for holiness and how others thought of them. In other words, even years after their deaths, were they still revered by others?

Also, the stories and legends about their lives were viewed from the perspective of imitability. Were these individuals exemplars of Christian virtues? Did the tales of their lives and deeds inspire others to be good people? The stories of their lives were not considered from a purely historical perspective. They were looked at differently, as models of virtuous behavior toward which followers could aspire. It is for this reason that the true, historical accounts of some saints are unknown, and it is why some individuals were canonized who most likely never even existed. One example is St. Christopher, whose historical existence is extremely doubtful (since there is no evidence whatsoever about him in historical sources).

However, making a saint of a historically dubious person is of little apparent concern to the Church, as some non-humans were actually declared saints. One famous example is St. Michael the Archangel. According to *Lives of the Saints*:

> The name Michael signifies "Who is like to God," and the war cry of the good angels[4] in the battle fought in Heaven against Satan and his followers. St. Michael the Archangel, whose feast is observed September 29, is one of the three principal angels venerated by the Church — Michael, Gabriel, Raphael. Holy Scripture describes him as "one of the chief princes," and as leader of the forces of Heaven over the powers of Hell [Hoever, 1955, p. 381].

This saint was never a human. He was an archetypal figure known in Catholicism as an archangel. There were various different types of heaven dwellers that were thought to exist in early Christianity. The ideas about some of these angel-like creatures were delineated in the book *The Celestial Hierarchy*, written by Dionysus the Areopagite in c. 500, which orders different types of angels based on their perceived importance. The highest angels were the seraphim, followed by the cherubim, and then the thrones. The middle category were composed of the dominions, virtues, and powers, and then, closest to human beings, were the last category of angels, including principalities, archangels, and then, finally, normal angels.

The Catholic idea of the archangel is seemingly an angel above the status of a normal angel, who serves in the capacity of a general or another high-ranking soldier on the battlefield of heaven (on the side of the "good angels"), fighting against other (evil) angels who fight alongside Lucifer, who was also an angel. Archangels, angels, and humans alike could be given the title of saint by the Church if they were deemed important enough to the faith.

The last element that was considered in the canonization process, after analyzing the lives of the potential candidates, was the existence of miracles. If an individual did not perform any miracles during life, this was not necessarily a problem, as miracles granted after the death of the individual were equally respected. Followers could travel to the graves of people whom they honored as exemplars of holy individuals, where they would pray for assistance either in life or in death. If their prayers were answered, they could submit these miracles to the Church for consideration and the organization could then go ahead with the process of canonization.

17

Stigmata and Other Miracles

St. Augustine said, "Miracles are not contrary to nature, but only contrary to what we know about nature." Miracles are interesting phenomena. They provoke wonder and excitement, and they kick-start the imagination and inspire spiritual consideration. Just what a miracle is, however, is still not understood. For an event to be considered miraculous, it does not just have to be inexplicable, but it also has to be credited to God or to other lesser deities, known as saints in Catholicism. This seems perfectly clear on the surface, but if its depths are explored, it demonstrates itself as a very confusing phenomenon. There are many occurrences that defy explanation in this world and yet they are not deemed miracles. For example, unexplainable lights in the sky that resemble spacecraft are hardly ever considered miracles, but people still find them interesting and there are many television shows and documentaries about the phenomenon. The appearance of such lights is not considered to be miraculous because many people think that they are due to the activity of extraterrestrials. A thousand years ago, however, the same phenomenon might have been considered a miracle. It is for this reason that from a linguistic standpoint, the term "miracle" cannot be defined. It cannot be quantified, so it cannot be accurately defined.

For example, people in different parts of the world consider different things to be miraculous. A priest from one part of the world may have a vision of the Virgin Mary and all the members of his parish will hear about it and consider it a miracle. The story will spread, and over time information could be submitted to the Vatican that a miracle has taken place and they will then investigate the occurrence. In such cases, others will typically begin to claim that they have had similar visions, even though they may not have. It is possible that such people actually believed that they had experienced a vision, but the idea of the vision was suggested by the experience of a local religious leader. Once the mind has something in its grasp, it can come to pass (within the mind).

The way that the mind works is inexplicable, and it is powerful. There have been many books and articles written about mind power, especially in the field of sports and sports psychology, but such information can also be found in business literature as well. In all of these fields, the lesson in simple: If you can control your mind to instill confidence and determination, you can be more successful. If the mind can see something, it can occur. It is for this reason that we must be skeptical about visions. Once individuals believe that visions in an area are common, they have the idea in their minds and they are on the lookout for potential visions. Strangely, visions are now more apt to occur. Such is the inherent power of the mind. This does not hold true in religious visions and experiences alone, but it can be documented in many other forms of group brainwashing. If UFO sightings have been especially common in a particular area, people in that area will be much more likely to witness a UFO. It is for this reason that people in miracle-rich areas are more likely to experience miracles.

Sainthood is only bestowed upon people who have miracles credited to them. Non-martyrs need two. So, places that have a large number of native saints must have a correlational amount of perceived miracles. The majority of saints in the Catholic tradition come from Italy and from Spain. In Italy, the majority of saints and miracles alike stem from towns in southern Italy. This could be because, as Woodward (1996) has suggested, southern Italians feel close to their local saints and ask various favors of such individuals. If individuals do not have enough money, if their families are not getting along well, or if a child is sick, they might decide to pray to a local saint for assistance. For such people, if any of those situations is remedied they may believe that it is a miracle and tell those around them about the new evidence of the divine that they have experienced. The neighbors around them would then become more likely to also experience similar miracles.

Outside of southern Italy and outside of places that share a similar obsession with saints and miraculous occurrences, such changes might not be thought of as being miraculous but as being mere secular changes alone. Getting a job, instead of being a gift from God, might be thought of as occurring as a result of a good interview. When a family starts getting along better, they might think of it as due to a positive effort by those involved in order to better all of their lives, rather than as a divine power changing it for them. A sick child getting better, outside of popular miracle areas, might be explained through medical reasons — perhaps the child had the flu, his or her system eventually dealt with it, and his or her health improved. In heavy miracle areas, the same recovery could be viewed as evidence of divinity. Just what makes a miracle is difficult to determine, and the idea of what a miracle is differs from person to person. It is for this reason that the Catholic Church is skeptical when it comes to viewing and determining the validity of miracles.

Miracles performed by Catholic saints include a number of diverse phenomena, including raising people from the dead, curing incurable diseases, levitation, causing food and other objects to appear out of thin air, and bilocation. Bilocation is a phenomenon that is reportedly common, and it refers to certain individuals appearing in two places at once. Padre Pio (1887–1968) was one such individual. He was credited with numerous episodes of bilocation. "Without leaving his friary at San Giovanni Rotondo, Padre Pio was frequently seen and addressed in different parts of the world. While he was observed by colleagues in his room, he was seen simultaneously in such diverse places as Uruguay, Hawaii, and Wisconsin" (Ruffin, 1991, pp. 16–17). In addition to his ability to appear in two places at once, he was afflicted with a phenomenon that many people think is miraculous. This is the appearance of stigmata: the sudden and unexplainable appearance of wounds that mimic the wounds of Jesus crucified. Wounds would appear without explanation on the hands, feet and side of the afflicted, wounds that cannot be medically explained or treated. One well-known stigmatic was St. Francis of Assisi (c. 1181–1226).

St. Francis was born Giovanni Francesco di Bernardone, a wealthy individual whose father was a cloth merchant. He grew up privileged, with anything he could possibly want. At a young age, he joined the armed forces. When he was headed out to war one day, he had a religious vision, a vision that directed him to return to Assisi. There he began a religious life. This was against the wishes of his father, who tried to change St. Francis's mind with beatings and other punishments, but he was not dissuaded. In sharp contrast to the wealthy Church, he renounced all of his worldly goods and embraced a life of poverty. He traveled to many places, including Egypt, where the Christian Crusaders were destroying the city of Damietta, killing all those in their path. He founded the Franciscan Order, and it received official support from the pope. This meant that individuals could join the order and not be excommunicated by the Roman Catholic Church. Other similar situations came about in the past, in which one charismatic individual wished to worship God and follow the teachings of Jesus in his own way. Such individuals attracted followers who wished to emulate the kindness and charity shown by the founder. However, no one was allowed to worship God or follow Jesus without the intervention of the Church. No one was permitted to interpret scripture for themselves either, so when groups such as these appeared they were not given papal approval, which meant that all members of the group were excommunicated. This effectively signifies for Catholics that they cannot go to heaven and that they will be sentenced to an eternity in hell. However, St. Francis was lucky to have received papal approval, and so his order could remain. He devoted more and more time to its growth, and he became increasingly more spiritual throughout the years.

He became known as an individual especially drawn to nature, and there are many tales that involve him preaching to birds and to other creatures. He recognized God in nature, and as St. Francis aged he increasingly associated with animals, potentially due to his spiritual beliefs. There is a famous tale involving St. Francis and a wolf that is found in the *Fioretti*, an anonymous Italian work that chronicles different occurrences in the life of

St. Francis of Assisi (c. 1181–1226) was afflicted with stigmata. His hands, feet, and side would bleed without (scientific) explanation. He was known to have been able to communicate with animals, and he is one of the most frequently prayed-to saints in Italy. This statue is located at the Church of the Immaculate Conception (Rome, Italy).

the saint. Apparently, a wolf who lived near the town of Gubbio was extremely hungry and he attacked and ate both domestic animals and human children. Everyone feared the wolf and St. Francis did not like this situation, so he wandered off into the wilderness to find the beast. According to the account in the *Fioretti*, once St. Francis saw the wolf he made a magical sign with his hands and asked the creature to come to him. The wolf followed him, and St. Francis led him into town, where the saint functioned as an intermediary between the townspeople and the wolf. He explained that the wolf had committed his crimes out of hunger alone and, therefore, he was not evil. St. Francis arranged a truce between the wolf and the townspeople. Provided that they fed the wolf regularly, he would no longer attack them. In a final act to put the townspeople at ease, St. Francis blessed the wolf. Since the people believed that the sign of the cross and words of benediction could work like magic, they no longer feared the wolf. Obviously, the historicity of this tale has to be questioned, but it should be remembered that historical accuracy was not important in the saint-making process.[1] What was important was whether or not the tale inspired people. "A medieval hagiographer wrote the life of a saint, not to tell his readers anything about the subject's personality or individuality, but rather to demonstrate how the saint exhibited those universal characteristics of sanctity common to all saints at all times" (Geary, 1978, p. 10).

St. Francis certainly did serve as an inspiration to all. This only increased in 1224, two years before his death, when the stigmata first appeared. St. Francis was praying on the mountain of Verna, engaged in a 40-day fast for the Christian holiday of Michaelmas: the feast of St. Michael the Archangel. He had a vision of a seraph, an angel with six wings that was on a cross. After this image materialized, he developed the stigmata. The account as written in *Lives of the Saints* is the following:

> St. Francis had been spending the days meditating on the Sacred Passion and now the Almighty sent a flaming angel in the form of a cross to pierce his hands and feet and side with wounds that never were to heal [pp. 391–393].

St. Francis had a wound on his right side that corresponded to the wound that Jesus supposedly received when he was pierced by a spear while on the cross dying. St. Francis also received wounds on his hands and feet — wounds that were thought to be similar to crucifixion wounds. The wounds were in the center of his hands. According to Habig (1973):

> [They] seemed to be pierced through the center with nails, the heads of which were in the palms of the hands and the upper part of his feet outside the flesh, and their points extended through the back of the hands and the soles of the feet so far that they seemed to be bent and beaten back in such a way that underneath their bent and beaten-back point — all of which stood out from the flesh — it would have been easy to put the finger of one's hand as through a ring. And the heads of the nails were round and black [pp. 1450–1451].

St. Francis is thought to have been the first bearer of the stigmata, but there were many others like him, including some of his contemporaries: Dodo of Hascia, who died five years after St. Francis, displayed a wound on his right side and wounds on his hands and feet. A nun named Lutgarde of Tonges, who died in 1246, also bled from the same locations, although the wounds themselves were not pronounced. St. Catherine of Siena also bled from her hands, feet, and side, although there were no visible wounds.

Other stigmatics had wounds on their heads that seemed to have been caused by nonexistent crowns of thorns. St. Rita of Cascia was one such stigmatic. She had a wound in

The body of St. Catherine of Siena, encased in marble, is below an altar in Rome, Italy.

the center of her forehead that appeared suddenly and without explanation and would not heal. The wounds of some stigmatics were fragrant and emitted pleasing scents, but the wound that St. Rita had emitted such an awful stench that she had to be separated from the rest of her convent (Ruffin, 1991).

There was a young girl in Woonsocket, Rhode Island, who also displayed the stigmata. Marie Rose Alma Ferron (1902–1936) was a native of Quebec. She had terrible arthritis, and she died of myocarditis when she was 34 years old. Beginning in 1927, the stigmata of scourging appeared. Her "outer arm was lacerated with red and purple stripes about one-half inch in width" (Boyer, 1958, p. 81). A day later, she began bleeding from her hands, feet and side. She also had a red mark around her head that resembled the shape of a crown of thorns, from which she also bled. Occasionally, blood leaked from her eyes as well.

The most famous case of stigmatism in modern times has to be that of Padre Pio, who had lesions on his hands, feet and side. Unlike the stigmata of St. Francis and other stigmatics, however, the (spear) wound was not located on Padre Pio's right side, but on his left. This is an interesting phenomenon when it comes to stigmatics: The wounds are not generally in the right places. In the case of the wound on the side, depending on the stigmatic, it is found on either the right- or the left-hand side. When it comes to the wounds found on the hands, most stigmatics have red marks, actual wounds, or they simply bleed from a point in the center of the palm. However, there is no way that the historical Jesus would have been nailed to the cross with nails through the hands, as the body could not have been supported. The nails would have been hammered into the forearms. One has to be skeptical about the claim that these wounds have some sort of divine origin. Even the Church is very skeptical about these matters, as it seems that the wounds that all stigmatics have perfectly match the wounds on the statues or pictures of Jesus crucified in their vicinity. People with stigmata copy the crucifixion that they see. If the wounds are in the wrong place on the statue, they are in the wrong place on the body. Individuals who spend days focused on various images of Jesus on the cross tend to develop the same wounds that are depicted on such images. The images are not always historically accurate. But still, stigmatics display the characteristics of the icons that they meditate on.

It should be noted that Christians are not the only individuals who develop stigmata. Muslims also develop wounds on their backs that correspond to those that Mohammed received. The same phenomenon is found in other religions as well. Since this is the case and because the stigmata are often not historically accurate, the Church does not readily endorse any claim of stigmatism as a miracle. The power of the mind is something that must be considered as a possible explanation of such so-called miracles. It has been said that the power of the mind is unlimited. Although it cannot be completely explained through science yet, it is possible that intense concentration on such images can cause a bodily reaction.

A similar thing happens with spiritual visions. Different countries depict Jesus's mother, Mary, in different ways. In some countries she is depicted as wearing blue and white robes, and in other countries she wears red and blue robes. When religiously inclined individuals have visions of her after prolonged bouts of prayer and meditation, the images seen in the visions correspond to the way St. Mary is depicted in images and statues that they would have seen and meditated on. It is therefore possible that all of these occurrences are products of the mind and that they do not have divine origins.[2] It is for this reason that the Church is suspicious of such claims, and they are reluctant to deem things like stigmata and visions miracles. However, miracles are still necessary in order to canonize someone. A person cannot be declared a saint due to moral conduct and charity alone.

18

Modern Saints

A saint is a person who should be an example to other Catholics. That is the simple version of the confusing canonization process. The Church states clearly that they do not make saints, that only God can make saints. Their function is determining who is and who is not a saint. This is confusing, because if this were actually true, then the Church could do nothing at all and the saints would still be saints. However, there is a lengthy process in which a saint is made that costs an incredible sum of money. In some cases, it costs almost $500,000 to make one. If the Church does not actually make saints, why would they need such a massive amount of money to confer the title? The truth is, holy individuals come and go. They live and they die. Some are so kind and spiritual that they serve as an inspiration to those around them, while others are buried and then soon forgotten. Holy people are recognized by others. The intervention of the Church is unnecessary. What the Church provides is nothing more than a title — a very expensive title.

The money that the Church requires in order to canonize someone is used for a variety of things. It should be remembered, too, that the process of canonization takes decades, if not centuries, to complete. Money is needed every step of the way. Most individuals who choose a religious life do not make an income through outside sources, so supporters have to give them money for living expenses, vacations and retirement. Everyone involved in the saint-making process typically gets paid for his or her work. The Vatican also charges large amounts of money as rental fees for the religious ceremonies that will be held once an individual is canonized. According to Woodward (1996), the Church charges approximately $7,500 for seats that are used during the ceremony. They charge an additional $12,000 for prayer booklets and a great deal of money for other works of art and rental fees. Before it even gets to this stage, however, there are a number of great expenses that have to be paid.

First, every potential saint requires a positio. This lengthy document must be printed at Tipografia Guerra, located in the Piazza di Porta Maggiore, and they charge between $13,000 and $25,000 per printing. The Vatican could save some money by going to a different printer, but they have an arrangement with this specific printer and it is the only company used for anything that the Vatican prints. After the positio, miracles have to be confirmed. In order for this confirmation process to begin, they need to print positiones — one for each miracle. These cost $4,000 each. So in printing costs alone, one can expect to pay the Church or its partner corporations more than $30,000. Once a positio is printed, money has to be paid to each person who reads it. Typically, people are paid approximately $500 each to read a single document. The Vatican then usually also brings in outside consulters, which costs almost $7,000. In all, the procedure costs hundreds of thousands of dollars.

The canonization of Mother Elizabeth Bayley Seton in 1975 cost $250,000 (Woodward, 1996). Of that $250,000, it took $225,000 for her to actually be called a saint. The rest of the money was paid to the Vatican for rental fees and other miscellaneous charges. The canonization of Katherine Drexel in 1990 cost a grand total of $333,250, and this fee is average. Some causes have cost much more money, totaling approximately $500,000 each. All of this money is spent in order to declare a person worthy of emulation. For Catholics, this title is important, and some of them do not believe that the money would be more appropriately used to assist the poor. The function of the saint and the corresponding process of canonization is important to them.

The first step in the canonization process is basically a promotional phase. Before 1917 it was required that 50 years pass before initiating any kind of action and they are still hesitant to start the process immediately after the candidate's death, but there are some types of promotional activities that can be started. Usually, a book about the candidate will be written and published, funds begin to be collected, prayer cards that feature the individual are made, and reports of divine favors granted in the name of the candidate are collected. This is all done because the local originators of the cause will eventually have to convince the Vatican that even after the death of the individual, a consistent and enduring reputation for holiness continues.

After this initial phase, the local bishop gets involved, and he begins the Ordinary Process. The candidate begins to be called a Servant of God at this stage. Basically, the bishop sets up a tribunal where witnesses come and testify about the life and deeds of the candidate. The testimonies are all transcribed and they are studied in order to determine whether or not the candidate should be considered holy or a martyr. It is important, too,

St. Peter's Basilica in the Vatican. This is the seat of the Roman Catholic Church, the only organization capable of declaring someone a saint in Catholic Christianity (Rome, Italy).

that the individual is not the center of a cult, and there have been individuals in the past who were denied sainthood because they were the subject of adoration and prayers by a number of followers. This type of worship is acceptable if it is through the blessing of the Church, but such a following outside the Church is not acceptable. Pope Alexander III (1159–1181) declared that no one was to be venerated without the authorization of the pope. The Church took other actions to stop the veneration of holy individuals without Church sanction. They prevented the publication of books about holy individuals who had not been canonized by the organization, and they banned artwork that depicted such individuals with halos or light emanating from their heads (Woodward, 1996).

In recent times, the canonization of Padre Pio was delayed an extraordinary amount of time because of the cult that surrounded him.[1] He was extremely popular due to the stigmata that he had and the many miracles that were credited to him, and immediately after death his cause was initiated. The Church determined that he was too popular, and so they delayed his canonization until recently. Although he died in 1968, he was not canonized until 2002.[2]

The next stage after the Ordinary Process is one in which all writings of the candidate, both published and unpublished, are collected and then studied. The Church must make sure that nothing in the writings of the potential saint goes against their teachings. There have been potential saints in the past who wrote about the Virgin Mary, for example, but the description that they provided was different from the Church's description. In such cases, the cause is immediately halted and the written work is placed in the Vatican's Index of Forbidden Books.

Provided that there is nothing that contradicts the teachings of the Church in the writings of the potential candidate, they pass to the next stage, where they receive a *nihil obstat* from Rome. This means that there is nothing objectionable in the files on the individual that the Vatican keeps. There have been causes halted in the past because some potential candidates had molested children. The file in the Vatican was checked to make sure that they had formally repented. If they had not, they could not become saints. Once the file at the Vatican was checked, it became clear that the candidates had not formally repented. Therefore, they were not declared saints (Woodward, 1996). They remained known as Servants of God or Blessed instead, and they were unable to ever become saints. This meant that they could only be venerated locally and not worldwide (Society of Jesus, n.d.).

If the candidate makes it through all of these processes, he or she moves on to the next step, which takes place in Rome. Money is paid to the Vatican so that it will look into the cause, and a type of trial is set up, in which there are people arguing for the candidate and there are others asking questions and bringing up possible elements of his or her life that may be against the cause. All of the information available about the candidate is (supposedly) read and judged, and a positio is created that documents the life and deeds of the candidate in detail. A decision is then made on the worthiness of the candidate. If it is determined that the individual in question is an exemplar of Catholic faith and virtues, he or she is declared a venerable and the body is unearthed.

The body is dug up primarily for identification purposes; if the individual is eventually declared a saint, but his or her body is not located in the grave, the Church will tell people not to go to the grave. Many followers believe that the power that saints have is stored in their remains. When these followers pray for assistance, they often travel to the grave site to be next to the saint. It is for this reason that the Church verifies where the candidates are actually buried. In the past, when bodies were unearthed they occasionally showed little or no signs of decay. Sometimes, their bodies emitted pleasing scents, like flowers, and the skin was still flexible and pliable, as it had been when the candidates were alive. Finding a body in this state often pushes the cause forward even more quickly. In the history of Catholicism, finding a body in this state was considered to be miraculous and certain individuals were canonized primarily because their bodies had failed to decay naturally after death (Cruz, 1977). This preservation could not be explained by the early Church and so it was generally declared miraculous. Such bodies were called Incorruptibles.

This lack of decay in the past could have been considered a miracle, and since a miracle is required for a person to be considered a beatus, meaning "blessed," the opening of the tomb was a definite shove toward sainthood. Today, things have changed. Scientific understanding is greater, and although the lack of decay is still considered miraculous by other Christian organizations, such as the Russian Orthodox Church, the preservation of the body is not considered miraculous anymore by the Roman Catholic Church. Therefore, a different type of miracle is required for beatification and a second is required for canonization (unless the person is a martyr of course). After these potential miracles are scrutinized, the committee comes to a decision regarding whether or not they are in fact miracles. If so, the person can be canonized.

The process of saint making has been changed several times, and many individuals who were declared saints at the beginning of Christianity would likely not have been canonized today. However, they are still revered by Roman Catholics. Just because the policies and procedures of the Church have changed does not mean that the beliefs and practices of followers have changed. For many individuals in Italy, the preserved bodies of saints on display in churches and in cathedrals are still considered to be miraculous.

The reasons behind this are multifaceted. One of the important concepts that must be understood is the medieval notion of the body in a religious and spiritual context — a notion that has carried over to present religious practices. However, it is no longer on the surface. Over time, although the admiration and awe shown toward physical remains are still present, the reasons behind such beliefs are hidden. In order to properly understand the importance of bodily remains, it is necessary to understand the function of the body in spiritual pursuits. Looking at asceticism in Catholicism can help to clarify these concepts.

19

Asceticism in the Catholic Faith

Padre Pio was a Capuchin friar. The Capuchins were a mendicant order whose existence came about because of St. Francis of Assisi. All members took vows of poverty and gave up their individual possessions. One of their practices, however, provoked ridicule. Although the individual members were not supposed to have any possessions or wealth, the organization itself could have as much money and possessions as it wanted. Therefore, many of these monasteries became extremely wealthy and the Capuchins lived luxurious lives. Since it became known that their claims of poverty were nothing but a joke, changes were put into place in the Middle Ages that limited the wealth of the organization, as well as the wealth of individual members.

Individuals that joined the order were expected to give up all of their worldly possessions and embrace a life of poverty and spiritual dedication. They often made use of various forms of ascetic practices. Self-flagellation was one such practice. After having joined the friary, when Padre Pio was a young boy, he and the other initiates were often forced to strip naked and whip themselves with a chain. The head of the friary at the time, Padre Tommaso, would make them do this at various times without warning. He would make them whip themselves until blood dripped down to the floor. Although this might seem odd today, the idea was to literally follow in the footsteps of Jesus, as much as it was possible. While whipping themselves, they were supposed to think of the tortures that Jesus endured. Therefore, one of the goals of the practices was to get closer to God by means of physical and mental practices performed in unison. According to Ruffin (1991):

> [The head friar] seemed to be very fond of doing this at mealtimes, requiring the hapless youth to go into a corner, strip, and flagellate himself until his back was a mass of bleeding flesh. The slightest infraction of the rule was an occasion for harsh reproofs, mortifications, and heavy punishments. Sometimes Tommaso would fasten a wooden collar around the neck of a boy who displeased him, sometimes he would blindfold him, and sometimes he would make him eat off the ground [p. 51].

Padre Pio came to believe that mortification of the flesh was necessary for spiritual advancement, and he advocated the use of such torturous practices in his own writings. He wrote a letter to someone in which he referenced a statement found in Galatians: "Those who belong to Christ Jesus have crucified the flesh with its passions and desires" (5:24). Referring to this statement, Padre Pio wrote:

> From this it is apparent that anyone who wants to be a true Christian must mortify his flesh for no other reason than devotion to Jesus, who, for love of us, mortified His entire body on the cross. The mortification must be constant and steady, not intermittent, and it must last

for one's whole life. Moreover, the perfect Christian must not be satisfied with a kind of mortification which merely appears to be severe. He must make sure it hurts ... for ... all the evils which hurt your soul can be traced to the failure to practice due mortification of the flesh, either through ignorance or lack of the will to do so. If you want to [unite with God] you must master the flesh and crucify it, for it is the source of all evil [McGregor, 1985, pp. 102–103].

Ascetic practices are encouraged elsewhere in the Bible. "The Christian's citizenship is in heaven (Phil. 3:20), and the Christian's duty is the crucifixion of his flesh (Rom. 8:13; I Cor. 9:27; Gal. 5:24)" (McGiffert, 1909, p. 17). In addition, there have been various Christian leaders who have also praised such practices. Pope John Paul II once wrote the following in a letter entitled Salvifici Doloris:

> Christ did not conceal the need for suffering from his listeners. He clearly stated, "If any man wishes to follow me ... he must pick up his cross daily." In addition, in front of his disciples, he demanded [that they have] a moral nature that can only be fulfilled if they "deny themselves." The path that leads to the Kingdom of Heaven is "hard and narrow," and Christ contrasts it to the "wide and easy" path that "leads to destruction."

There are multiple reasons why people engage in self-injurious practices. Two of them are important in Christianity. The first has to do with following Jesus in the flesh. He was scourged and tortured before being nailed to the cross. It is only natural that some of his followers wish to share some of that pain, if even just on a spiritual level. It is this initial concept that leads certain individuals to scourge themselves or to wear barbed chains around their thighs. The Church, too, encourages this behavior, and a large number of religious ascetics have historically been canonized.

In a sense, this was the most logical transition from the martyrs. Sainthood began with martyrs — individuals who gave up their lives for the faith. Those individuals gave up their entire bodies in order to follow Jesus into death. Once Christianity was accepted and became legal, there were fewer martyrs for the faith. People did not give their lives for Jesus, so the next best thing began to be honored and considered during the canonization process. Individuals who put themselves through the same tortures that Jesus would have endured became a source of respect and emulation for other Christians. People who would have shed their blood on the cross with their lord still chose to shed it, although they did not have to. For this reason, they were admired and many were canonized.

Pope John Paul II canonized more individuals than any other pope. He himself was recently declared a beatus (Blessed), and this large image of him was put up outside of the Vatican in St. Peter's Square. Pope John Paul II emphasized that the pathway to sainthood is not easy and that austere practices are important (Rome, Italy).

There is another reason why

certain people engage in ascetic practices. It is the reason behind all sorts of self-injurious practices that are found in religions throughout the world. Asceticism takes diverse forms depending on the traditions in which it is found. In some traditions, asceticism is not too severe and adherents might fast for extended periods of time or deprive themselves of certain luxuries temporarily. But in other traditions, extreme ascetic acts are performed. There are certain Buddhists who have burned either fingers, hands, or their entire bodies in homage to their deity, and there are other individuals in various traditions who performed similar austerities. The idea of martyrdom is in nearly every tradition. While Buddhists used to burn themselves to death, others threw themselves from mountaintops, fed themselves to wild animals, or buried themselves alive. Of those who buried themselves alive, two of the most extreme practices are found in the Shugendo faith in Japan and in Indian ascetic traditions.

In the former, individuals engaged in self-injurious practices for years, such as meditating under freezing waterfalls and disfiguring themselves by cutting off appendages or cutting out their eyes, all the while reducing their food intake. Eventually, when they felt that death (by starvation) was near, they buried themselves in underground tombs. There, in complete darkness under the surface of the earth, they died.

The Indian ascetic known as *asannyasi* did something similar. He lived in solitude for years, performing austerities that resemble those carried out by Shugendo followers. Eventually, when he felt that he was spiritually ready, he would announce his intention to bury himself alive. He would announce the time and the place of his burial, and others would come to watch the event. "The holy man exhibits complete tranquility and dissociation from the world around him. Not a muscle moves as a grave is solemnly dug in front of him and he is lowered — still alive — into the hole and the earth is closed over him for all time" (Yalman, 1962, p. 315).

When outsiders hear about such actions, they are thought of as suicide. However, those performing the actions do not consider them to be suicidal. They think of it differently — as though they are simply entering another state of existence. It is not that they are ceasing to exist. It is only that their state of existence is changing. There are definite parallels between such practices and Christian traditions. Back at the beginning of the faith, when martyrs were common, they could have renounced their beliefs and lived. But they chose to die instead. Their choice was suicidal, and yet it is not thought of as suicide. In addition, such martyrs likely did not think that they would cease to exist. Rather, they would pass through a metamorphosis and arrive at another state of existence: in a heavenly realm perhaps, in which they are in the presence of God.

Giving one's life for God is an extreme act, an act that modern faiths deem anachronistic to their teachings. But the desire to perform such acts is still there, buried deep into the subconscious of individuals prone to austerities. Rather than end their lives, they perform other less extreme ascetic practices, such as scourging themselves, engaging in extended periods of starvation, and the like. One Christian saint who engaged in such self-injurious practices is especially revered by members of the Catholic sect, and he was a source of inspiration to Padre Pio. He was called St. John of the Cross (1542–1591), although his given name was Juan de Yepes.

He received an early education from the Jesuits but joined the Carmelite Order in 1563. There he met another (future) saint named St. Teresa of Avila (1515–1582), who convinced him to help her restore the order to its original precepts, which included living a life of strict asceticism.[1] He recited prayers daily, abstained perpetually from the consumption of meat, and often fasted and tortured his (physical) body in a number of other ways. The types of penances that he endured are similar to those practiced by Buddhist monks. This similarity is interesting, as is the similarity between the two faiths when they both initially came into being. There have been numerous studies done that compare the two faiths, and it seems that at the beginning of Christianity the two religions could have been viewed as two branches of the same overarching tradition. This connection might not be arbitrary, and it will be discussed in more detail in forthcoming chapters.

St. John of the Cross, possibly as a result of his ascetic practices, began to perform unexplainable phenomena. He often levitated while praying intently, and there were many people who witnessed this miracle (Cruz, 1977). After living a pious and religious life, he died of illness when he was 49 years old. St. John of the Cross is not famous today because of the events in his life. It was something that occurred with his physical remains that called attention to the holy man.

Nine months after his death, it was decided that his bones be moved to a location in Segovia, Spain, and legal documents were drawn up that permitted the move. They dug up his remains but were shocked to find that the body had not decayed at all. The skin was still supple and flexible, and a fragrant smell emanated from the body. The documentation that they had called for the removal of bones and not an intact body, so they did not want to move it.

Not knowing what to do, they decided to cut off one of the saint's fingers so that they could prove that the body was incorrupt. When they cut off the finger, fresh blood flowed from the wound, as though he were still alive. This sparked curiosity and awe, and it led to his eventual canonization in 1726. His body was then thought of as a whole-body relic — a source of miraculous occurrences and evidence of the divine. It was exposed for the last time in 1955, and although it had discolored, the body itself was still flexible and moist (Cruz, 1977). This body and others like it draw individuals on religious pilgrimages. There is a fascination with relics in Christianity, just like in Buddhism. A relic could be a single bone or even a piece of clothing worn by an especially holy individual. What inspires the faithful most of all, however, are whole-body relics — typically only found in Buddhism and in Catholic Christianity.

20

The Importance of Physical Remains

The veneration of physical remains in Italy is integrally linked to the cult of the saints. Thomas Aquinas (1225–1274) explained this in the book *Summa Theologica*: "In memory of [the saints], we ought to honor any relics in a fitting manner, principally their bodies, which were temples of the Holy Spirit dwelling and operating in them, and destined to be likened to the body of Christ by the glory of the Resurrection" (Aquinas, 1947). The saints are thought to function as intermediaries between living beings and God. They bridge the gap between this world and the next, and due to their function and their necessity to Roman Catholics it is as though the saints are not really dead. They are liminal beings, functioning between this realm of existence and the next.

Families used to travel to the grave sites of saints, whether crypts or catacombs, where they would have religious ceremonies. Sometimes, they would eat dinner within the proximity of saintly remains. This practice is not unique to Christianity, and it is found in many other cultures, including Chinese, Vietnamese, Japanese, and ancient Egyptian cultures, in which ancestor worship was prevalent. In a sense, this Christian practice is ancestor worship. They pray to individuals who have preceded them in life, invoking their spiritual presence beside their earthly remains and asking for guidance into the afterlife.

The cult of the saints, as it is known, developed from "two fundamental antecedents: the pagan cult of heroes, and the Christian belief in the resurrection of the body" (Geary, 1978, p. 33). The mythical heroes of ancient times are still sources of inspiration today, and students continue to read about their exploits — stories about their superhuman feats of strength, communion (or even their familial relationship) with gods, and bravery. The cult of the martyrs came about as a natural development of this already present, culturally inherent cult of heroes.

The Christian belief in the resurrection of the body also influenced the development of the cult of the saints. Bodies of martyrs and the bodies of later saints were preserved as much as possible due to such soteriological reasons. The modern viewpoint of the death and life continuum from the perspective of Roman Catholics has to do with a distinction between the physical body and the spiritual self. When the body dies, the spirit lives on in the afterlife. However, for early and modern Christians alike this is not the end of the body. There will come a time when all of the pious dead, especially saints and martyrs, will be resurrected. It is the perspective of many Christians that in the future the dead will be reunited with their physical bodies, provided that they are in God's good graces. Since the martyrs had already been accepted by God (according to the Church), in early Christianity, believers wished to be in the proximity of the martyrs' remains in both life and death. This

The pagan cult of heroes was instrumental in the development of the Christian cult of saints. This is a statue of Perseus displaying the severed head of Medusa (Florence, Italy).

was because when the martyrs' bodies were reanimated these own believers' bodies would be much more likely to be granted the same favor.

> The bodies of the martyrs, unlike those of heroes, would not remain dead forever. Early Christians took literally Christ's promise of the resurrection and thus expected that on the last day the martyrs' physical bodies would be taken up by their owners [Geary, 1978, p. 33].

This concept causes one to reconsider the relationship between the soul and the body in this life, in the afterlife, and at some point in the distant future when the bodies of pious individuals are reanimated and reinfused by the same soul. This concept is unique, but it has been influenced by other traditions. Thinking of this connection and the inextricable relationship between the spirit and earthly remains provides insight into the nature of life and death, an insight that is at the very core of Christian practices.

Death, when viewed in this manner, is a strange thing, and it can be overcome. When a person dies, the physical body is discarded and the soul lives on in the afterlife. The early Christian idea of the soul was initially not concrete, and there were many theories about the true nature of the spiritual side of an individual. The early Christians, in other words, did not dismiss the possibility that the soul had multiple parts. This was already an accepted idea in many preexisting religious traditions that influenced the development of Catholic Christianity, including the Egyptian idea of multiple parts of the soul. The Egyptian religious traditions accepted the existence of many aspects of the spirit. There were eight spiritual parts that were connected to a single individual. The Ba and the Ka were two of these aspects.

The Ka is an unusual phenomenon, as it was thought of as almost a spiritual shadow that followed a person around throughout his or her life. In a sense, it is sort of like the Catholic idea that every person has a guardian angel (known as a *daimon*) that watches out for him or her during life. The Ka gave a person spiritual power, and it could take power through offerings. For example, if food or other similar offerings were placed before statues of Egyptian gods, the gods were not expected to eat such offerings but to utilize the energy that was inherent in such offerings. The Ka was thought to gain energy in a similar manner. It was this part of the soul that traveled into the afterworld when death arrived. It rejoined the spiritual world while the second half of the soul, the Ba, remained behind with the body.

The Ba is more closely related to the modern perception of the soul, but it is connected to the physical body. The term basically referred to all aspects of an individual with the exception of his or her physical form. The Ba was connected to the physical body, though, and it was due to the needs of the Ba that the Egyptians went to such trouble to preserve the remains of the dead. The Ba contained the character and personality of the deceased, while the Ka was the independent spiritual being that gave life energy to the individual while he or she was alive. To utilize a Chinese and Japanese concept in order to explain this concept, the Egyptian Ba is the spiritual being that provided *chi* (in Chinese) or *ki* (in Japanese). These two terms refer to the same concept. They are different names for the universal life energy that all living creatures are thought to possess. The energy infuses the physical body only temporarily. While it is there, there is life. When it dissipates, death ensues. In the Egyptian idea of death, the Ka instantly returns to the nether realm, but the Ba lingers around the body. The Ba contains the personality of the individual. Therefore, for a person to live on spiritually in the afterlife once he or she discards the body, the two parts of the soul have to be reunited (David and Archbold, 2000). Otherwise, all of the things that make a person who he or she is would no longer exist. In order to perpetuate the existence of the individual, the two parts have to be rejoined, and this cannot happen if the body is not preserved. The body must be preserved for as long as possible in order to allow the Ba and the Ka to reunite, so that the individual could continue to exist, albeit in a different state of being.

It is possible that this complex Egyptian concept of multiple parts of the spiritual half of an individual influenced the Christian concept of the same phenomenon. The early Christians did not dismiss the notion of multiple parts of the soul. Plutarch (46–c. 120) even wrote that the soul is not one singular substance but a composite of many different layers. Although the idea of multiple parts of the soul was accepted in early Christianity, in time the idea of the soul began to refer to a singular essence. It was later in the development of Christianity, during the first and second centuries, that the idea of a single soul became commonly accepted.

However, older notions persist. Christians clearly believed that saints were still present in their bodies and in their tombs after their physical deaths. Cultic practices were therefore carried out in the tombs. Some ate with the dead, while others slept in their vicinity. Such actions were carried out in order to gain the spiritual and corporeal protection of the saints. Many individuals also wished to be buried next to saints, so that the saints would help them gain entrance to heaven. This was perceived as a growing problem by the Church, and so they propagated the belief that one did not have to be close to the physical remains of saints in order to gain their assistance and protection in the afterlife. It is probable, though, that the Church simply said this to stop the practice, even though they themselves did not believe it. Augustine did say, "Maybe martyrs did remain close by, foraging for souls and assisting the afflicted at their tombs" (Kaufman, 1994, p. 7).

When determining where the Christian practice of mummification came from, it is interesting to note the similarity between Egyptian religious notions of the soul and the corresponding Christian concepts. If it was important to be in the proximity of the physical remains of saints in order to gain their protection, the spirit must have also been perceived as remaining with the body. Although ideas may differ today, the earlier concepts still remain. They linger in the believer's psyche, and they can be found in the depths of modern cultic practices in the Roman Catholic tradition.

The bodies of martyrs and saints were considered especially numinous. It was for this reason that believers wanted to be in the presence of such remains. They gathered up the bones of dead martyrs and other saints because of their belief in the miraculous powers of such remains. Eunapius of Sardis (349–c. 414) wrote about the end of paganism: "For they collected the bones and skulls of criminals who had been put to death for numerous crimes ... made them out to be gods, and thought that they became better by defiling themselves at their graves. Martyrs the dead men were called, and ministers of a sort, and ambassadors with the gods to carry men's prayers" (Eunapius of Sardis, 1921, p. 472).

Whole-body relics were valued, but so were parts of bodies, and even clothing that touched holy bodies. The importance placed on such objects led to a relic trade. People manufactured fake relics, and they stole relics from one location in order to sell them in another. Some clergy members stole relics from one church only to have them translated to their own. These relics were in high demand, and a site was not even considered holy if it did not have a relic. At the Council of Nicea in 767, for example, the Church declared that every church altar must house the relics of a saint. Up until 1967 the Church continued to provide certificates for relics, and even today the definition of an altar according to the Code of Canon Law is a tomb that contains the relics of a saint. Relics were extremely important, and they continue to be an integral part of Catholic religious beliefs.

Such items were thought to be infused with divine powers, and the mere presence of such objects could effect miracles and other magical phenomena. "These relics are miraculous, giving off pleasant odors when touched, healing the sick, and otherwise expressing the will of the saints whose remains they are" (Geary, 1978, p. 4). The obsession with the dead and with the remains of the dead, and the interrelationship between the cult of the saints and the cult of relics, can be more adequately defined as a cult of the dead.

21

The Cult of the Dead

There is certainly a cult of the saints, and there are more than 10,000 total saints according to the (18-volume) *Bibliotheca Sanctorum*. But why is it that their physical remains are so important to followers? Why is it actually a cult of the dead? At the beginning of Christianity, early believers worshipped saints for the powers that they were thought to possess. The believers thought that being close to the remains of such holy individuals was beneficial and that prayers could be answered while in such proximity. This is because followers believed that the (magical or mystical) powers that saints had were somehow accessed through the bodily remains. It was as though the remains themselves were infused with divine powers.

There was a theory about life and death and the function of the saints proposed by the Church, but most of the followers did not consider such things in detail. They did not attempt to understand concepts that cannot be easily understood. Instead, most of their practices ended up being based upon nothing more than popular superstition (Geary, 1978). Hume (1875) summed up this common trait that is found in nearly all religions: "The vulgar, that is, indeed, all mankind a few excepted, being ignorant and uninstructed, never elate their contemplation to the heavens ... so far as to discern a supreme mind or original providence" (p. 334).[1]

It is possible, too, that the entire Catholic organization is infused with superstition, and the current teachings are more superstitious than theological. Much of what is thought of as current Church doctrine is not compatible with either logic or ethics. "The arguments for much of what passes as current church doctrine are so intellectually contemptible that mere self-respect forbids a man to voice them as his own. The very fact that the intellectual level of the church has been raised makes it harder for [even] a priest to swallow the scriptural fundamentalism reverted to by Rome when it claims that priests must be celibate or that women cannot be priests" (Wills, 2001, p. 10). The practices of the faith have little to do with self-reflection and (theological) consideration of the divine. Many of them are relegated to the practice of superstition instead, which runs contrary to logic. The uneducated rely on superstition because "they tend to explain and interpret all natural phenomena either by the intervention of saints if the effect is good, or by some magico-supernatural power, such as the evil-eye, if the results are harmful" (Zammit-Maempel, 1968, p. 1).

The notion of the evil-eye (*mal'occhio*) is still present, and there are some individuals in Italy who display their superstitious beliefs by wearing a cattle horn on a necklace in order to ward off the curse. Sometimes, individuals wear this horn and an amulet of a saint on the same chain—evidence of religious ideas and superstitious beliefs being blended together. Superstitious practices and other customs found in diverse religious traditions are often incorporated into new faiths. Many "pagan customs and folk-ways that were too deeply rooted to be eradicated became adapted to the new religion after being given a different interpretation by the Church. A case in point is the old pagan custom of wearing protective amulets, which, under the strict censorship of the Church, became substituted by the wearing of medals bearing the image of some protective saint" (Zammit Maempel, 1968, p. 2). Early superstitions did not go away; they were simply altered to fit into the changing structure of the new religion.

The Catholic cult of the relics and the veneration shown to the dead bodies of saints do display a great deal of superstition. The dead were considered magical beings, capable of changing fate and circumstance in order to assist the living. The bodies had little to do with the people who once inhabited them. The remains of saints had more to do with the emotional and psychological needs of the living, and it was for this reason that there were many relic thefts reported in the Middle Ages. In a way, the practices of the Church actually served to promulgate this unusual practice of dealing out the dead. According to canon law, it was wrong to sell relics, but it was acceptable for clergy members to buy such relics.[2] The theft of such items, along with the practices performed in the vicinity of such remains, demonstrates the importance that believers placed upon the remains of the dead.

Although this veneration was likely influenced by other, earlier religious traditions, there are also scriptural reasons why it exists. In the Book of Kings, a miracle is reported to have come about when the body of a dead man touched the bones of a holy individual: "Elisha died and was buried. Now Moabite raiders used to enter the country every spring. Once while some Israelites were burying a man, suddenly they saw a band of raiders; so they threw the man's body into Elisha's tomb. When the body touched Elisha's bones, the man came to life and stood up on his feet" (I Kings 13:19–21).

According to accounts found in the New Testament, it was not just the bones of the deceased that could work miracles but even objects that had touched the bodies of holy individuals. Here is an example regarding Paul, one of the followers of Jesus: "God did extraordinary miracles through Paul, so that even handkerchiefs and aprons that had touched him were taken to the sick, and their illnesses were cured and the evil spirits left them" (Acts 19:11–12).

This quote states that objects that touch the bodies of saints can cure people of illnesses and can likewise cast out demons that were apparently living within people. This is also an interesting concept: that a human soul and an evil spirit can inhabit the same physical body. If this is the case, a divine spirit can also inhabit the same body as a human soul. This concept explains how God could actually use the body of a saint in order to work miracles. The belief in the magical power found within saintly remains was expounded in the eighth century by St. John of Damascus (c. 676–749) in his book *Expositions of the Orthodox Faith*: "These [saintly remains] are made treasures and pure habitations of God: For I will dwell in them, said God, and walk in them, and I will be their God. The divine Scripture likewise saith that the souls of the just are in God's hands and death cannot lay hold of them. For death is rather the sleep of the saints than their death."

Death in Catholicism is viewed as a temporary state alone. It is a state in which the soul leaves the body, but one day it is destined to return and to inhabit the same remains. This is a strange matter, because although this is one belief, another has to do with the inseparability of the soul and the physical body. If the soul were completely gone, then miracles and the like that occur in the presence of such remains could not be explained (through Catholic religious beliefs). It has to be remembered that the soul of the saint is forever connected to his or her body. This concept is not clearly explained anywhere, but both phenomena exist in Catholic religious ideas: The body is discarded by the soul temporarily, but it still remains with the flesh. This confusing idea can be perfectly explained by looking at the concepts of the soul that exist in some other religious traditions—traditions that likely influenced Christian beliefs about life and death. These concepts and connections will be explored more fully later. For now, it is sufficient to know that early Christians literally thought that the spirits of holy individuals were inextricably bound to their bodies.

The power that relics were perceived to have had is evidenced by the cult that surrounded them. Actual physical remains were accorded more respect and spiritual value than objects that had merely touched holy individuals, or even objects that they may have worn while alive. Churches and cathedrals that house individual bones are sites still frequented by pilgrims and are known as especially holy sites primarily due to the presence of such relics at these locations. The most valued relics, however, are whole-body relics. There are many bodies on display in Italy. Some have decayed naturally and are little more than skeletons. Others, however, are bodies that have failed to decay naturally.

The preservation of some of these bodies can be easily explained. Some of them were embalmed. Others were treated in various ways to withstand decay and to essentially effect preservation. Still others were not treated in any obvious way yet due to environmental factors did not decay. The presence of certain fungi in the earth has been known to cause mummification, and the right combination of humidity and temperature can also effect preservation. A body buried in volcanic soil without a casket, for example, will naturally be drained of its fluids, and it will desiccate and be preserved, provided that it is not eaten by insects or rodents. It was this same natural process that was used to preserve bodies in predynastic Egypt.

However, there are a number of bodies on display in Italy that cannot be adequately explained. They have been preserved, but the cause of the preservation is still a mystery. Many credit the phenomenon to the preservative power of the spirit, and such bodies are actually considered to be evidence of the existence of God. It is thought that if someone in life is infused with divine grace, his or her body may fail to decompose after death. Thus, the state of the body after death is indicative of a person's spiritual advancement.

These bodies display some characteristics that other mummies do not. Typically, the conditions in which the bodies are preserved are not conducive to such preservation. The skin does not dry out and tighten, but it tends to remain loose and flexible. Sometimes, it does not become pale but maintains a rosy complexion, as if the individual were still alive and merely sleeping. Some of the bodies are moist for an extended period of time after death, while others sweat, secrete strange fluids, or even bleed years after the deaths of their owners. One famous example of this phenomenon is the body of St. John of the Cross, who bled when his finger was cut off nine months after his death. These bodies are a source of wonder and religious devotion, and they are considered miraculous by many individuals all over the world. Collectively, they are known as the Incorruptibles.

IV. Incorruptible Bodies

Christ gives us the relics of saints as health-giving springs through which flow blessings and healing. — St. John Damascene

22

The Incorruptibles

According to Giuseppe Fallica (2009), the term "Incorruptibles" refers to bodies that were miraculously preserved by faith without any type of embalming or other treatment. Such preservations are typically unexplainable by science and, according to most authors on the subject, cannot be classified as either artificial or natural mummification. Even when looking at Vreeland's (1998) classifications of mummy types, it is difficult to put the Incorruptibles neatly into any specific category. Class I mummification is preservation that occurs naturally by a number of preexisting environmental factors. Class II preservations are intentional mummification through the enhancement of natural processes, and Class III mummification is artificial preservation, using such techniques as evisceration, smoke-curing, or embalming with things like resins, oils, or herbs. For a body to be called an Incorruptible, it was not supposed to have been treated in any way. Since the preservations cannot be explained by science, it is deemed that the bodies were preserved by God and it is thought to be indicative of the high spiritual advancement of the individuals during life.

Of course, there are some scientists and other disbelievers who propose a number of theories in an attempt to explain (and discredit) the preservation.[1] Some say that the preservations occurred due to environmental factors, such as fungi in the soil that functioned as a preserving agent. Fallica (2009) wrote that this is not possible because the bodies were often found around other bodies that had decayed. If the preservation were due to an environmental factor, then all of the bodies should have been preserved. One example of this is the body of St. Andrea Bobola (1590–1657), which was found perfectly preserved in a crypt underneath a Jesuit church in Pinsk. Forty years after his death, his remains were found preserved, even though the bodies around him had decayed normally. He had met his end as a martyr in the hands of the Cossacks, who put him through unimaginable tortures. He was dragged by horses, burned, stabbed, and eventually put to death with a saber (Harney, 1941). The body had been mutilated, which normally would have hastened decomposition, but the body was miraculously preserved. "The condition of the body, which has never been embalmed, treated, or conditioned, has many times been declared a miraculous preservation in spite of its mutilated condition, which of course resulted from the Saint's cruel martyrdom" (Cruz, 1977, p. 245). Those who examined the body during the canonization process noted that his skin had normal coloring, was flexible, and looked lifelike, despite the mutilated appearance of the body. It is a preservation that cannot be explained. If there had been something in the soil that functioned as a preserving agent, the other bodies around it would have been likewise preserved. The corpse was unearthed in 1896 and redressed. Parts of it were taken and sent to various locations that desired a piece of the saint. The Bishop of Mohilow even took a large piece of the spine as a relic for his own church. How St. Andrea's body was preserved while the others around him decayed naturally is unknown.

Others think that the preservation of the Incorruptibles may have occurred due to the ascetic practices of the individuals. Ascetics in various cultures are often found naturally preserved after their deaths, and it is thought that such mummification occurs due to their regulated diets and intake of strange substances. The individuals in Yamagata, Japan, for example, who intended to mummify themselves cut out all grains and ate pine products, such as pine needles, bark, and sap. They believed that such products functioned as preservatives and that the substances helped them to mummify. The mummies of Guanajuato, Mexico, which were found preserved in grotesque positions, were likewise thought to have been created by a combination of soil conditions and their diet. However, there is no scientific evidence that proves that dietary changes can result in bodily preservation. Therefore, even if some of the Incorruptibles in Italy were ascetics, such a lifestyle cannot be shown scientifically to encourage bodily preservation after death.

Others say that the bodies were deliberately preserved and that the Church is defrauding people, but Fallica (2009) again thinks that this is unlikely, since a fraud like this would be completely contrary to the practices of the Church. People who choose a religious lifestyle, he wrote, would likely not be deceitful. However, the Church historian Mosheim (1842), in his book An Ecclesiastical History, Ancient and Modern, from the Birth of Christ to the Beginning of the Modern Century, wrote: "The Christian Fathers deemed it a pious act to employ deception and fraud" (p. 247). In this statement, he was referring to the act of forging documents and rewriting history in a way that would lend more evidence to the historicity of Jesus, but the deception of the Church does not stop with forging historical accounts. In recent times, a number of deceitful activities of the Roman Catholic Church have been brought to light, including its role in protecting child molesters and hiding their crimes, rather than turning them in to the authorities (Pedote, 2010; Plante, 2004). In addition, Wills (2001) pointed out the many immoral and deceitful activities that were carried out by popes in order to maintain the illusion of papal infallibility. But such knowledge is not new. Foote and Wheeler (1887), in their book *Crimes of Christianity*, explicitly pointed out crimes committed by popes and by other members of the Church from the beginning of Christianity through the Crusades. It seems that, as a whole, the Church does not have a problem hiding information from outsiders, and deceit seems to be an acceptable practice to the organization.

In fact, there have been various authors who have written about the evil and deceitful practices of both the pope and the Church, including Dante Alighieri, the famous author of the *Divine Comedy*, who put popes in hell in his masterpiece. In *Inferno*, he wrote: "Here Popes and prelates butt their tonsured pates, mastered by avarice that nothing sates" (7.46–48). Dante was apparently angered by the fact that many popes were extremely rich. He did not think that religious figures should be some of the most wealthy individuals in the entire country (Wills, 2001). Artists also depicted popes and the Church as evil and deceitful. "Painters of the Last Judgments—Andrea Orcagna (c. 1308–1368), for instance—used to include a figure wearing the papal crown in the fires of hell, presenting the pope as a terminal sinner damned forever" (Wills, 2001, p. 1). This was not intended to be an attack on the Church, only a lesson for the faithful. Such depictions demonstrated that no matter how authoritative the pope might be, "he is not impeccable as a man — he can sin, as can all humans" (Wills, 2001, p. 1). Therefore, the Church, and the Church leaders, can still continue to be deceitful as they have in the past. As the evidence demonstrates, it is not inconceivable that they have intentionally mummified many individuals and then passed them off as Incorruptibles.

Another common critique used by non-believers to discredit the phenomenon is that the bodies had mummified or saponified naturally and the events were erroneously interpreted as being miraculous. Fallica (2009) suggests that this is unlikely, because there are telltale signs that signal that such kinds of natural mummification have occurred. The skin is usually the best indication. In cases of natural mummification, there is often a reduction in the total size of the bodies and the skin hardens. Both of these occurrences come about as the body desiccates. In addition, the body usually begins to smell bad, and it often takes on a deformed and irregular shape. The body then stiffens, and it becomes nearly impossible to bend the arms or the legs into different positions. The Incorruptibles, however, display none of these signs. When unearthed even years after their deaths, the bodies look as though they were still alive. The skin is still rosy, as though blood still flowed beneath it, and the remains are fresh, flexible, and (sometimes) moist.

In the case of bodily saponification, it can be more difficult to determine if a corpse had saponified or if it was miraculously preserved. This is because such bodies do tend to maintain their coloring, moisture, and flexibility. However, when it is impossible to determine for sure whether the preservation was miraculous or not, a group of experts is often called in to examine the remains. "In the case of the Beata Mariana Navarro of Jesus, for example, a commission of 11 surgeons studied the cadaver (a century after death) in order to determine if the cause of such a wonderful preservation was natural or artificial. Well, what they found was not a mass of adipocere,[2] but internal organs and viscera that were still fresh and moist" (Fallica, 2009, p. 44). In addition, in cases of saponification the body often emits a horrible stench, and the Incorruptibles never smell bad. They always have a fragrant smell, like flowers, according to most witnesses. This scent is called the Odor of Sanctity (L'Odore della Santità) by believers.

Another claim from non-believers is that the bodies may have been intentionally preserved and then forgotten in time. This particular claim is not easily refuted because of the recent discovery by pathologist Ezio Fulcheri, who was invited by the supervisor of the Vatican Egyptian Museum to examine the body of an Incorruptible. He examined the body of St. Margaret of Cortona (1247–1297), and he found that there were large incision marks on her thighs, abdomen and chest. The internal organs had been removed, and the body was embalmed with a solution that gave the remains a pleasant scent. It was this scent, misinterpreted as the Odor of Sanctity, along with the remarkable preservation of her body, that led to her eventual canonization (Vago, 2007). After Fulcheri's discovery that the body had been purposefully eviscerated, records were searched in order to determine whether this was done with the knowledge of the Church. In some of the old documents, it was recorded that after the saint died many citizens of Cortona had asked the local bishop for permission to embalm the body. The saint was so important to the people that they wanted her preserved for all time. After a century or two, people forgot that the body had been embalmed, and the records were never consulted. Therefore, for centuries, individuals had believed that her body had been miraculously preserved, but it had actually been accomplished artificially.

As a result of this discovery, incorruptible bodies of people who died centuries ago are now under more scrutiny, as it is not sure whether the preservations are miraculous or the remains were artificially preserved.

Believers in the miraculous nature of the Incorruptibles, however, do not think that all of the bodies on display in Italian churches and cathedrals had been deliberately mummified in the past and then forgotten about as time progressed. They believe that many of the bodies on display are truly miraculous, having been preserved by God.

23

Miraculous Preservation

It seems that the preservation of such bodies did not occur secondarily to climatic conditions or the manner or place of burial. They also did not seem to be affected by the time elapsed before burial, by moisture in their tombs, or by the temperature of the grave sites. The Incorruptibles were deemed miraculous because the bodies had (supposedly) been preserved without any embalming or other preservative treatments. Most of the bodies were found lifelike and flexible, and many of them had a floral fragrance that permeated the remains. This again was considered evidence of sanctity. Making the phenomenon even more inexplicable is that many of these bodies were found next to other skeletal remains that had decayed normally. Another mysterious phenomenon that accompanies such miraculously preserved bodies is the presence of blood or other clear liquids that issue from the remains. This phenomenon is not generally recorded in cases of intentional preservation.

Typically, bodies left in open air mummify eight times faster than bodies that are buried, so bodily preservation occurring in fresh air is rare and difficult to explain scientifically. St. Coloman (d. 1012) was taken captive near Vienna when he was on a pilgrimage to Jerusalem. He could not understand the language of his captors, who were engaged in a battle at the time. They took him for a spy and hung him from a tree, where the body remained for months. Strangely, it was said that his body did not decay at all during this period of time — that it remained fresh and pliable, as though he had only recently died. St. Bernadino of Siena (1380–1444) was laid out in open air for 26 days before his funeral so that people could continue to visit from faraway places in order to pay their last respects to him. During that time, his skin complexion and flexibility did not change at all, and it is said that on the 24th day a stream of blood flowed out of his temporarily closed casket. When the coffin was opened, it was seen that the blood was coming from his nose and covered the habit and pillow inside (Hofer, 1943). Catholic believers soaked small pieces of cloth in the blood and took them home as personal relics.

The body of St. Angela Merici (1474–1540), similar to the corpse of St. Bernadino, was laid out for a full 30 days before her eventual funeral because of the unceasing number of individuals who wished to touch her remains. During that time period, the body did not change color or stiffen. A doctor cut out one of her bones in order to make relics before her burial, and those relics were sent to various other churches. Today, the body is located at the Casa S. Angela in Brescia, Italy. It has clearly been mummified, and the skin is a dark brown color, a color that can likely be attributed to a treatment performed on the remains in 1930. The body was decaying and this was seen as a problem to the Church, so a priest at the Catholic University of the Sacred Heart in Milan made an embalming solution in order to treat the remains. Since the embalming, the body has remained fairly well preserved.

St. Teresa Margaret of the Sacred Heart (1747–1770) was likewise laid out for a full 50 days, but this occurred after her funeral, not before (Fallica, 2009). The circumstances following her death were unique. Immediately after her death of gangrene, she began to decay, so the funeral was scheduled for only a day or two after her death. Her skin changed to a dark purple color and her abdomen began to swell: evidence of internal chemicals breaking down her bodily tissues. She did not look like she was still alive, like some of the other Incorruptibles, and the body took on a grotesque appearance. Still, visitors did not stop coming to visit her and to be close to a body that they believed could work like magic. She was thought of as a saint before her canonization, much like St. Angela Merici and St. Bernadino of Siena, and therefore crowds of people wished to be near Teresa's holy body, hoping for miracles. They wanted to make physical contact with the body in order to make use of the divine power that they thought inhabited it, and they wanted relics. Church officials cut up pieces of the clothing that she was wearing in order to give them to the visitors who were looking for such miracle-working items. After her funeral, however, as soon as the corpse was out of sight, it is said that her body began to inexplicably change. Newcomb (1934) wrote:

> When her body was being carried below ground to be buried underneath the monastery, it was discovered that the lividly purplish hue of her face, hands, and feet had changed to a faint rose-like color, which gave her a more angelic beauty than she had when alive. The nuns decided to put off the burial for a while. The ninth of March, that is, two days after her death, the religious [sic] went to her uncovered tomb again, and were astonished to see that the lifeless and pallid color of her hands and feet had now changed to the glow of living flesh; her cheeks, now rosy, gave a heavenly look to her face ... she seemed, truly, to be alive, just quietly sleeping. The Father Provincial and Doctor Antonio Romiti, the monastery surgeon, marveled at the beauty of her countenance ... even the eyelids were dewy and in color, even her lips seemed fresh and naturally red. They returned to see the corpse two days later, when their astonishment reached its peak on discovering that the face was even more beautiful and that the body had regained its former size and shape without exuding a drop of moisture. Her limbs had become so pliable and so easily moved as to give the impression of being animated. It was at this time that a new and most delightful odor, not to be compared with any earthly fragrance, clearly revealed what had been brought about in these precious remains.... God had glorified them by the gift of incorruption [pp. 219–220].

Another phenomenon that accompanied this corpse cannot be easily explained—a phenomenon that occurs frequently with the Incorruptibles. There was moisture forming just underneath the nostrils of the body. When the moisture was removed with a cloth, it was found to have a floral fragrance that the archbishop called the Fragrance of Virginity (Newcomb, 1934). Just what virginity smells like is unknown, but it is likely that the archbishop was referring to the odor of sanctity that other witnesses have described: a flower-like scent that permeates the remains.

When reading accounts of saints like the one quoted earlier, it should be remembered that they were written as hagiographies, not biographies, and so historical accuracy was not as important as creating an account of the saint that other believers would want to read. The primary aim in writing about the lives of saints was not to give a completely accurate historical account but rather to provide an example for believers to emulate. The problem with hagiographies is not the flowery language but the interpretation of historical events through a pre-set lens. In other words, if a person begins to write an account of the life of a saint and already believes that God worked through the individual, events that might not have been normally considered miraculous will take on a new light. If the account is to be considered historical, then the writer cannot make any kind of judgment that he or she may want.

"The historian is not free to make any interpretation, and so arrive at any facts he likes; what he has before him are *data* not *desiderata*; and he is bound, in so far as he recognizes historiography to be a search for truth, to take care that his interpretation, as well as his inevitable suppositions, are continually checked by the data and not imposed by them" (Peter, 1965, p. 111). Many hagiographers have been guilty of imposing their own judgments and evaluations on available historical evidence, and it is for this reason that the critical reader must be weary. Take the following example from the hagiography of St. Teresa Margaret: "It was at this time that a new and most delightful odor, not to be compared with any earthly fragrance, clearly revealed what had been brought about in these precious remains.... God had glorified them by the gift of incorruption" (Newcomb, 1934, p. 220). Take away the flowery language and the meanings imposed by the writer and we are left with this amended account: "The body was fragrant and did not decay." Certainly the second example is not as powerful (for believers) as the first, but it is precisely this type of stripping away (of flowery language) and extraction of the truth that must be undertaken.

It should be remembered, too, though, that the aim of such hagiographies in Catholicism was not to present an entirely historical picture but to provide an embellished account that other Christians might aspire toward. That is why expressions like "she died a holy death" and "the infallible Church" show up in reports. The accounts are meant to inspire believers, not to provide accurate historical accounts. Keeping this in mind, we can read the hagiographies and still gain important information. Take away the flowery language and the conjecture and we still have an account of a strange occurrence that likely took place after the death of this saint — an occurrence that cannot be easily explained.

Even more unusual are those bodies that remained preserved and flexible in extremely humid conditions. The body of St. Josaphat (1580–1623), for example, remained submerged in water for a full week before being pulled out, and yet his body was still remarkably well preserved. He had angered the Orthodox Christians, and they beat and hacked him to death. When the body was found it was mutilated, but it had not substantially decayed. King Sigmund of Poland wanted Josaphat to be named a saint, so he asked the Vatican to begin the process of canonization. Pope Urban VIII granted his request and had Josaphat's body unearthed (five years after his death). The body was said to have been found in a perfect state of preservation, even though his clothing had rotted away.

Many people wanted parts of his body as relics and wanted to see his miraculous preservation, so the body was removed from its tomb, redressed and propped up on the episcopal throne for believers to see. Although it was decided that the body would not be chopped up for relic seekers, some religious individuals decided to take some anyway. They cut off the little fingers of both hands and one toe from the left foot and absconded with the artifacts.

While the body was on display, a strange liquid resembling sweat dripped from its face. This liquid was wiped off with handkerchiefs, and then pieces of the cloth were sent to various locales as (secondary) relics. An extremely expensive reliquary was made for the saint. It was made entirely from silver and mother-of-pearl, and it included a life-size image of the saint in a reclining position, supported by six silver angels who were kneeling, and the sides of it were lavishly decorated with scenes of his martyrdom. It is said that when his body was being prepared for its translation into the reliquary the wound on his forehead, which had been inflicted 27 years earlier, began bleeding again (Boresky, 1955).

St. Catherine of Genoa (1447–1510) was another example of a body being unusually preserved despite having been buried in humid conditions. She had been buried in the Pammatone hospital chapel. After 18 months, however, it was discovered that she had been buried right next to a water source. Upon hearing the news, people feared that her body might have decayed. The preservation of bodies is extremely important in Catholicism, and so the thought of this potential rapid decay was disheartening. Those concerned unearthed her in order to verify if her body had been damaged by the burial conditions. It was found incorrupt, although the moisture around her had rotted away her coffin. St. Madeleine Sophie Barat (1779–1865) was found in a similar state of preservation despite having been buried in extremely damp conditions for 28 years. "When the debris of wood and the mildewed garments were removed, the body was found entire, the features quite recognizable, the veil [over her face] well preserved, the slender fingers still clasping a small crucifix" (Ward, 1925, p. 638).

The body was so well preserved that the Church decided not to cut it into pieces. Normally, the bodies of holy individuals are cut up so that pieces of the remains can be sent to other churches and cathedrals as relics. This did not happen to the remains of St. Barat. Instead, a costly housing was created to display the corpse and the face and hands of the body were covered with silver. It is likely that the face mask and the silver gloves are covering substantial decay today, but it is inexplicable how the body was well preserved when unearthed after being buried in humid conditions for so many years.[1]

Other bodies that were found preserved despite similar humid conditions include St. Teresa of Avila (1515–1582) and St. Catherine Laboure (1806–1876), who remained buried for an amazing 56 years before being unearthed. In her case, however, the moisture that surrounded her body was not a problem. This is because she was buried, like popes and other high-ranking members of the Church, in three distinct caskets. The outer coffin was elm, followed by a middle coffin made from lead, and the coffin that immediately surrounded her body was cypress. The aim of three caskets is obviously to prevent decay, and when her body was unearthed it was found perfectly preserved. Once fresh air touched the remains, however, the body began to decay. It started to darken. In order to prevent further putrefaction, the Church decided to mummify her. They removed her heart and other organs, and they took out the ribs and the clavicle for use as relics. They also disconnected her arms and removed them from the body for relic purposes. Then, they injected her body with an embalming solution of formaldehyde, glycerin and carbolic acid (Crapez, 1933). Her thus-preserved body was positioned for public viewing under the altar of the Our Lady of the Sun Church. Her hands, which were cut off by preservers, were placed in a special reliquary, and her preserved heart was put in another reliquary made from gold and precious gems.

The preservation of individuals deemed holy is important to Catholics in Italy and in other European countries, and the lack of decay is considered to be evidence of God by some believers. There are hundreds of corpses on display all over Italy in churches and in cathedrals. There are so many of them that it is impossible to come up with an exact number.

Fulcheri (1996) had put the figure at 315 bodies, but there are likely many more. Some of the remains of the saints, beati and venerables in small towns are only locally known to exist. Other bodies exist but have been forgotten or even lost over the centuries. In an interview with Heather Pringle, Fulcheri said, "I don't think that any count is possible. Not even the bishops know how many there are. You see, there are so many churches that have been closed and are neglected now" (Pringle, 2001, p. 249).

It is even more difficult to determine the number of body parts from saints, venerables and beati that are preserved in churches and cathedrals. It was (and still is) a common practice to cut off pieces of the body and to send them to diverse religious centers for enshrinement as relics. How many there actually are in Italy will unfortunately remain unknown. The large number of bodies and relic body parts attests to the importance of the physical body for Catholics. A large number of the bodies of holy people that are on display are found in Rome, Florence, Naples, Genoa, and Palermo.

24

The Preserved Bodies in Rome, Assisi and Mantova

The preserved bodies of saints, beati and venerables are found in more than 25 different churches and cathedrals in Rome. Beside the whole-body relics, there are an incalculable number of relics—body parts—on display or at least enshrined in locations all over the city. The remains of Anna Maria Taigi (1769–1837) rest at the Basilica of St. Crysogono. She married and had children, and after her death in 1837 her body was buried in the cemetery of Verano. Eighteen years later, it was decided that her body be translated to the Church of St. Maria of Peace. As was the custom, when a body was moved to another religious locale it was inspected. The examiners were amazed to find that, in her case, the body had not decayed and it seemed to be in a perfect state of preservation. It was "as fresh as though it were buried the day before" (Fallica, 2009, p. 428). The body did not remain at the new location for long, though. Another location wanted it, so another transfer occurred in 1865, 28 years after her death. Again, the body was examined, and it was still found to be amazingly well preserved. Primarily due to the state of her corpse, she was officially recognized by the Church three years later, in 1868. She was named a Blessed, and her body was put on display for more than a week so that the inhabitants of Trastevere could come to see her. Her skin was flexible and it had a red coloring. After another inspection by a doctor, it was determined that her internal organs had not putrefied, but that they were whole and still preserved.

Francesca Romana (1384–1440) was another saint who was thought of as an Incorruptible. She was born to a very prestigious and rich family, like most other saints, and when she was 13 years old she married a rich man named Lorenzo Ponziani. They had three children, but two of them died at a young age. Francesca was known for her generosity, often giving money to the poor and assisting displaced women and the sick. It is said that she experienced a number of strange phenomena during her periods of prayer — phenomena that were considered miraculous, including visions and ecstasies. The presence of such visions, although none of them were visible to others, led people to suspect that she was blessed. After her death, her body was displayed for several days before burial at the Church of Santa Maria Nova. Her body was exhumed more than four months after her death and appeared fresh and was fragrant. The condition of her remains pushed her into sainthood. Two centuries later, in 1638, only her bones were found.

Most of the time when people write about the Incorruptibles, they only write about the well-known individuals whose bodies are still seemingly preserved and on display in churches or in cathedrals in Italy and France and in other churches throughout all of Europe. However, focusing on just one or two famous Incorruptibles does not provide an accurate picture of the majority of such cases. The initial bodily preservation of Francesca, and then its subsequent decay, however, is typical when it comes to the Incorruptibles. When the bodies of important religious personages were unearthed, they were initially found to be preserved. This amazed some people, and the fragrant smell that accompanied such bodies caused some people to hypothesize that they were cases of miraculous preservation. However, the preservation was typically not permanent. The preservation of such bodies was only temporary, and after the bodies were unearthed, unless they were treated, they often quickly deteriorated. For this reason, some of the bodies that were initially unearthed were then treated in order to ward off inevitable decay.

Sometimes, this involved the removal of organs and treatment with balms or chemicals. In other cases, the organs were left in place and the treatment consisted only of the application of preservative chemicals. Some of the Incorruptibles have been damaged by the faulty application of such chemicals. The body of Arcangela Girlani of Mantova (1460–1495) for example, was dug up almost 300 years after her death and treated with an embalming solution (in 1782). It was unearthed and treated again in 1932. However, the mixture had been improperly applied and it stripped away part of her flesh. In order to hide this deformity, a facial mask made from silver was created, along with a matching covering for her hands. The body was examined again in 1960 and found to still be flexible and intact.

The application of masks and other bodily coverings is common when it comes to corpses of saints, venerables and beati in Italy. Bodily preservation was attempted by many different means, and sometimes such preservation was successful. However, in other cases,

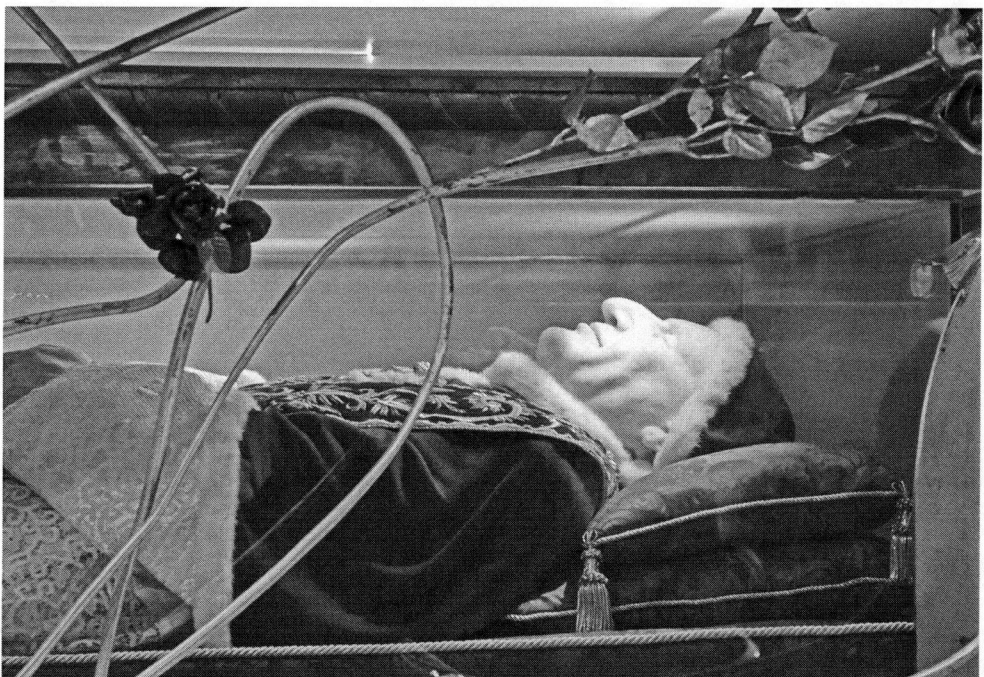

The body of Pope John XXIII, located at St. Peter's Cathedral in the Vatican. A mask hides the decomposition of his body and preserves his likeness (Rome, Italy).

the bodies could not be completely preserved. Sometimes, decay set in and the bodies deteriorated. When this happened, rather than hide the bodies from public view, masks were put into place to hide the decay. In many cases, wax masks were used that look like human flesh from a distance. In other occurrences, silver masks were made to cover the faces instead.

The body of St. Clare of Assisi (c. 1193–1253) was thought to have undergone a similar treatment, as her face was covered with a silver mask and then displayed at the cathedral in Assisi. Professor Fulcheri and his colleagues were going to examine this body to see how well she was actually preserved underneath the mask. They were shocked to find that there was no body there at all (Pringle, 2001). Years ago, the body had completely decayed. Not wanting anyone to know, the Church gathered together her bones and then covered them with a mannequin made from silver. It was redressed in the saint's clothing, and no one knew about the deception. People saw the outline of the body and believed that it was whole. Although the preservation of the flesh is important, sometimes it is nearly impossible to prevent decay. Eventually, all beings are reduced to dust. This occurrence, though, is indicative of the importance placed on the physical remains by the Roman Catholic Church and the need to venerate the actual corpses of important individuals.

St. Philip Neri (1515–1595) was the son of a well-known and wealthy Florentine man. Philip moved to Rome at the age of 18, and due to his fascination with the physical remains of the saints and early martyrs he often prayed in the catacombs at night. He became increasingly more religious, and he began practicing austerities. He began catechism classes and other religious activities, and he actually became well known in Rome for his religious organizational pursuits. He died in 1595, which is when, like the other Incorruptibles, his history became all the more interesting. According to Church doctors, two of his ribs had been broken and they were forced upward above his enlarged heart, in the shape of an arch. Since the individual did not complain of any pain during life, it was deemed a miracle.

The body was placed in a small chapel attached to the Chiesa Nuova in Rome after a few days, and it was uncovered about four years later. When they uncovered the coffin, there was a large crack in the cover, and due to this fissure, the body was covered with cobwebs and dust. His clothing had also rotted away, along with other objects that were placed into the tomb with him, and the body was therefore covered. It took those present some time to remove all of the materials that hid the body. When they did, however, they found that his body was in a perfect state of preservation. The body had been initially treated with a preservative solution when the autopsy was performed, which likely explains the condition in which the body was found. The face had decayed, however, and so it was covered with a silver mask before being displayed in the Chiesa Nuova. Initially, the body was going to be displayed in a coffin made entirely of silver, but the display design was changed. It is now displayed in a reliquary made from gemstones and other expensive materials. The Church decided not to chop him up to make relics. Instead, they took bits of his skin alone and gave these relics to other churches and individual believers.

The Venerable Pietro della Madre di Dio (1565–1608) was born in Spain and died in Perugia, but today his body is found in Rome at the Convent of Santa Maria della Scala. After having joined the Carmelite Order, he went to Rome as an assistant to the Attorney General (*Procuratore Generale*) of the congregation in Rome. He was such an able preacher, though, that he caught the attention of the pope, who nominated him Apostolic Preacher

Often, the bodies of saints were covered with silver or other expensive materials, so that they would endure forever. They were then displayed in ornate coffins in prominent positions in cathedrals or churches. This is the body of St. Ranieri (Pisa, Italy).

(*Predicatore Apostolico*). The pope also asked Pietro to start a new convent of Scalzi, in Rome. This convent came to be called the Convent of Santa Maria della Scala. He lived there for many years, known first as the prior and then later as the General Superior (*Superiore Generale*).

When preaching to his congregation, he stressed devotion to Mary, the mother of Jesus, and the diffusion of scapulars to the public. A scapular most likely originated from an apron-like garment worn by some Christian monks. It is still worn, in various forms, by priests, friars, monks, and nuns, but the term also refers to smaller objects of devotion that signify allegiance to an order. These devotional scapulars could be necklaces with cloth patches fashioned so that when the wearer puts them on one of the patches will be in the front of the body, while the other will be on the back. Just what is on the patches can differ. Sometimes it could be a picture or symbol of a saint or religious order, and it signifies the acceptance of a way of life or devotion to a particular religious order. In the *Catholic Encyclopedia* (1914) it was written: "Like the rosary, the brown scapula has become the badge of the devout Catholic." The importance that Pietro placed on this piece of cloth was likely to strengthen the faith of his congregation and to bind them tighter.

Aside from the political advancements made within the Church itself, he also had a number of spiritual abilities, such as the gift of prophecy and the ability to see spiritual entities. It was also said that he was able to drive demons away (Fallica, 2009). After a long and painful illness, he died and was buried. The body was unearthed four years later when his process had begun, and like the other Incorruptibles, his body was found whole.

The life of Pietro della Madre di Dio (Peter of the Mother of God) is an example of a pattern common to many venerables, beati and saints. Of course, there were some saints who were poor and who had little to do with the internal politics of the Church, but the majority of saints were born into wealthy and influential families. It was often through the connections already established by the family that the child was able to join an order and be promoted up through the ranks of the Church in Rome. George and George (1955) conducted an academic study in which the financial backgrounds of the saints were analyzed. They compiled a list of saints for whom they were able to access historical documentation about the relative wealth of their families and put together a list of 2,494 saints from the first century up until the twentieth century. They found that in the entire history of the Church, 78 percent of saints were from upper-class families, 17 percent were from middle-class families, and only 5 percent were from lower-class backgrounds (p. 87). This schism was even more pronounced between the seventh and the 13th centuries. In the seventh century 96 percent of all saints were from upper-class backgrounds. In the eighth century it was 97 percent, in the ninth 94 percent, and in the tenth century it was back up to 97 percent. Between the 11th and the 13th centuries, 88 percent of all saints were from wealthy families.

The best chance someone had to be named a saint by the Church was if he or she had been born into a wealthy family and if he or she became politically active within the Church in order to receive promotions. High-ranking members of the Church were more likely to be beatified and canonized. The reason wealthy individuals were more likely to be canonized has to do with such individuals deciding to give up their wealth in order to pursue a religious lifestyle. "The way of the saint is the way of voluntary poverty [and] is accomplished by the fact that a man or woman of high social status and wealth rejects these privileges in turning to a life of religion or in accepting some type of heroic self-sacrifice for the sake of his [or her] Christian devotion" (George and George, 1955, p. 92). Again, it seems that even here the unofficial requirements for canonization include some type of martyrdom. The importance of the martyrs has not dissipated, but the idea of what constitutes martyrdom has been broadened to include giving up a wealthy and privileged way of life in order to live a life in the Church, albeit a very comfortable life.

If one is an active member of the Church organization, his or her efforts and lifestyle will be known by the saint makers. Therefore, it is only natural that many saints are affiliated with the Church. This is also why the majority of saints are from Italy and other European countries. The bodies on display in Italy, Spain, and France, in particular, are primarily the corpses of priests, friars, and nuns. The service to the Church was important, as was service to the poor and displays of religious devotion. The preservation of bodies in churches and cathedrals was likely desired by friends of the individual, so that they could still look upon him or her and feel close to the person. This is only one of many reasons why the bodies were preserved and displayed, and it is a reason that is not unique to Catholicism. The relic bodies of important Buddhist monks in China and Tibet, for example, are literally used as living shrines: constant reminders of the teachings of the individuals thus mummified.

Human beings, by nature, are all the same. They may learn different languages, develop diverse values, and hold different metaphysical views, but at the very beginning everyone starts off pretty much the same. The preserved bodies on display in Italy are needed for other aspects of the Roman Catholic faith — needs that will be discussed more fully in subsequent chapters — but they are desired by the living first and foremost. This bodily preservation has more to do with those people who are still alive than the deceased individuals who are prominently displayed. It might help some people to deal with both the uncertainty of life and the certainty of death. This is one of the reasons why the cult of the dead is so large and why bodies (and pieces of bodies) are found in just about every church and every cathedral in Italy.

25

Mummies in Florence, Naples and Sicily

St. Francis de Geronimo (1642–1716) was born to a wealthy family, and he became ordained as a priest at a young age. He then got a degree in theology and was therefore able to enter the Jesuit Order. He spent much of his life preaching and converting people to the faith, and he died at the age of 74. One of his brethren, named John, arranged St. Francis's body for burial. John wrote:

> His cadaver was fresh and flexible, and his face was as beautiful as a live man's, not horrifying to those who saw him. Even I, who often get a weak heart upon seeing corpses, stood next to him. I treated and dressed him with my hands, and upon seeing him I received satisfaction and consolation. I noticed an accommodating gesture that he made toward me while I (with two other brethren) were trying to place his hands across his chest (in order to receive the chalice), but they fell right back down. Therefore I said to him, "Father Francesco, hold those hands still where I put them!" And in fact, they remained there without falling down again.
>
> With the two [other brothers], we decided to cut off the callouses from the underside of his feet in order to keep them as relics, and upon cutting off the callouses that he had on the bottom of his right foot, if I am not mistaken, it began to drip fresh and ruddy blood, so much that it stained many towels, and it continued to issue forth from 4:00 that day until nighttime."[1]

The appearance of blood issuing from the bodies is unusual, even when it comes to the Incorruptibles, but there are a handful of cases in which bodies bled years after death. Besides the body of St. John of the Cross, which was previously mentioned, a famous example of such postmortem bleeding is the body of St. Germaine de Pibrac (1579–1601). After death, like the other Incorruptibles, she was found flexible and lifelike. Forty-three years after her death, the body was being moved so that the Church could enshrine another corpse at the same location. One of the workers dropped a tool. It struck the face of Germaine's body, and she began bleeding. It was this event, along with the miraculous state of preservation in which her body was found, that led to her canonization.

Mary Magdalen de' Pazzi (1566–1607) and Mary Bagnesi (1514–1577) are both enshrined at the Carmelite Church in Careggi, Florence. Mary Magdalen de' Pazzi was born to a very wealthy and well-known family in Florence, but she decided at an early age to pursue a religious life. She is said to have experienced a number of unusual religious phenomena, including levitation and visions of saints. When she was 42 years old, she died after a painful illness and was buried beneath the church in the monastery where she had lived. Her body was infused with a strange floral scent that was thought to be of divine origins. It was called the Odor of Sanctity. This scent issued from the tomb in which she was buried, and it was thought of as miraculous by believers. A year after her death, the tomb that held her body was opened, and the remains were found to have been preserved. "When the casket was opened the corpse was found to be still entire, fresh-looking, and fleshlike in its softness. Blond hairs still adhered to the head; the whole body was flexible. The Saint appeared as one recently deceased. Yet the clothing was wet, for the place of burial was a damp one with running water nearby" (Minima, 1958, p. 348).

After she was unearthed, the body continued to be fragrant and a strange liquid, which had the same fragrance, began seeping from behind the knees of the corpse. The nature of this liquid was (supposedly) unknown to the nuns who inspected the body, but they sopped it up with cloths and then distributed pieces of the fabric as relics. For the next decade, this liquid is said to have issued from the remains. Her body is today on display in a reliquary made from bronze and crystal, and it is still fairly well preserved.

Mary Bagnesi, enshrined at the same location, knew St. Mary Magdalen de' Pazzi. Bagnesi's story is a strange one. It seems that she was so opposed to marriage that when her father arranged one she became severely ill. She fainted, and her condition steadily worsened. She became bedridden and was unable to rise for years. For 34 years she remained in bed, and she had a strange affinity for cats, who stayed with her in her room, slept on her bed, and even supposedly got her food from time to time when she was hungry.

In time, she began to have visions and her neighbors began to think that she was possessed by the devil. A local priest came to visit her, and he told the neighbors that she was not working with the devil. This pacified them, and they began visiting her in her room for spiritual guidance. She is said to have frequently levitated. Her beatification was in 1804, more than 220 years after her death, and her remains are currently located in Careggi, Florence.

The Incorruptibles are known to occasionally display some odd characteristics, but in the case of Antonio Vici (1381–1461) the reported occurrences are truly bizarre. His parents were wealthy individuals, and both of them were members of the Franciscan Order. After Antonio requested admission several times and was turned down, the Franciscans finally accepted him. After his initiation he devoted the rest of his life to the Church, and after 68 years in the order he passed away at the age of 80. He was buried beneath the floors in the Church of San Damiano.

About a year later, a flame was seen burning on top of the slab of his tomb, and James of the Marches said that it was definitely a miracle (Cruz, 1977). Antonio's body was unearthed immediately and found to be incorrupt. It was also fragrant. Since the flame was spotted and declared a miracle, the Church decided that he deserved a better resting place, so they moved his body to a ground-level location near the main altar.

In 1599, the body was exhumed a second time and it was moved to a crystal enclosure — an urn. While the remains were at this location, it is claimed that an inexplicable event occurred. Some people heard knocking from within the urn. This was also determined to be a miracle (Canonici, 1961). Therefore, they decided to move the body to an even more exalted resting place, where in 1649 another miracle reportedly took place. "The body, which was always prone, with the right hand resting against the left, raised itself when a girl possessed by the devil was brought before the shrine" (Cruz, 1977, p. 138). How any of the miracles were verified is unknown, but what is important is not whether or not they actually occurred. What is important for this study is the Catholic belief that such occur-

Pope Innocent XI (St. Peter's Basilica, Rome).

rences did take place and that it was decided that they were of divine origins. It is because of these so-called miracles and the condition in which the body was found that Pope Innocent XI declared Antonio Blessed (a beatus) in 1687, more than 225 years after his death.

The body of Andrea Avellino (1521–1608) is located at the Church of San Paolo Maggiore in Naples. During his life, it was said that he was able to see the future and perform various other unnamed miracles. One of those future predictions involved the treatment of his own body. He predicted that his body would be buried four days after his death. It is reported in his hagiographies that he was in fact buried after four days by individuals who had known him and were familiar with his prophecies. This was deemed miraculous (Fallica, 2009). He died when he was 87 years old after a long and painful illness. After three days, his body was still flexible, and when doctors later cut into his body fresh blood flowed from the incisions that were made. This again was deemed a miracle, and the body was buried in a special location. One year later, it was unearthed and found incorrupt. These events led to his eventual canonization.

The corpse of Francis of Naples (1763–1841) can be found at the Basilica of Saint Peter. Francis suffered for many years from a painful disease. This is a reoccurring element in the lives of the Incorruptibles. Whether or not it is only a coincidence is unknown, but many individuals whose bodies have not decayed normally suffered throughout much of their lives. They dealt with painful diseases, and then later their bodies were found to be preserved by unknown means. The body of Francis of Naples, like most of the other Incorruptibles, was found to be flexible and preserved, and it exuded a sweet fragrance.

26

Mummies in Other Parts of Italy

Egano Lambertini and Castora Galuzzi gave birth to a daughter named Imelda in 1322. When she was young she had an unusual fascination with communion wafers. However, it was not permitted to have them until the age of 14. She desperately desired to have one, though, and she decided to enter a religious order. She joined a Dominican convent, and she did work for the other sisters there. She scrubbed floors and cleaned rooms. One day, however, a strange phenomenon was observed. She was looking at the tabernacle, and other nuns turned to face her when they noticed something in the air above her head (Catholic Apologetics, 2010). It was the host. Those present interpreted the unique phenomenon as an indication of God's will to let the young girl eat the wafer. According to hagiographies, the nuns plucked it out of the air, placed it on a paten, and gave it to her. However, it turned out that this wafer actually killed her. "The rapture with which she received Our Lord was so great that it burst her heart" (Catholic Apologetics, 2010). It is unlikely that her heart actually exploded upon eating this item, but that is how her hagiographies were written. She fell to the ground, dead. Later, her body was found incorrupt. It was prepared for enshrinement, and it is currently on display at the Church of St. Sigismund, in Bologna.

St. John Bosco (1815–1888) was born in Becchi, a small town near Castelnuovo, Piedmont, and he joined a seminary in Chieri when he was 20 years old. There he studied for six years, until he was ordained as a priest by the Archbishop of Turin, named Franzoni. John Bosco worked in Turin, and he ended up taking care of children without homes. Apparently, he was dressing for Mass one day and he heard a priest chasing away a homeless boy. Don Bosco called the child back to the church and offered him a place to stay. "More and more young boys without homes began flocking to Don Bosco's church, and in February of 1842, the 'oratory' (as it had come to be called) numbered 20 boys. In March of the same year, the oratory numbered 30; and in March of the year 1846, 400. Don Bosco soon had to find more room for all of these homeless boys and obtained one building after another in an effort to keep them off the street" (Catholic Apologetics, 2010). He started a number of houses for homeless boys, which are today called Salesian Homes. Don Bosco's preserved body is now on display in the Basilica of Maria in Turin, although it is unknown if it were naturally or artificially preserved.

Next to his remains is the preserved body of another saint, Maria Mazzarello (1837–1881), who, like Don Bosco, began a school, this one for girls, which eventually turned into a boarding school. She was responsible for the female side of the Salesian Homes, and she is the founder of the Salesian Sisters. Maria Mazzarello was born in Mornese, in what was once a part of northern Italy, and she joined a religious organization called the Association of the Daughters of Mary Immaculate when she was 15 years of age.

When she was 23, typhoid hit her town and many people became sick. A lot of them died. She cared for many of them but soon caught the epidemic herself. She survived, but the disease took its toll. It took a lengthy amount of time for her to recover, and she was left weak. She never regained her former strength. Like Don Bosco, she had an initial experience with a young girl who did not have a place to live, and Marie founded the Daughters of Mary Help of Christians. This organization helped young Christian girls who did not have homes.

Maria died while on a mission to France. She fainted and was in bed for 40 days, diagnosed with pleurisy. Feeling that the end was near, she decided to return to Italy; she did not want to die outside of her own country. Eventually, she made it back to her hometown of Mornese. She received her last rites and then said to those around her, "Good-bye. I am going now. I will see you in heaven."

The story of Maria Goretti (1890–1902) is a strange and sad one, but it is informative with regard to Christian terminology and the bestowal of titles by the Church. She moved to Ferrire with her parents at a young age. They were looking for work, and they believed that there was a better chance of earning money in this town. After arriving, they met a local family there: the Serenellis, who had a 19-year-old son named Alessandro. Marie was said to have become extremely religious throughout the years, and she therefore turned down the sexual advances of Alessandro. She kept turning him down, but he finally decided to take action. When there was no one else at home, he decided that he was going to have his way with her, whether she wanted him to or not. He entered her room, intent on raping her, but she fought him off. His plans foiled, he took a knife from his belt and stabbed her repeatedly. She fell to the floor of her room with 14 stab wounds.

The father of the house entered the room later and found her. He took her to the hospital, where she died soon after. Before her death, she was visited by a priest to whom she made her last confession. The priest asked her if she forgave her attacker, to which she responded, "Yes, I forgive him with all my heart, and I cannot wait to see him in heaven."[1] After her death her cause was begun right away, and within 50 years she was named not just a saint but also a martyr. Her body was intact for many years, but now only her bones are left. They are located at the Sanctuary of Madonna delle Grazie, in Nettuno. They are still visited by many pilgrims yearly. The fact that she was made a martyr is unusual, and it forces one to wonder what the true meaning of the term was in her case. The word was not utilized with the meaning of "one who died for the faith." She did not die by the hand of someone who hated her faith but by the hand of someone who wanted her virginity. She was named a martyr because she kept her virginity. In this sense, the term "martyr" loses its real meaning and it becomes something different for Catholics. It is a title alone, devoid of true definition.

The term "martyr," in the way it is used by members of the faith, has no real meaning. It is just a term. Some saints were considered martyrs because they died for the faith, others because they suffered for the faith. Some were named martyrs because they met with some difficulties while in positions of power within the Church. And, in the case of Maria Goretti, some were martyrs because they kept their virginity. This is not logical. However, maybe it is not meant to be logical. In some traditions, logic takes a backseat to faith (Geary, 1978). Gilbert (2007) explained:

I embrace in advance what I am presently incapable of understanding. There's a reason we refer to leaps of faith — because the decision to consent to any notion of divinity is a mighty jump from the rational over to the unknowable, and I don't care how diligently scholars of every religion will try to sit you down with their stack of books and prove to you through scripture that their faith is indeed rational; it isn't. If faith were rational, it wouldn't be — by definition — faith. Faith is belief in what you cannot see or prove or touch. Faith is walking face-first and full-speed into the dark [p. 175].

Logic is not a primary concern for some individuals who are religiously inclined. Such people choose to shut off rational thought and to simply believe what they are told to believe. Since there is no rational explanation behind the beliefs, they cannot be explained to inquirers. For example, some Catholics get angry when asked to explain such aspects of their faith. They do not like to be questioned about their beliefs, and they do not think critically about the reasons behind some of their practices. They also do not logically consider the meaning of titles bestowed upon individuals by the Church. This indicates that certain aspects of their faith are not meant to be logical but based on spirituality alone. In other words, shutting off thoughts and simply accepting what they are told is truthful helps individuals to live in a manner deemed appropriate. Everyone needs direction. If some people cannot find their own, they look for such guidance elsewhere. This is likely why stories of saints do not need to be historically accurate but imitable. It may also be why Catholics spend such a large amount of money on the bestowal of a title like saint. The term "martyr" conjures up an image of a holy individual who sacrificed his life for others, like Jesus himself. Jesus was the first martyr. The others who followed him into death were also considered martyrs. When considering such individuals, followers are inspired. They are hagiographical accounts of individuals who should be followed and emulated.

However, martyrs today are rare. If enough time passes, many things are forgotten. Events in history begin to lose their importance in time. Therefore, new martyrs are needed in order to promulgate the faith. A modern martyr, who can be looked upon as a source of inspiration, is therefore important. The hagiography of the individual can be altered in order to provide an account of the person's life that perfectly accords with the Church's idea of an ideal Christian, and the individual's death can be given importance by the conveyance of the martyr title. In this way, the term "martyr" loses its real meaning in Catholicism. It is a title of sanctity alone. This same type of thing has occurred with the Incorruptibles, as the meaning of the term is no longer clear.

27

The Importance of the Incorruptibles

What does the term "incorrupt" actually mean to Roman Catholics? Initially, the term was said to refer to bodies that had been preserved miraculously. Such inexplicable preservations were thought to be evidence of God and evidence of the sanctity of the individuals whom he worked through. However, the term "incorruptible" seems to be used in a variety of other cases in which bodies had not been naturally or miraculously preserved but artificially preserved. Some were preserved with chemicals. Others were embalmed or even eviscerated, and yet they are still called Incorruptibles.

The word "Incorruptibles" refers to the bodies of saints that are displayed, no matter the method of their preservation. Strangely, though, the term is also used to refer to the remains of holy individuals that were not preserved. It is used to describe individuals whose bodies just did not decay right away. There are many hagiographies of Incorruptibles that describe how the bodies were incorrupt for some time, but now they are only bones. In other words, the term is used for corpses that decayed naturally. However, it gets even stranger, as the term is often applied to individuals who were not preserved at all. Here is an example: "St. Clare died in Assisi on the eleventh of August in the year 1253. On September 23, 1850, her coffin was unearthed and opened. The flesh and clothing of the saint had been reduced to dust, but the skeleton was perfectly incorrupt" (Catholic Apologetics, 2010). In this example, any bones that were found that had not disintegrated (into dust) can be referred to as incorrupt. However, this does not make any sense from a linguistic point of view. If skeletons can be incorrupt, what would distinguish the Incorruptibles from any other body that has been buried? Again, like terms such as "martyr" and "saint," it seems that the word "Incorruptible" has no real meaning. It is a title that is simply given to individuals in order to let believers know that the person referred to is worthy of emulation.

People with the titles of saint, martyr, and Incorruptible are important in Italian religious traditions. Each city has numerous bodies on display in churches and cathedrals. Every town has at least one patron saint, and different saints are prayed to throughout Italy. Some cities have many guardian saints. Naples, for example, has more than 50 official patron saints. Just what this means and why it is important to residents is difficult to explain. The saints themselves, as described in their hagiographies, are examples to be followed in life, and their physical bodies are a source of miracles and divine protection: They are good luck. At the Council of Trent it was declared: "The bodies of holy martyrs and others now living with Christ, bodies which were His members and temples of the Holy Spirit, which one day are to be raised up by Him and made glorious in everlasting life, are to be venerated by the faithful; God gives men many benefits through them."

This is the relic body of St. Bernardo da Corleone (1605–1667). In reality, only his bones are left and they have been encased in this statue made in his image (Palermo, Sicily).

St. Teresa Margaret of the Sacred Heart (1747–1770) said, "Everything comes to an end; therefore take heart, for we pass from one thing to another until at last we arrive at eternity. Even seeing how things of this world end so quickly ought to console us, because the nearer and more quickly are approaching that end toward which all our activities should tend." Perhaps bodies of holy individuals are primarily a reminder of the transitory nature of life and of the inevitability of death. Life is short, and no one can escape death. Therefore (from a Catholic viewpoint), what is done in life is only important as it relates to the afterlife. The bodies of holy individuals can assist believers in their lives due to the power that such remains are thought to have. They also serve as a constant reminder of the finite nature of life. The hagiographies are examples of how to live an admirable and pious life.

A cult has sprung up around many saints, beati, and venerables. In cases where the bodies were later found incorruptible, the cults often grew even larger. Just one of many such examples is the cult surrounding the beatus Giacomo da Bitetto (c. 1400–c. 1485), whose body is currently located in Bitetto, Bari, at the Convent of Saint Francis. Although Giacomo is virtually unknown in the United States and in countries outside of Europe, there are many websites about him and his still extant cult. Such websites include pictures of him, stories about his life and miracles that are credited to him, and information about his ongoing process of canonization, which may not even happen. According to the official site, www.beatogiacomo.it, the preservation of his body forced a revival of his canonization process. It was the condition of the body that was the impetus for his consideration for sainthood. On Tuesday, November 30, 1999, the Congregation for the Causes of Saints in the Vatican approved his positio, the extremely long and expensive document that chronicles the virtues of the candidate. Therefore, canonization might be possible in the future.

This individual, like many other Incorruptibles, worked with the poor and sick during some of the darkest times in all of Europe. He was assisting individuals during the plague, when people all around him were dying and when the human body was a source of misery and torment. Pringle (2001) wrote: "Seldom in humanity's long history has the body been held in such pitifully low esteem as it was in medieval Europe" (p. 247). However, amidst all of this suffering and all of this decaying human flesh, there was one exception — those miraculous bodies that did not decay like mere mortals. During such dark periods in human history, the preserved bodies of saints were obviously thought of as miraculous. They were worshipped as reservoirs of divine energy, and they were symbolic of the very essence of God. With individuals dropping dead everywhere and disease touching nearly all of humanity in Europe, it might have seemed to some that God was absent had it not been for the miraculous preservations of the bodies of saints, beati, and venerables.

After the death of Giacomo da Bitetto, his body was kept in a common sepulcher where the rest of the brothers of his order were buried. His body was placed there in 1485, and it was uncovered about 20 years later. Like hundreds of other potential saints, his body was found unusually well preserved. It still had color, and it was flexible. It also gave off a fragrance deemed to be the Odor of Sanctity.

The preservation of the body was deemed miraculous because of the strong humidity and the total absence of ventilation that surrounded the corpse (Fallica, 2009). This is an odd statement, because for a body to remain preserved an absence of ventilation is often a contributing factor to mummification. There are cases when bodies are completely preserved while entombed, but when exposed to fresh air they rapidly decay. The body of St. Bernadette Soubirous (1844–1879), which has been previously mentioned, was initially found preserved. It had been buried in multiple caskets, one of which was a lead casket that had been soldered shut. When first exposed, the skin color was pale, but once it was touched by fresh air, the complexion quickly began to turn black. Another example (of such rapid deterioration due to the introduction of fresh air) found in Italy has been nicknamed the Grottaresca Mummy. When the tomb was first opened, the mummy was in an incredible condition. It was nearly perfectly preserved, according to the reports of individuals who first opened the tomb and saw her body. However, once it was exposed to fresh air, the body rapidly dried out and darkened. Typically, in cases of both artificial and natural mummification a tight seal on a crypt or other enclosure will help to preserve bodily remains. This is because fresh air does not touch the corpse.

The fact that examiners of the bodies of Incorruptibles were unfamiliar with this fact is indicative of the type of people who performed such examinations and the lack of knowledge about mummification that they may have had. They must have been uneducated individuals (in this regard), looking upon the remains of corpses and trying to decide whether or not the remains were naturally or unnaturally preserved. They were likely unfamiliar with the natural chemical processes of decay and the treatments needed in order to effect artificial preservation. Since they were unfamiliar with preservation techniques, it stands to reason that they would not know what to look for when searching for evidence of artificial preservation. Members of the clergy, when performing such (medical) examinations, also did not like to undress the bodies of saints. Therefore, any signs that the bodies had been previously treated would likely have gone unnoticed.

This does not mean that all of the incorruptible bodies were artificially preserved. It only means that no one can know for sure if they had been treated. However, the majority of the bodies that have been recently examined had been intentionally embalmed.

28

Preservation in Christianity

St. Margaret of Cortona (1247–1297) did not marry, but she lived in Montepulciano with a man for nine years and had a son. One day, her boyfriend did not come home. She followed her dog into the trees, where she found his dead body covered with leaves. Margaret took this as a divine sign. She gave all of her boyfriend's possessions to his family, and she and her young son returned to her father's home. She needed a place to stay, but her stepmother convinced Margaret's father not to take her in. With no place else to turn, she asked the Franciscans in Cortona for assistance. Following their suggestion, she found work in town but later gave this up so that she could spend more time assisting the poor and praying. She kept this up for three years, at which time the Franciscans came to think that her conversion was sincere. (The illicit love affair at this time was considered a sin, and she therefore was not readily accepted into the faith.) After she had been accepted, she lived an extremely religious life and she engaged in ascetic practices, including mortifying her flesh, in order to atone for her earlier (perceived) sins. She continued this severe ascetic discipline until her death at the age of 50, which she predicted. After her funeral, the body was entombed.

Years later, the remains were found to be in an amazing state of preservation and they had a sweet, aromatic fragrance. The body was examined, and it was determined that it had not been deliberately preserved, so it was deemed miraculous. It was thought that her body was so infused with divine grace that it failed to decay like a mere mortal. The body is on display in the Basilica of Cortona. It rests in a reliquary studded with precious jewels. In 1977, Joan Cruz described the preservation: "The body is light in color and dry, but completely whole. Even the eyes are full and all of the nails of the feet and hands are still in place — truly a miraculous preservation which has existed for almost seven hundred years" (p. 94). However, a recent examination has determined that the body of the saint had definitely been eviscerated and embalmed. She had been deliberately mummified by clergy members. According to Pringle (2001):

> Those who preserved St. Margaret had done so remarkably thoroughly, excising her internal organs and drenching her skin in fragrant lotions. Their handiwork reminded Fulcheri of the techniques employed by the ancient embalmers in Egypt. Mulling this over, the pathologist wondered whether the resemblances were merely coincidental — the results of independent invention by two different cultures at two different moments in time — or whether at some point in the distant past, the Catholic Church had borrowed something from the great Egyptian tradition of mummification, adapting it to its own purposes [p. 257].

St. Clare of Montefalco (1268–1320) was cut open after her death by her fellow sisters. While alive, she had said, "If you seek the cross of Christ, take my heart; there you will find the suffering Lord" (Cruz, 1977, p. 103). The women took her suggestion literally, and they cut out her heart, looking for a cross. Upon inspection of her heart, they claimed that there was in fact some tissue that resembled a cross. The heart was divided and kept in different places as relics, and it is said that the pieces were incorrupt. Her entire body, too, did not decay, and it was investigated and determined to be a miraculous preservation. Joan Cruz (1977) wrote: "Clad in exquisitely decorated robes with a veil covering the face and a crown adorning the head, the relic was found during its last examination in 1968 to be dry but perfectly flexible. The exposed hands of the saint, only slightly darker than normal, appear perfectly formed" (p. 105). This miraculous preservation was investigated again recently by Fulcheri and other doctors and members of the clergy. It was found that she, too, had large incisions running across her body. She had been eviscerated and embalmed just like St. Margaret (Pringle, 2001).

It is said that after the death of the Blessed Margaret of Metola (1287–1320) more than 200 miracles occurred that demonstrated her holiness. Various people planned to initiate her canonization process at different times, but it was always forgotten. Her cause was finally opened in the 17th century, however, when her body was found in a state of perfect preservation. The body was examined by doctors who declared that no chemicals or other substances had ever been used to preserve it. Cruz (1977) wrote:

> The body of Bl. Margaret, which has never been embalmed, is dressed in a Domenican habit, and lies under the high altar of the Church of St. Domenico at Città di Castello, Italy. The arms of the body are still flexible, the eyelashes are present, and the nails are in place on the hands and feet. The coloring of the body has darkened slightly and the skin is dry and somewhat hardened, but by all standards the preservation can be considered a remarkable condition, having endured for over 650 years [p. 112].

However, a more recent investigation again revealed the presence of large incision marks. There is no doubt that the body of Margaret of Metola, like those of St. Clare and St. Margaret of Cortona, had been embalmed. The Church purposefully mummified her (Fallica, 2009).

St. Bernardino da Siena (1380–1444) was also intentionally mummified, along with St. Rita of Cascia (1381–1457) and St. Catherine of Siena (1347–1380). St. Catherine is quite possibly one of the most beloved saints in Italy. It was said that she had the stigmata, but only she could see them (Cruz, 1977). After her death, her body was found to be preserved, although it is known today that it was actually embalmed (Pringle, 2001). Some time after her death, though, the body was divided into pieces. Her head was enshrined at the Hospital of St. Lazarus, her arm was sent to Siena, her fingers were given to Venice, a rib was sent to the Convent of St. Mark in Florence, and her shoulder blade was sent to the Dominican Sisters of Magnanapoli in Rome.

St. Rita was another beloved saint. In 1627, the pope pronounced Rita's beatification and her body was examined. It was said that the remains looked as though she had just recently died, even though she had been dead an amazing 170 years. The skin was still flexible and it was a natural color. The body also was infused with the Odor of Sanctity, and it was said that this scent, along with the miraculous preservation of the body, was evidence of her sanctity and evidence of God. It was not disclosed at the time that the body had been intentionally mummified. Her internal organs had been removed, and the body was treated with an embalming fluid made of various preservative plants and flowers, thus infusing the remains with the scent described as the Odor of Sanctity. The "otherworldy scent" that many witnesses described is therefore likely evidence of embalming and not evidence of miraculous preservation. (Interestingly, although embalming involves treating the body with herbs and spices, materials that function as preservatives, the archaic meaning for the phrase "to embalm" was "to give a pleasant fragrance to.")

Embalming solutions that are known to have been used in Italy, including the formula used to preserve the body of Rosalia Lombardo, whose small body is on display in Palermo, gave the bodies a lifelike appearance. Arsenic, which was used in many embalming solutions, infused the body with a rosy, lifelike coloring. Dr. Tranchina from Naples was a well-known embalmer who advocated the use of arsenic in embalming solutions, and Dr. Salafia, who mummified Rosalia Lombardo, was influenced by his methods (Johnson, Johnson, and Williams, 1993). Besides the mummification of this young girl, Dr. Salafia also mummified a number of other well-known individuals, including high-ranking members of the Church. He preserved the body of Cardinal Michaelangelo Celestia in 1904. Five years later, the body was viewed and said to have been perfectly preserved. "The features, color, and form had been so carefully preserved that the Cardinal looked as if he were asleep" (Quigley, 1998, p. 51). His embalming procedure was well known, and he taught other embalmers how the procedure was supposed to be performed. Typically, he did not drain the blood of the deceased. He injected approximately 15 gallons of his embalming solution into the carotid artery, which was sufficient to effect near-perfect and relatively permanent bodily preservation. Other embalmers who were hired to mummify holy individuals also injected embalming solution into the brachial and femoral arteries, in addition to the carotid arteries (Quigley, 1998).

Some embalming solutions also served to keep the body flexible and moist. Therefore, when considering the Incorruptibles this evidence should be weighed as evidence of embalming. If the bodies were moist, flexible, or reddish in color, they were likely embalmed. If they had a "divine scent"—a floral fragrance—it was also evidence that they had been embalmed. This is because the embalming solutions were reported to be fragrant like flowers. Since the discovery that a number of these bodies had without a doubt been embalmed, all of the phenomena that were previously used as evidence of sanctity are now more appropriately considered evidence of embalmment.

How is it that previous examinations of the bodies did not reveal any evidence of evisceration or embalmment? Doctors and clergy members alike were present during such examinations, and yet they concluded many times that the bodies showed no evidence of being embalmed and the preservations were therefore deemed miraculous. How could they have missed such blatant evidence? This is simply explained. Those examining the bodies, who were typically all Catholics and believers in the spiritual attributes of the saints, did not feel comfortable undressing them. They did not remove the clothing when performing their investigations, and therefore, they were unable to find evidence of embalming (Pringle, 2001).

There are other Incorruptibles that were not visibly embalmed. There were also those that displayed extremely unusual attributes, such as bleeding years after the deaths of their former occupants. It should be noted, though, that arsenic-based embalming solutions do not require the drainage of bodily fluids. Therefore, a body thus preserved could, in effect, bleed after death if the skin was cut or damaged. There are also ways to hide embalmment.

"Embalming historian Edward C. Johnson points out that embalming can be concealed in a number of ways; cavity fluid may be introduced through the navel, which is then closed with a circular stitch, arterial fluid may be injected in the popliteal artery behind the kneecap so that the incision won't show from the front, or the body may simply be covered with a preservative-saturated cloth" (Quigley, 1998, p. 196).

In another possibility, some popes and other saints were embalmed using a technique that required neither incisions nor injections. This embalming technique and solution was developed by Oreste Nuzzi and first applied to Pope Pius XII. It made use of osmosis, and the preserving chemicals were drawn into the body of the deceased, thus effecting mummification. It is probable that bodies that had no incision scars or evidence of injections were preserved in this manner, even though the procedure was not made public.

Supporting the idea that some Incorruptibles were secretly embalmed is the body of St. Mary Magdalen de' Pazzi (1566–1607), which smelled of embalming fluid. A strange but fragrant fluid (i.e., embalming solution) issued from behind the knees of the body—one of the easiest places to hide an injection. "From the knees of the sacred body trickled a liquid of exquisite scent. It looked like oil, but it was not. It was examined [by nuns], but its nature could not be ascertained" (Minima, 1958, p. 326).

It is possible that individuals hoping for the canonization of potential saints took action to artificially preserve their bodies. Since the absence of decay was considered a miracle until recently, it might have pushed the candidate into sainthood—possibly being the last of the required miracles needed for sainthood. It should be remembered that for Italian Catholics saint is an important title, as is the availability of relics. St. John Damascene said, "Christ gives us the relics of saints as health-giving springs through which flow blessings

Statue of Pope Pius XII, located at St. Peter's Basilica, in the Vatican (Rome, Italy).

and healing." However, it seems more likely that the Church, and not Christ, is responsible for many of such relics, as it arranged the preservation of such bodies. Handling relics that were not preserved would have been a problem to the Church. Relics that decayed would have been a health hazard, and they would have disgusted those around them — not the type of correlation that Catholics would want to have with their hero saints. Therefore, with regard to the relic cult, bodily preservation was necessary. The Church mummified many bodies, and the mummification of holy individuals was extremely important to the sect. Such practices have not dissipated, and even today mummification is carried out by the organization.

In 1984, for example, the Church hired a number of mummification experts to preserve the body of a Ukrainian cardinal named Josef Slipyj (1941–1984). They wanted him preserved for political motives.[1] They wished to discourage the political ideas of Communism and therefore sought to preserve the body of an influential figure who took the same stance as Rome. They also wanted to make sure that another religion did not become popular there, as Catholicism is an intolerant faith, opposed to other beliefs. "The Vatican worried that as Communism faded in Ukraine and a new era of religious tolerance dawned, other religions might gain a strong foothold in the country" (Pringle, 2001, p. 252). They thought that the incorruptible body of a religious figure who supported the same ideas as the Vatican would assist them in their political motives.

The team of people employed to mummify the cardinal, besides pathologist Ezio Fulcheri, included Nazzareno Gabrielli, who is the director of scientific research at the Vat-

The bodies of saints, beati, and venerables are important to Catholics. For this reason, the Church sought to preserve such bodies. This is the body of St. Victoria, a martyr. It had been treated to withstand decay, wrapped in a protective covering, and then sealed in this coffin under the altar (Florence, Italy).

ican Museum, and Gianfranco Nolli, an Egyptologist and past director of the Vatican's Egyptian Museum. The Church wanted the body mummified, but it did not leave the method of preservation entirely up to the assembled team. Rather, the Vatican wanted the body preserved using the same methods utilized by the ancient Egyptians. Their religious practices necessitated this particular style of preservation.

The team created an embalming solution and then set to work. They cut the cardinal open and removed his internal organs. They also removed his brain using the method employed by Egyptians and cleaned the internal cavity of his body, anointing it with preservative solutions. They then dipped the body into a chemical bath, and they continued various chemical treatments for the next few months. Decay had been halted, and the body was well preserved. Once the treatment had been concluded, the team informed the Church that the job had been completed and that it was successful and the Vatican then began planning his burial. The body was transferred to Lviv and entombed in a crypt.

His canonization is planned, however. The first step in the Roman process of canonization is the identification of the body of the potential candidate. In the past, when bodies were unearthed and found to be incorrupt the cause itself was catapulted forward with more speed than those causes in which bodies were found to have naturally decayed. When the body of the cardinal is unearthed, it will obviously be found to be incorruptible. This should push the canonization process forward, and after the necessary fees are paid to the Church he will likely be named a saint.

The preservation of bodily remains is extremely important to the Roman Catholic faith, and there are numerous examples of preservation carried out not just by individual monasteries and churches but by the Vatican itself. The practice of mummification cannot explicitly be justified or necessitated by Christian scripture or related historical documents. Just where the practice originated from is therefore not straightforward. In order to determine where this practice started, it is necessary to look at the origin of Christianity and at the other faiths and historical occurrences that influenced its development.

V. Influences from Other Cultures

If you believe what you like in the gospels, and reject what you don't like, it is not the gospel you believe, but yourself. — St. Augustine

29

Mummification in Roman Society

Although mummification was not a standard practice in pre–Christian Roman culture, there were some cases of mummification. One famous example (of a preserved body) has been nicknamed the Grottarossa Mummy due to its discovery in the Grottarossa district just outside of Rome. The discovery was made in 1964, when construction workers began digging for a project. They found a white marble sarcophagus that was decorated with elaborate carvings. There were masks on the corners, and the sides were decorated with various hunting scenes. On one side was a deer-hunting scene, while on another was a boar-hunting scene. On the top of the lid was a depiction of a lion hunt. Elsewhere on the sarcophagus were carvings of deities, notably Venus, a Roman goddess associated with fertility, beauty and love.

The mummy inside the marble sarcophagus was the body of an eight-year-old girl, nicknamed the Grottarossa Mummy. The body was found adorned with gold earrings, gold rings, and a gold necklace embedded with sapphires. There were also various objects placed into the sarcophagus with her body, including a doll made from ivory, a box and shell-shaped pot both made from amber, and another small box that had a handle. Examiners determined that she likely lived during the second century C.E., during the time of the Antonine emperors (160–180). The strange thing about this particular find is that the body had been embalmed, following Egyptian methods of preservation, and embalming was not a Roman custom.

When the body was first exposed to fresh air it was well hydrated and had pale, white skin, but the exposure effected quick deterioration. The body soon turned brown and the skin hardened. The sarcophagus had previously been airtight, which assisted in preserving the remains. The sudden exposure to oxygen, however, caused the body to desiccate and decay rapidly. Today the skin is dark brown and it has hardened, taking on the texture of parchment. The weight of the mummy is 4,960 grams and it is 120 centimeters in length (Ascenzi and Bianco, 1998).

The body was embalmed and then wrapped in linen. It was treated with various substances in order to prevent decay. There was no evidence of sectioning, and there was no residue to suggest that the body had been covered with natron. (Natron is a natural substance found in Egypt that is composed of sodium chloride and sodium bicarbonate.) The internal organs had not been removed, and when the sarcophagus was opened there was a fragrant smell, not unlike that of flowers, which indicated to researchers that it was in fact treated with balms (i.e., embalmed). Analysis of the body revealed the presence of abietic acids, which supports the conclusion that *Cupressaceae* products, especially *Juniperus*, were used in the bodily preservation process. "This technique was commonly applied in Egypt during the last period, including the Roman era when the Grottarossa girl was alive" (Ascenzi and Bianco, 1998, p. 264).

At first it was thought that the girl must have been of Egyptian descent, due to the method used for her bodily preservation, but after careful analysis it was determined that she was not Egyptian and that she was most likely of Italian heritage. There are also no records available that describe where the mummification took place, and it was initially thought that she was mummified in Egypt and then later relocated to Italy. However, further analysis again demonstrated that this was not likely the case. Due to the manner in which the linen was spun, it is most likely that she was wrapped in Italy, using Italian linens.

This find is particularly important when considering the influence of Egyptian beliefs and practices on the Christian religion. This mummy demonstrates that Egyptian funerary practices were utilized in Rome, and at the time that this particular mummification was performed there were many foreign religions that were entering Rome and becoming popular. Christianity at that time was not the Christianity that is here today. Many of the customs and beliefs had not yet been concretely formed, and it was from some of these other faiths that were known about in Rome that modern Christian beliefs and practices were adopted. In other words, Roman Catholicism is an amalgamation of various other faiths and practices. This is not a negative thing. Customs and explanations that were useful or deemed important were adopted for use in a quickly changing new religious movement. People being the same all over, it was logical for such adoption to take place.

Many of the known practices in Christianity, and even the standard version of Christian history, were developed later. They were not put into place at the onset of Christianity. Part of this, at least with regards to the historical aspects of the faith, had to do with a lack of information found in historical texts about Jesus and his followers. The first portions of the New Testament were not written until approximately 50 years after his death, but most of the information that appears in the Bible about Jesus was not written until approximately 100 years after his death. There was no information about him at all in Roman historical sources, even though they kept extensive accounts. This fact has led some individuals to suggest that he did not exist at all and that all of the practices of Christianity, along with its history, were actually just absorbed from other traditions (Wood, 1938; Robertson, 1949; Wells, 1975; Wilson, 1984).

Wells (1971) wrote:

> The writer of the epistles of John admits that many people at the time of these early Christian records denied that Jesus had "come in the flesh," and he is quite unable to produce any realistic proof that he had. Other very early Christian documents are Paul's epistles addressed to the Romans, Corinthians, Galatians, Ephesians, Philippians, Colossians, and Thessalonians. All of these are unanimously agreed to have been written before the gospels, yet they exhibit such complete ignorance of the events which were later recorded in the gospels as to suggest that these events were not known [p. 3].

The earliest records of Jesus in the epistles of Paul mentioned no miracles. Nor did they provide information on Jesus's relatives or history. They only mentioned a Jewish cult that centered around a crucified man called the Messiah. This would have been nothing unusual, because there were other known religious traditions that centered around a crucified savior, such as the cults of Dionysus and Horus (Weigall, 2003). There was no information about the time and place of the crucifixion. There was also no biographical information about Jesus, including when and where he was born. The information that is considered factual about him today is found in the Bible alone, a text that did not exist at the onset of Christianity. As such, the information found in the Bible cannot necessarily be considered accurate. If one was inclined to believe such stories anyway, there would still be a problem. This is because the accounts in the Bible are contradictory. The birth of Jesus is just one example.

According to Luke (2:1–7), Jesus was born during the census of Quirinius, which began in 6 C.E. However, the Gospel of Matthew (2:1) states that he was born in the reign of King Herod, who died in 4 B.C.E. And when readers critically analyze the Gospel of Luke, they will become completely confused. According to this gospel, John was conceived during the reign of Herod and Jesus was born six months after John (Luke 1:36). However, Mary was still pregnant with Jesus during the census (Luke 2:1–3). This means that her pregnancy lasted at least 10 years (Wilson, 1984). This glaring inconsistency has been present, and readily visible, for centuries. It could only have been overlooked by individuals who cannot see what is right in front of them. They do not consider things clearly, and they do not read critically. Therefore, they are blind.

Despite the contradictory explanations found within, there are some people who believe that the Bible is the "infallible and inerrant word of God" (Konig, 2006). For such individuals, the 10-year pregnancy is likely regarded as just another Christian miracle. However, for historians, such inconsistencies demonstrate the need to gather historical information about Jesus from other, earlier accounts. The problem is that there was little information about him in early Christian records and there was no information at all in outside (e.g., Roman) sources.

If the earliest Christian records did not contain facts about him, it is likely that such information was unknown. And if later versions contained more information, despite the fact that new historical evidence did not emerge, the information had to have been made up. The accounts found in the gospels are therefore not historical in nature; they have been edited, distorted, and embellished to create an interesting and inspiring tale (Wells, 1971). "Most scholars have now accepted the fact that the Bible is a blend of history and fiction" (Gadalla, 2008). The gospels are not historical books. Even the earliest one, the Gospel of Mark, was not written until after the fall of the Judean state (Zeitlin, 1965). Therefore, there is no reputable source for historical information about Jesus.

It is likely that no one who had ever known Jesus personally actually wrote anything about him. This is one of the reasons why many scholars have suggested that he may not have actually existed. There are two factors that support the suggestion that there was no historical Jesus. One is that there is a lack of historical evidence of his existence; what evidence there is cannot be completely trusted since they were not eyewitness accounts. The other factor is the availability of some historical documents that suggest that Jesus was a myth alone (Wood, 1938; Robertson, 1949). There are some accounts of Christians in Jewish and pagan records. This is one by Tacitus (XV:44):

> They derived their name and origin from Christ, who, in the reign of Tiberius, had suffered death by the sentence of the procurator Pontius Pilate. For a while this dire superstition was checked; but it again burst forth, and not only spread itself over Judaea, the first seat of their mischievous sect, but it was even introduced to Rome, the common asylum which receives

and protects whatever is atrocious. The confessions of those who were seized discovered a great multitude of their accomplices, and they were all convicted, not so much for the crime of setting fire to the city, as for their hatred of the human race [Gibbon, 1960, p. 104].

This passage states that a number of Christians set fire to the city and that they hated humankind. This might refer to Christians who did not like non-believers—those who thought that non-believers were not in God's good graces and who would go to hell. Julius Firmicus was a Christian writer who lived during the reign of Constantine I. He explained this belief: "To be a member of the [Christian] community was to be in reality, and not merely in conception, a child of God and heir of everlasting salvation: to be excluded from the community was to pass again into the outer darkness, the realm of Satan and eternal death" (Hatch, 1890, p. 63).

The most interesting point in the passage, though, is that the idea held by the Christians, that their savior was crucified under Pilate, was wrong. It was a "dire superstition" that had been "checked." Although there is little to no credible evidence of the historicity of Jesus, there was a Messiah who was killed shortly before his time—the Messiah of the Essenes died, shedding his blood for humankind, c. 63 B.C.E. There are other similarities between the Essenes and the later Christians, including the idea of a ritual meal and the use of water for purification. The Essenes, for example, had a "ritual meal that began with the blessing of bread and wine by a priest" (Wells, 1971, p. 259). The Essenes were in existence during the first century, and it is likely that John the Baptist was a member of the sect (Atkinson, 2010). It has therefore been suggested that perhaps the early Christians were confusing some historical information and their Messiah was actually an earlier one, who may have existed before the reign of Tiberius.

The lack of evidence of the historicity of Jesus, and the fact that many Christian traditions and legends are found in earlier religions, has led many individuals to question whether or not he actually existed. However, just because nothing was recorded at the time that he was alive does not mean that he did not exist. Sometimes, things are not instantly perceived as being important. It takes years before some people are able to reflect upon events that took place in the past and then determine their historical significance. This is likely what occurred regarding the historical documentation of Jesus, which did not exist at the onset of Christianity. Peter (1965) wrote:

> No one is really born great; it is because of subsequent happenings that the circumstances of this or that person's birth are considered worth noting. This sort of thing has to be said concerning every "significant event" in history: it is seen to be significant *after* it had happened. If indeed a contemporary event is said to be a significant one, this is an interim judgment based on an opinion about what will follow from it; and it is often the case that what is thought at the time to be an epoch-making event is considered from the perspective of later years to be of quite minor significance, or may even pass from human memory altogether [p. 99].

Therefore, those things in history that are considered especially important today were generally only considered important after the event had taken place. The Christian religion was already taking a definitive shape when the first texts about Jesus were written and the Church already had established some of its teachings and its philosophy. It is likely for this reason that the Bible was edited in the way that it was.

The gospels in the Bible were likely based upon earlier accounts, and they were probably not written by anyone who had actually known the historical Jesus (Wells, 1971; Gladden, 2004). That is why there are so many discrepancies regarding the historical occurrences. For example, if the texts were written by people who had actually known him and who were with him when he died, they would likely remember what his last words were. However, there are discrepancies in the accounts.

> The gospel writers, who we are supposed to believe were Jesus's close disciples, cannot even remember their master's last words correctly! According to Matthew and Mark, Jesus quotes Psalm 22 as his parting words, asking "My God, my God, why have you forsaken me?" But Luke has Jesus quote Psalm 31: "Father, into your hands I commend my spirit." For those who don't like either of these, there is always John's account, in which Jesus says simply, "I am thirsty," and then, "It is finished" [Freke and Gandy, 1999, p. 142].

The gospels were likely first put together while making use of earlier texts and oral traditions. Then, the names of the most probable disciples to whom the texts could be attributed were added. At the first Council, the Church decided which books to include and which books to discard, based upon which books supported their teachings and which ones ran contrary to their preexisting beliefs. Again, this is altering history in order to support the existing belief and not altering the beliefs according to new information uncovered. Editors of the Bible made their own contributions, and translators altered parts of the text in order to comply with their existing beliefs and their standard of morality (Gadalla, 2008).

Early versions that described Jesus being hanged, for example, were changed in later versions to reflect crucifixion. This did not just happen in the first few centuries of Christianity alone, but it continues to occur today. Acts 5:30 in the King James version of the Bible states that Jesus was "hanged on a tree," while the same line in the New International Version states that he was "hanged on a cross." The earlier versions explicitly state that he was hanged on a tree and not crucified, but such accounts were edited in some translations. (This was possibly done in order to separate Christianity from some preexisting pagan faiths that centered around a hanged deity.) In addition, Luke 2:43 in the American Standard Version of the Bible talks about Joseph and Mary as the parents of Jesus, while the same passage in other versions, including the King James Edition, switched the reference of his parents to "Joseph and his mother." This change was likely first put into place to reflect a new dogmatic addition to the Christian faith: the concept of a Virgin Birth, which did not exist in the first century (Wells, 1971). Many other changes were made in different translations, so it is impossible to view the New Testament as being historically infallible. In other words, the stories in the book cannot be accepted as historical accounts. The Bible, as it is known today, was edited and put together during the Council of Trent in 1546, and during this meeting it was decided that only four of the many gospels would be included: those of Matthew, Mark, Luke and John. It is readily accepted, though, that none of these individuals had ever known Jesus. "Mark was not an eyewitness to the events that he describes in the Bible. Neither were Matthew, Luke or John" (Gadalla, 2008).

In order to truly understand who Jesus was as an individual and where the modern Catholic religious traditions were born, it is necessary to look at the available evidence with an open mind. This is not easy for some people, as their preexisting beliefs, in part, determine who they are as individuals. However, if one is able to disregard previously held beliefs and to see historical evidence anew, he or she will be able to learn more about the true nature

Jesus and Joseph, his earthly father. After the dogmatic addition of a new concept in Christianity, the Virgin Birth, Joseph was, in a sense, edited out of the picture (Palermo, Italy).

of Jesus of Nazareth and about the differences between the historical truths and the standard version of truth as created by the Roman Catholic Church.

It has already been previously established with regards to saints and martyrs that historical accuracy was not important in the canonization process. "Accounts of saints' lives are by their very nature subject to shaping and distortion by the prejudices of the age in which they are written; accretions of legend are readily added to whatever slim core of fact there may be" (George and George, 1955, p. 96). The records of saints and martyrs did not have to be historically accurate. It was for this reason that the histories of various saints were edited to remove anything negative, and it is why certain individuals were canonized who probably never even existed. What was more important than historical accuracy was that the story of the saint inspired people. If the hagiographies of saints were altered for this purpose, why wouldn't Church historians do the same with regards to the son of God himself? In other words, if the hagiographies were not designed for historical accuracy but for inspiring awe and admiration from followers, it makes sense that the same concept and philosophy would be applied to all historical records in Christianity.

In fact, this same thing occurred regarding the official creation of Church history. Eusebius (263–339), employed by the Roman emperor Constantine, created the first history of the Church in the fourth century, and it is this history that is still propagated today. Eusebius's job was to create an admirable account, and in so doing he did not place much importance on truth. He put things into the history that would glorify the Church, and he eliminated from it anything that would disgrace the Church. He exaggerated the number of Christian martyrs and created biographies for the martyrs that had no historical truth whatsoever — at least not insofar as they related to the martyrs whom he described. He based such historical accounts on the legends of pagan saints (Freke and Gandy, 1999). Unfortunately, it is this biased and non-historical account that remains the history of the Roman Catholic Church. He was the only Church historian from the first three centuries whose account still survives. Therefore, his account has been "adopted by all Church historians after him, thereby perpetuating the lies, which have become the traditional history of Christianity" (Freke and Gandy, 1999, p. 242).

The tendency of the Church to edit history, whether it be Church history as a whole, the hagiographies of saints, or the holy scriptures themselves, makes it necessary to seek confirmation of facts and suppositions using outside sources. Luckily, many of the stories found in both the New and the Old Testaments originated from much older accounts. There sources are historical in nature. As previously explained, historical accuracy was not the aim of the Church when compiling and editing the Bible. Their aim was to create a divine, metaphysical figure — one who would attract followers and serve as an inspiration to all. Therefore, we must look at the older sources in order to approach the truth. We must verify the information found in the Bible in order to determine what is historical and what is not.

30

The Old Testament

Many stories recorded in the Bible as it is currently known actually have origins in other, older texts. The Bible was meant as a history book, and thus its authors incorporated information from other known textual sources as well as oral traditions. It is for this reason that stories printed in other forms appear in the Old Testament. A well-known example of this is the story of the great flood — the inundation that was meant to destroy all life on this planet. The story about this event shows up in the Bible, but it likely originated from the Epic of Gilgamesh, one of the earliest texts on this planet, which was written between 2100 and 2000 B.C.E., long before the Old Testament was compiled.[1] The tale was recorded by the ancient Sumerians, whose civilization suddenly appeared approximately 6,000 years ago.

Modern research suggests that the deluge occurred approximately 13,000 years ago, in c. 10,970 B.C.E. (Sitchen, 2010). The historical account of this occurrence as recorded by the Sumerians closely matches the Bible in its description of the flood and in the construction of an ark-like vessel. However, the Sumerian account tends to make more sense logically. According to the ancient Sumerian account, there were multiple gods who effected the creation of mankind. One of them, named Enlil, said, "The uproar of mankind is intolerable and sleep is no longer possible by reason of the babel" (Sandars, 1972). The gods met, and they decided to exterminate all of humankind. However, there was one silent dissenter. A goddess named Ea wished to save humans from this extermination, so she approached a man named Utnapishtim (known also as Ziusudra), who was close to the gods, and she told him how to survive the incoming deluge. She said, "Tear down your house, I say, and build a boat. These are the measurements of the barque as you shall build her: let her beam equal her length, let her deck be roofed like the vault that covers the abyss; then take up into the boat the seed of all living creatures."

He set to work immediately in order to build this boat. After seven days, it had been completed and the DNA of all known creatures was stored on board (Sitchen, 2010). The flooding began soon after. The Epic of Gilgamesh reads: "Then the gods of the abyss rose up; Nergal pulled out the dams of the nether waters, Ninurta the war-lord threw down the dykes, and the seven judges of hell, the Annunaki, raised their torches, lighting the land with their livid flame." The flooding lasted for six days and subsided on the seventh. At this time, the oceans became calm, but there was no life and no land to be seen. Gilgamesh wrote:

> I looked at the face of the world and there was silence. All mankind was turned to clay. The surface of the sea stretched as flat as a roof-top; I opened a hatch and the light fell on my

face. Then I bowed low, I sat down and I wept, the tears streamed down my face, for on every side was the waste of water. I looked for land in vain, but fourteen leagues distant there appeared a mountain, and there the boat grounded; on the mountain of Nisir the boat held fast, she held fast and did not bulge.

The boat remained there and did not move. On the seventh day, Utnapishtim let a dove loose, seeking land. The bird flew off but found no place to set down and so returned. Then, Utnapishtim unleashed a swallow, but it, too, returned, having found no place to land. Finally, he let a raven loose, and it did not come back. Knowing that the bird had found land, he prayed to the gods. "Seven and again seven cauldrons I set up on their stands, I heaped up wood and cane and cedar and myrtle. When the gods smelled the sweet sacrifice, they gathered like flies." In this way, the human race continued, as did the seed of all other living creatures.

The biblical account is similar to the Sumerian account, but it is likely that the polytheistic elements were edited out in order to fit the account more appropriately into the Judeo-Christian tradition (Sitchen, 2010). In the biblical version, God, who created humankind, became angry. He decided to kill everyone. He said, "I will blot out man whom I have created from the face of the land, man and animals and creeping things and birds of the heavens, for I am sorry that I have made them" (Genesis 6:7). Angry and wrathful, God decided to kill all living creatures. However, he then displayed a small bit of compassion and decided to save a select few. He approached Noah, who was close to God, and told him to build an ark. "For behold," God said, "I will bring a flood of waters upon the earth to destroy all flesh in which is the breath of life under heaven" (Genesis 6:17).

After instructing him in the method of creating the ark, God asked Noah to gather together two of every creature in order to perpetuate their existence. In the Sumerian account, only the seed of each animal is required. Two of each animal requires a much larger vessel, one that would not be easily constructed. However, this is the biblical version, which differs from the Sumerian original. God said to Noah, "Take with you seven pairs of all clean animals, the male and his mate, and a pair of the animals that are not clean, the male and his mate, and seven pairs of the birds of the heavens also, male and female, to keep their offspring alive on the face of all the earth. For in seven days I will send rain on the earth forty days and forty nights, and every living thing that I have made I will blot out from the face of the ground" (Genesis 7:1–4).

Seven days later, the deluge came and wiped out all living creatures, save those that were protected aboard the ark. The flooding lasted for 150 days, at which time God remembered Noah and the animals that were with him and so he stopped the deluge. In the seventh month, the ark came to rest upon the mountains of Ararat. Noah opened a window and let loose a raven, which could not find a place to land. Then he sent out a dove, which also could not find a place to land. He waited another seven days and again sent the dove out to search for land. This time, although the dove returned, it had an olive leaf in its mouth. This was how Noah knew that the floods had subsided from the earth. According to the Bible, this is how humankind continued on this planet with animals and other creatures.

Obviously, these two accounts are similar. Since the Sumerian account was written thousands of years before the Bible, it is likely that the Bible is based upon the preexisting historical account: the Epic of Gilgamesh. In the Sumerian account, the man called upon is asked to keep the seed of living creatures aboard, which would not take up much room.

This might not have been understood by compilers of the Old Testament, who interpreted it as meaning the actual creatures, along with their mates — because otherwise, the animals would have been unable to reproduce. The other thing that does not make a ton of sense in the biblical version is the intent of God.

> The tale of the Deluge and its hero is told in both sources along similar lines, except that unlike the monotheistic Bible where the same God first decides to destroy mankind and then saves it through Noah, the Mesopotamian version clearly identifies Enlil as the angry deity — while it is Enki,[2] defying Enlil, who saves the seed of mankind [Sitchen, 2010, p. 154].

The Judeo-Christian God initially wants to destroy all living things but then decides that he doesn't want to kill all creatures. Rather than call off the flood, he helps a human to survive it.[3] It is odd that he does not call off the destruction but simply guides a person, helping him to survive it. The Sumerian account is more logical in this respect, in which there was one deity intent on destroying humankind and another who was intent upon saving it.[4]

This flood was one of the most important and influential occurrences to have happened during this cycle of existence. It is only natural that the story shows up in various historical accounts. It is also human nature to amend the account so that it makes more sense within the confines of the culture in which it was translated. Therefore, it is probable that the biblical account came directly from the ancient Sumerian account. Other accounts of the Old Testament were also likely taken from Sumerian texts, including the account of Adam and Eve at the beginning of it all. One example is a description of an oncoming famine that will last seven years. The Bible has the following account:

> The seven good cows are seven years, and the seven good ears [of corn] are seven years; the dreams are one. The seven lean and ugly cows that come after them are seven years, and the seven empty ears blighted by the east wind are also seven years of famine. It is as I told Pharaoh; God has shown to Pharaoh what he is about to do. There will come seven years of great plenty throughout all the land of Egypt, but after them there will arise seven years of famine [Genesis 40:26–30].

The Sumerian account has a divine being named Anu talking to another named Ishtar (Sandars, 1972). Anu says, "If you do what you desire there will be seven years of drought throughout Uruk when corn will be seedless husks. Have you saved grain enough for the people and grass for the cattle?"

Ishtar replied, "I have saved grain for the people, grass for the cattle; for seven years of seedless husks there is grain and there is grass enough."

The Bible describes the famine when it finally came and how people were saved due to the preparation of Joseph (Ishtar in the Sumerian account): "The seven years of plenty that occurred in the land of Egypt came to an end, and the seven years of famine began to come, as Joseph had said. There was famine in all lands, but in all the land of Egypt there was bread" (Genesis 41:53–54).

These two accounts are similar, and there are many other connections between the texts. It is probable that the stories of the Old Testament have roots in these earlier tales. The Old Testament, one of the most important historical documents of this existence, compiled known information that originated from much older sources. A similar thing most likely occurred during the process of compiling the New Testament as well.

31

Historical Evidence

Much of what is thought of as history regarding both Jesus and Christianity does not stem from the Bible and from other historical references. Instead, it comes from artwork that was created over 1,000 years after the death of Jesus of Nazareth. One specific example is the crucifixion of Jesus. The image that many individuals have of this event does not come from historical sources but from works of art by artists such as Leonardo da Vinci. In art, the crucifixion of Jesus was depicted in a specific manner—a manner unsupported by historical evidence. He is depicted as being nailed to a cross with large nails through the palms of the hands and the soles of the feet. The only archaeological evidence of a crucifixion involving nails, though, was the anklebone of a person who had been crucified that had been discovered in a tomb. This find was especially important because the nail used to secure the individual to the cross was still in the bone. However, it was through the side of the bone and not the front. So, the individual's ankles would have been nailed into the side of the cross and not secured into the front of it.

Due to (morbid) experiments that have been performed over the years, it is now readily accepted that nails through the palms of the hands would not have supported the weight of a body, which led many scholars to determine that the nails were driven into the forearms instead. However, most of the historical evidence that has been unearthed suggests that nails may not have been used at all to secure the upper body. It seems to have been much more common to tie the individual's upper body to the cross by rope and to only nail the ankles into the side of the cross.

There are some very old examples of graffiti in Rome that depict standard Roman crucifixions, too, and the depictions presented in such archaeological finds also run contrary to what some people assume was historical fact about the event. In such depictions, the cross was not a cross at all but a T-shaped structure and there was a footrest in place on the bottom of the center beam. Following the historical evidence available from archaeological finds, Jesus may have only been tied to the wooden structure, with his feet resting on a foot platform. There is no way to know for sure, and the Bible is unfortunately of no assistance. It gives no details about the manner of crucifixion. The Gospel of John in the New Testament states that they crucified him. It does not describe the actual method of securing him to the beams. There are even some who have pointed out that maybe he was not crucified at all but hanged. The cross was not adopted by the Christians right away, although it was a symbol used by earlier pagan traditions. In the earliest New Testament texts, the descriptions given of the death of Jesus could refer to him being hanged. In the Gospel of Luke, for example, the reader is informed that Jesus was crucified between two thieves and that all three individuals died in the same manner. However, Luke went on to describe one of the robbers, writing: "And one of the malefactors which were hanged..." (23:39). In addition, during the life of Origen (c. 185–254) Christians were known as "the followers of the god who was hanged" (Mangasarian, 2004). The accounts of Peter in the King James translation of the Bible also indicate that Jesus was hanged and not crucified (Acts 5:30). The actual text is as follows:

> Then came one and told them, saying "Behold the men whom ye put in prison are standing in the temple, and teaching the people." Then went the captain with the officers, and brought them without violence: for they feared the people, lest they should have been stoned. And when they had brought them, they set them before the council: and the high priest asked them, saying "Did not we straitly [sic] command you that ye should not teach in this name? And, behold, ye have filled Jerusalem with your doctrine, and intend to bring this man's blood upon us." Then Peter and the other apostles answered and said, "We ought to obey God rather than men. The God of our fathers raised up Jesus, whom ye slew and hanged on a tree" [Acts 5:25–30].

According to this passage, Jesus was clearly hanged from a tree and not crucified on a cross. The first time Jesus appears on a cross in any kind of image is not until more than 400 years after his death. Such archaeological finds and theories contradict the ideas that some contemporary Christians hold. This is because the modern faith is not based entirely on historical (Christian) accounts. There are a number of other cultural and social aspects that influence historiography and the writing of history—aspects that must be considered when interpreting the current beliefs that form the basis of the modern Roman Catholic faith. The beliefs that modern Catholics have in many instances cannot be traced neatly back to any specific historical document, as the ideas are a mixture of practices and beliefs from various different faiths. Like many great religions, it adopted what was good from other existing traditions and built upon it, creating Christianity as it is known today.

There is much that is unknown about the life and death of Jesus of Nazareth. Part of this is because at the beginning of the Christian movement there were no written documents about the man. Of documents that sprung up later, and of historical writings in general, it should always be remembered, too, that they cannot be completely accurate. "History, in fact, is more a matter of rough guessing from all of the available facts" (Peter, 1965, p. 90). There is nothing wrong with this and it is still commonplace, but it must be kept in mind. History is a work of art by the historiographer, who takes known, recorded facts, adds his or her own conjecture, and then joins such facts together to create a smooth-flowing narrative.

Christian historical sources, like Jewish sources, were put together in this manner. Facts that were known were fused together using intelligent guesses based on logic and available evidence in order to create historical accounts that read smoothly and inspire. The problem with this is that once the narrative was put together any evidence found later that did not fit neatly into the same story was discarded. It was for this reason that many gospels were not included in the Bible as it is known today. The book was edited in a specific manner in order to create a story that could be easily read and understood.

There is another potential problem with the way the New Testament was written and edited. The primary goal of stories about Jesus in the New Testament was not historical accuracy (Geary, 1978). Like any hagiography, the aim of the account was to produce a history that would inspire and amaze readers in order to influence their actions and decisions. The accounts of martyrs were modified to make them perfect depictions. The positios of potential saints are also edited to provide a perfect example of one perfection of Christ that other religious individuals could follow. All of this must be kept in mind when sorting through the historical evidence that forms the basis of Christian thought and practices.

Many Catholics are taught from a young age that Jesus was born in a stable in Bethlehem in year one on December 25, the winter solstice according to the Julian calendar. However, most archaeologists and historians would disagree with all of this. The idea that Jesus was born in a stable comes from one line in the Bible that states that Jesus was placed in a manger, which is an animal feeding trough. There is nothing whatsoever in the Bible that says that he was born in a stable. The wood needed in order to build a stable was virtually non-existent in the arid desert. For this reason, it is now generally agreed that Jesus was born in a cave. This cave, located under the Church of the Nativity, has become a place of pilgrimage for many Christians.

Cave dwelling was common in the area where Jesus was born, and there were many basement caves, which were basically lower levels of homes. Such caves were used to store food and animals, so a manger in such a cave would have been quite common. It is likely in one such cave that Mary gave birth to her son. Why she was in the basement, rather than in one of the rooms upstairs, can be explained by a mistranslated term in the New Testament. The New Testament was written about 100 years after the death of Jesus, and it was written in the language of learned scribes: Greek. The New Testament states that they laid him in a manger because there was no room at the inn. However, the term used for inn does not really mean "inn." Rather, it means "the guest room" or "the upper room" (Johnstone, 2009). So, it is more likely that she was in one of the rooms upstairs in a home, along with a number of other people. When she went into labor, they moved downstairs into the basement cave for privacy.

It is also unlikely that Jesus was born in Bethlehem. Bethlehem was 90 miles away from Nazareth. It is hard to fathom that Mary walked this distance so late in her pregnancy, especially since all of her friends and family were in Nazareth and not in Bethlehem. There would have been no reason for Mary to have made such a long journey (although the Bible states that it was for a census). There is a different, very logical reason why the birth of Jesus was placed in Bethlehem. It was to fulfill an Old Testament prophecy that the Messiah would come from the city. In this tradition, the Messiah must come from the House of David, and David came from Bethlehem. Since a birth in Bethlehem was necessary to match the existing message in the Old Testament, it is plausible that the gospel writers kept this in mind and wrote it to facilitate the spread of Christianity. There was likely no way to know the place of Jesus's birth anyway, since there were no known written records about Jesus before the texts of the New Testament were written. Among those texts, the earliest book was written approximately 50 years after the death of Jesus, but the majority of them were not written until at least 100 years after his death. Therefore, it is unlikely that anyone who had ever known him personally had written anything about him.

When he was born is technically unknown, but most scholars place it at c. 4 B.C.E. According to accounts in the Bible, he was born during the reign of Herod, so this date makes perfect sense from both historical and archaeological perspectives. The date celebrated today as Christmas, December 25, is not an arbitrary date, but it is likely not the date of

Jesus's birth, which is unknown. Christmas did not begin to be celebrated as a holiday until the fourth century, and when it first began it was celebrated on January 6. It was changed to December 25 later in that century in order to directly match the same date as the nativity of Mithra, the Zoroastrian god of the sun. Frazer (1961) explained this:

> What considerations led the ecumenical authorities to institute the festival of Christmas? The motives for the innovation are stated with great frankness by a Syrian writer, himself a Christian. "The reason," he tells us, "why the fathers transferred the celebration of the sixth of January to the twenty-fifth of December was this: It was the custom of the heathen to celebrate on the same twenty-fifth of December the birthday of the Sun, at which they kindled lights in token of festivity. In these solemnities and festivities the Christians also took part. Accordingly, when the doctors of the Church perceived that the Christians had a leaning to this festival, they took council and resolved that the true Nativity should be solemnized on that day and the festival of the Epiphany on the sixth of January. Accordingly, along with this custom, the practice has prevailed of kindling fires until the sixth." The heathen origin of Christmas is plainly hinted at, if not tacitly admitted, by Augustine when he exhorts his Christian brethren not to celebrate the solemn day like the heathen on account of the sun, but on account of him who made the sun [p. 305].

In this way, some of the pagan festivals were taken as Christian saints' days and other religious holidays. Practices found in Christianity can also be found in earlier traditions, and some of the preexisting savior stories and myths were most likely used to fill in the missing elements of the Jesus story.

The modern Church, along with painters and sculptors, generally depicts Jesus with his mother, Mary, and his father Joseph alone, but there is evidence to suggest that he grew up in a family with brothers and sisters (Meier, 1991). Some believe that Joseph was a widower and Jesus's brothers and sisters were actually Joseph's children from a previous marriage, but linguistic analyses tend to refute this idea (Johnstone, 2009). The brothers and sisters of Jesus were probably his actual brothers and sisters, as the Greek terms used can only refer to blood relations. "No embarrassment is evinced about the fact of these brothers. Nor is there any indication that they may be half-brothers, brothers by a different mother, or any such designation aimed at reducing their importance and minimizing their relationship to Jesus" (Eisenman, 1997, p. 74). The Bible only provides one of his sisters' names: Salome (Mark 15:40; Eisenman, 1997). However, it provides all of his brothers' names:

> Coming to his hometown, ... [Jesus] began teaching the people in their synagogue, and they were amazed. "Where did this man get this wisdom and these miraculous powers?" they asked. "Isn't this the carpenter's son? Isn't his mother's name Mary, and aren't his brothers James, Joseph, Simon and Judas? Aren't all his sisters with us? Where then did this man get all these things? [Matthew, 13:55].

There is other evidence in the Bible that Jesus did, in fact, have siblings. Here are just a few examples:

1. "While ... [Jesus] was still speaking to the people, behold, his mother and his brothers stood outside, asking to speak to him" (Matthew, 12:46).
2. "Then his mother and his brothers came to see [Jesus], but they could not reach him because of the crowd. And he was told, 'Your mother and your brothers are standing outside, desiring to see you'" (Mark 8:19–20).

3. "But I saw none of the other apostles except James the Lord's brother" (Galatians 1:19).
4. "It was Mary Magdelene and Joanna, and Mary the mother of James, and other women that were with them, which told these things unto the apostles" (Luke 24:10).
5. "After this ... [Jesus] went down to Capernaum, with his mother and his brothers and his disciples, and they stayed there for a few days" (John 2:12).

There are many other examples found in the Bible that demonstrate the once common knowledge that Jesus had brothers (and sisters). There is evidence outside of the Bible that points to the same conclusion as well, including references made by Flavius Josephus, who wrote about Jesus and his brother James. Flavius wrote: "Festus was now dead, and Albinus was but upon the road; so he assembled the sanhedrin of judges, and brought before them the brother of Jesus, who was called Christ, whose name was James" (Antiquities 20:199–200). James is probably the most famous of Jesus's brothers, and for people knowledgeable about Christian history he commands as much respect as his brother (Eisenman, 1997). While James was alive he was known as the most important figure in Christianity. He was the bishop of the Jerusalem Church, and he was known as James the Just because of his piety and righteousness (Eisenman, 1997).

Meier (1992) wrote:

> From a purely philological and historical point of view the most probable opinion is that the brothers and sisters of Jesus were his true siblings. This judgment arises first of all from the criterion of multiple attestation: Paul, Mark, John, Josephus, and perhaps Luke in Acts 1:14 speak independently of the "brother(s) of the Lord" (or of Jesus). The natural sense of brothers in all of these passages, as judged by the regular usage of Josephus and the New Testament, is sibling [p. 1].

The idea that Jesus had siblings was commonplace and accepted as historical fact during the first few centuries of Christianity. It was during the fourth century that this idea began to fade, possibly because the changing Church began to stress the idea of the Holy Trinity. This metaphysical theory was new to Christianity, and it was adopted from preexisting traditions (Mojsov, 2005).

The truth is, there is much that we do not know about Jesus and this was also the case when the Church (as it is known today) was established. It is unknown what town he even lived in when he was growing up. "The Bible makes no mention of where the young Jesus lived. In Matthew (2:23) and Mark (1:23), Jesus is called a 'Nazarene' and in other documents a 'Nazoraean.' But the town of Nazarene was not mentioned in Bible-related texts until some four hundred years C.E. Nazarene probably refers to another Jewish sect, also known as the 'Nazirites,' involving John the Baptist and Jesus's brother James" (Hanson, 2005, pp. 77–78).

Very little was known about the historical Jesus, and it is human nature to try to fill in the gaps. Written records were scarce until the Bible was put together in its current form, and most of the Church practices that are known today were non-existent. Such practices have origins not just in the historical teachings of Jesus but also in other traditions. There are explicit connections between Christianity and some of the older mystery religions, and scholars have posited that the teachings of Jesus were influenced by other traditions, including

Buddhism (Gruber and Kersten, 1995). Historical evidence supports the claim that Jesus was familiar with Buddhism, primarily because it was taught in Judea when he was alive and many of his statements and teachings have nearly identical counterparts in Buddhism. "The real historical question is not if he studied Buddhism, but where and how much he studied Buddhism, especially during his so-called 'lost years'" (Hanson, 2005, p. 76).

There are no biblical records about the life of Jesus between the ages of 13 and 29, but it is well documented in non-biblical accounts that he traveled extensively. Muslim records even call him the "traveling prophet." There are historical accounts about Jesus making it as far as India that are found in China, in many Muslim sources, in Persian texts, and in Kashmiri Hindu texts.[1] Historical evidence about Jesus visiting India also comes from Indian sources. The Western world knows about these sources mostly from author Nicolas Notovitch, who reviewed some unusual temple records and then published the information that he found in a book entitled *The Unknown Life of Jesus Christ*. He stated in the book that the information he was providing was found in documents located at the monastery of Himmis, near Leh, Ladakh, in Kashmir, which he came across when visiting in 1887. The accounts that he claimed to have studied talked about Jesus's travels throughout India, his sermons and preachings that were delivered there, and the problems that he had with Brahmans, Zoroastrians, and other religious officials along the way.

Once Notovitch had read and translated the accounts, he considered publishing the information. He approached some high-ranking members of the Church, asking for their advice regarding the possible publication of the information that he had come across. First, he spoke with a cardinal in the Vatican who was close to the pope. The cardinal suggested that Notovitch did not publish it — as it would do no good and would only serve to make enemies (Notovitch, 1894). The cardinal then asked if he could buy the translated manuscript, but the writer refused. Notovitch later sought out the advice of a cardinal in Paris. This man also suggested that Nicolas not publish the information — that it would be better if it remained hidden and unknown. The cardinal explained, "The Church suffers too much already from the new current of atheistic ideas, and you will but give a new food to the calumniators and detractors of the evangelical doctrine. I tell you this in the interest of all the Christian churches" (Notovitch, 1894). To put it simply, he wanted the account hidden so that it would not damage the Church. However, Notovitch eventually decided to publish it anyway. The book was first published in 1894, and it was met with controversy, as people as a whole do not like conflicting information. The Church instantly dismissed it as nonsense, but the organization was disturbed enough to employ an individual to find and destroy the original temple documents (Hanson, 2005; Serrano, 1972). The destruction of such documents by the Church was common. Hanson (2005) explained:

> By the second century C.E., the Church of Christ was destroying every piece of evidence of the life of Christ that did not support its doctrines, and the Church continued its purging with more or less fervor throughout the succeeding centuries. The activity continued at the turn of the twentieth century when the very question of Jesus's travels as a young man was raised first by Notovitch. Different Church authorities destroyed documents at the Himmis Monastery and later documents at the Tun-huang caves in central Asia. At stake throughout the centuries was the critical Church doctrine that Christ was a Jew who started his own religion as the Son of God. Any evidence not supporting this view was condemned as "apocrypha" and destroyed or rewritten. Even the four gospels were rewritten to provide the impression that Jesus never left Judea [p. 86].

Whether the account is true or not, there are definite parallels between Buddhist teachings and Christian teachings. Both Buddhists and Christians venerate relics, and both faiths utilize methods of bodily preservation, despite teachings that emphasize the relative unimportance of the physical body. In Buddhism, the practice of austerities is generally carried out in order to develop internal spiritual energy and to help the practitioner to realize the unimportance of the physical body. There is an unusual and rather disgusting form of meditation that involves meditating near a dead body. Sharf (1992) explained:

> These practices are thought to be particularly efficacious in eradicating attachment to the body, whether it be lust directed to another or vanity with regard to oneself. The meditations on impurity involve locating an abandoned corpse by the roadside or in a charnel ground, taking up a position nearby, and contemplating the inherent repulsiveness of the body. The Buddhist scriptures enumerate ten meditations on impurity, distinguished according to the relative stage of decomposition of the corpse at hand, be it bloated, livid, festering, cut up, gnawed, scattered, hacked, bleeding, worm-infested, or skeletal [p. 3].

This practice is utilized to help the meditator realize that this life is only temporary and the body is but a shell. It is shed at the moment of death, much like a cicada sheds its husk, and therefore is relatively unimportant. In Christianity, the same aversion to the physical body is expressed, despite the practice of mummification. "In both religions, there is a connection between the struggle against the corporeal, against the body, as the source of all harm and impurity, which with Luther led to the expression, 'This corpse, this sack of maggots'" (Otto & Almond, 1984, p. 92).

In addition, the miracles that are reported to have occurred in Buddhism and in Christianity are very similar and include such things as healing of diseases, protection from fire and other calamities, and the like. Bodies are also said to have been found miraculously preserved in both traditions. "Whole-body relics in both Buddhism and Christianity are usually fragrant and beautiful" (Bingenheimer, 2005, p. 14). Sometimes, there are miracles around their graves, indicating to followers that the deceased want

The crucified Christ flanked by Mary and John (Byzantine, late thirteenth century C.E.). This is common Christian symbolism, with Jesus in the center of the image, while two others stand beside him. All of the individuals have halos. Mary and John are both lower than Jesus (London, England) (© The Trustees of the British Museum. All rights reserved).

The Buddha with his attendants. This painting, by an unknown artist, has been mounted on a scroll. It displays Amida Buddha flanked by two Arhats, Buddhist saints. The figures all have halos, and the attendants are lower than the Buddha. Note the similarities between this image and the Christian image on the previous page (from a private collection in Rhode Island).

31. Historical Evidence

At first glance, this carving might appear to be Christian, due to the clothing, hairstyle, and familiar halo. However, this is a Buddhist statue, depicting an Arhat, a Buddhist saint (Kamakura, Japan).

to be found. The appearance of these phenomena is rare outside of these two traditions and can likely only be completely explained by exploring possible relationships between the two religions.

There are similar connections between the biblical version of the life of Jesus and the historical accounts of Siddharta Gautama, the Buddha. Both of their births, for example, were equally prophesized and deemed divine events. Both were born from virgin mothers, and they were attended to by angels. They were visited by wise men bearing gifts, and as children both of them amazed those around them with their incredible wisdom. Later in life, they both began ministry at the age of 30. They both attracted disciples, and both fasted in the wilderness for 40 days. In addition, both were consecrated in a holy river and both performed numerous miracles. The teachings that the two of them advocated were also similar in nearly every aspect, including the importance of universal peace and love for others. Finally, upon their deaths, miraculous events were witnessed by both groups of their followers.

Among connections between Christianity and other religious faiths and traditions, the relationship between Christianity and Buddhism is tenuous. But it is still there. The bonds between Christianity and other traditions, however, are much stronger and more difficult to dismiss. Strong similarities can be made between the lives of Jesus and Attis, Dionysus, Mithra, Krishna, and the Egyptian gods Osiris and Horus. For example, the birth of Horus, like the births of the Buddha, Jesus, and many other religious figures, was thought to be immaculate — their mothers were virgins. Horus was born on December 25, was visited by three kings, and was baptized at the age of 30, exactly the same as Jesus. He had 12 disciples, like Jesus and some other gods, and performed miracles, such as healing the sick. Horus was called the Lamb of God and the Good Shepherd, and he died in the same way as Jesus, Dionysus, and others — he was crucified, buried for three days, and then resurrected. It is obvious that Christianity, like other great religions, borrowed some concepts, ideas, and practices from earlier traditions. In order to determine where any of their practices originated, namely the practice of mummification, it is important to study the belief systems that influenced early Christianity.

32

Immaculate Conception and the Resurrection

There are certain motifs that keep appearing in various religious traditions. They are obviously considered important to people, which is why, throughout the ages, such concepts were not discarded. These include the idea of the immaculate conception and the idea of a life-giving deity who died and was then resurrected. The idea of an immaculate conception is not new, and in early Christianity it was not taken literally. At the beginning of Christianity, believers knew about Mary, Joseph, Jesus and all of his brothers and sisters due to oral tradition and (possibly from) some early written texts that were likely precursors to the Bible. There was no idea of a virgin birth in early Christianity.

The ancient document of the Mt. Sinaitic palimpsest states that Jacob begat Joseph, and Joseph, who was married to Mary, begat Jesus, who is known as Christ (Wells, 1971). There is conflicting information in the biblical accounts: Mary was betrothed to Joseph when she was impregnated, but the passage continued with, "And Joseph, her husband..." (Matthew 1:19). If they were already married, they would have consummated the marriage. In addition, there are various passages in the gospels that refer to Jesus as the son of Joseph. Some of the edits that were performed to the Bible also provide evidence that early Christians believed that Jesus was naturally conceived by Joseph and Mary. In one of the earliest versions of Luke a passage reads "and his parents knew it not" (2:43), but a later version has this edited account: "Joseph and his mother knew not of it" (Wells, 1971). This is clearly evidence of the later addition of the Virgin Birth concept and the corresponding alterations in the historical accounts to support it.

In early Christianity, there was no doubt that Jesus was conceived by Joseph and Mary (Eisenman, 1997). It is only if he were actually Joseph's son that Jesus would have been a descendant of David. This is because Joseph, and not Mary, was related to David. Jesus's connection to David was necessary if Jewish people were going to believe that he was the Messiah. However, a virgin birth would remove the connection to the family of David (Wells, 1971). For this reason, a virgin birth not only would have been regarded as nonsense to early Christians but a major theological problem as well.

The idea of the immaculate conception was added later. The Virgin Birth, originally not meant to be taken literally, was borrowed from other religions, "in the same way that pagan festivals were adopted as Christian saints' days" (Freke and Gandy, 1999, p. 6). One major example of this adoption is the celebration of Christmas, which was explicitly moved to December 25 due to the god Mithra. Traces of ancient faiths and ancient practices are found deeply embedded in Christian traditions, and a virgin birth is one such concept.

The Holy Family, by artist Gerard David (1460–1523). Initially, Christians believed that Joseph was the father of Jesus. Early versions of the Bible refer to Joseph and Mary as his parents. It was later, after the first century, that the concept of the Virgin Birth was added by the Church. After this occurrence, Joseph was often removed from artistic depictions of the holy family (from a private collection in Rhode Island).

An immaculate conception seems to exist in nearly every ancient faith. There was never a doubt that a god could impregnate a mortal. Such tales are found in ancient Greek and Roman traditions, as well as in Egyptian, Sumerian, and Christian religions. Frazer (1961) suggested that the idea of anyone being close to God in various traditions, such as a saint in Christianity and the awliyā' Allāh in Islam, is a remnant of this ancient belief.

Any holy person who can commune with God in ways that other mortals cannot could actually be a child of God. This would signify that the person's human father was not his or her actual father, and it would make the mother a potential virgin. The belief in a child resulting from a divine-human union (whether it be sexual or asexual) is common in many faiths, and it has not dissipated. Frazer (1961) wrote: "These modern saints, whether Christian or Moslem, who father the children of Syrian mothers, are nothing but the old gods under a thin disguise" (p. 79). He points out that many human beings (who are considered holy) actually have terms originally reserved for divinity in their names. This again supports the existence of a popular idea that a child can result from a woman being impregnated by God. This union results in an offspring that is not quite God and not quite human, but he or she has attributes of them both. Therefore, like the saints and the awliyā' Allāh, the individual can function as a perfect intermediary through which mere mortals can access God.

It seems that all of the known saviors were not completely human. Almost without

A more common representation of Jesus and Mary. Joseph has been edited out. This was done after a dogmatic addition to the changing Christian faith: the concept of the Virgin Birth. This idea did not exist in early Christianity (Florence, Italy).

exception, they did not have attributes of a mere mortal. This is because they were closer to God. They were not human but half-breeds: half God and half human. In almost every case of a god impregnating a woman, the woman was a virgin. Thus, in religions everywhere, there are holy individuals who were born after an immaculate conception. In all of these conceptions, the resulting offspring were consistently thought to be saviors. Such saviors include Attis, Ra, Krishna, Tammuz, Zoroaster, Buddha, Osiris, Horus, and Krishna. In the Judeo-Christian tradition, there are Jesus and possibly Moses.

Although the accounts of the birth of Moses in the Bible do not explicitly state that he was conceived immaculately, the facts immediately succeeding his birth are similar to the accounts of other immaculate conceptions leading to the birth of a savior. His birth was predicted by seers, and he was able to walk immediately after his birth, like the Buddha and other savior-gods. A strange and heavenly light filled the house, and the child had the gift of prophecy. He was able to speak immediately on the very day that he was born, evidence of a great deal of wisdom that he had either gained in previous existences or been given by God before his birth. The birth of Moses may not be considered to have resulted from an immaculate conception by some people, but the traits that he possessed and the signs that foretold his coming are consistent with such stories. It is therefore evidence that this tradition even existed among the writers of the Old Testament — that the idea of a miraculous birth was not only prevalent but also important.

Another miraculous birth in Jewish tradition is the birth of Isaac, whose mother was sterile. The most famous in the Judeo-Christian tradition has to be the birth of Jesus, which was foretold. The story appears in the gospels of Luke and Matthew, and it also appears in the Koran, in which Jesus is referred to as Issa. According to the Gospel of Luke, angels announced the birth to shepherds, who traveled to the town of his birth, where they found Mary and Joseph and the baby, lying in an animal feeding trough. The archangel Gabriel had appeared to Mary and said, "Do not be afraid, Mary, for you have found favor with God. And behold, you will conceive in your womb and bear a son, and you shall call his name Jesus. He will be great and will be called the Son of the Most High. And the Lord God will give to him the throne of his father David, and he will reign over the house of Jacob forever, and of his kingdom there will be no end" (Luke 1:30–33). Mary then asks how this was possible, since she was a virgin. And like many of the other saviors in different traditions, the messenger responds that God will put the child there.

The Gospel of Matthew provides a slightly different account. Mary became engaged to Joseph before he learned that she was already pregnant. Having learned this, he decided to quietly divorce her. She likely explained to him that she had not been impregnated by another man but by God himself. Joseph might not have believed this story initially, but according to the Book of Matthew, an angel appeared to him in a dream and confirmed this story. The angel said, "Joseph, son of David, do not fear to take Mary as your wife, for that which is conceived in her is from the Holy Spirit. She will bear a son, and you shall call his name Jesus, for he will save his people from their sins" (1:20–21). All of this (for the most part) matched with what a prophet had recently announced — that a virgin would give birth to a son and that the child would be called Immanuel. Although they were to name him Jesus instead of Immanuel, the name Immanuel means "God with us." Therefore, some believe that the prophecy did in fact refer to the birth of Jesus.

Another miraculous birth in the Judeo-Christian tradition is the birth of John the Baptist, a relative of Jesus. The Gospel of Luke reported that John was the son of Zechariah, who was an old man, and his wife, Elizabeth, who was sterile. The birth of John was also foretold by the archangel Gabriel, who imparted this information to Zecharia when he was in the Temple of Jerusalem. Zechariah did not quite believe the angel and asked, "How shall I know this? For I am an old man, and my wife is advanced in years" (1:18). The angel Gabriel became angry with Zechariah for questioning what he had been told and punished him. Gabriel took away his ability to speak. The angel said, "You will be silent and unable to speak until the day that these things take place, because you did not believe my words" (1:20). Mary, the mother of Jesus, was Elizabeth's cousin. The archangel Gabriel, when he was giving Mary news about the forthcoming miraculous birth of Jesus, also informed her of the miraculous pregnancy of her cousin Elizabeth, announcing two miraculous births in one visit. Gabriel said, "Your relative Elizabeth in her old age has also conceived a son, and this is the sixth month with her who was called barren. For nothing will be impossible with God" (1:36). Mary traveled to see Elizabeth, and upon hearing the news of her pregnancy, the baby in Elizabeth's womb "leaped for joy" (1:44).

There are two examples of miraculous births in Christian tradition, both of which were predicted and announced before they occurred, and there are two similar births in Jewish tradition: the birth of Moses and the birth of Isaac. However, this tradition of maintaining the existence of the miraculous birth of a savior, along with corresponding elements, such as a virgin mother and the birth being foretold, is not unique to Judeo-Christian ideas. It is found in other, much older traditions. Both Horus and Osiris were miraculously born to a virgin mother, for example, and the Egyptian statues and pictures of Isis with the baby

Horus were the precursor for Christian imagery of the Madonna and child (Gadalla, 2008). This relationship and the Holy Trinity of Osiris, Horus, and Isis were extremely important to people, so these elements of this ancient religion were transposed upon the newly developing Christian faith.

The second motif that keeps reappearing in various religions is the idea of a god who dies for the sake of humans and is then later resurrected. Tales of divine resurrection appear in Etruscan, Egyptian, Greek and Norse mythology.[1] They appear in religions in ancient Sumer, in the Aztec civilization, and in Roman and Phrygian[2] traditions. In addition, they are found in Arabian, Japanese, Australian aboriginal, and Native American faiths. One such example is Adonis. His actual name was Tammuz, but out of respect and awe he was called Adonis. The term stems from the Semitic word *adon*, which means "lord." The appellation Adonis was mistakenly applied to the god by the Greeks, who thought that it was a name rather than a title of respect (Frazer, 1961). As an interesting side note that is indicative of the influence that myths such as this one had upon Judeo-Christian traditions, Jehovah is often referred to in the Old Testament as Adonai, which was most likely originally Adoni, meaning "my Lord" (Frazer, 1961).

Adonis was worshipped by Semitic people, but it is likely that his cult began in earlier civilizations. In Babylonian accounts, he is an extremely important god, known as the spouse of Ishtar, the equivalent of Mother Earth in the Western tradition. Every year, worshippers would celebrate the birth, death, and resurrection of this god. The festival was an important religious occurrence. Incense was used, and a symbolic representation of the god was placed into a coffin and then pushed into a body of water. Worshippers wailed and provided offerings as though the god had recently died, but then later they celebrated his resurrection. Lucian (120–c. 190) wrote: "They make offerings to Adonis as one dead, and the day after the morrow they tell the story that he lives." The bodily representation of Adonis, before being placed into the water, was ritually treated as the actual body of the god would have been. It was washed, embalmed with aromatic spices, and then wrapped in linen. Basically, it underwent the same treatment as the corpse of Jesus, who was also embalmed and wrapped in linen (John 19:40). Then, like Jesus, Adonis was resurrected after his death.

Another figure that has similar attributes is Attis, the Phrygian god. His birth was miraculous, and his mother was a virgin named Nana. There are two versions of his death. In one, he died in the same manner as Adonis, killed by a wild boar. In the other history, however, Attis mutilated himself under a pine tree and bled to death on the spot. He showed true selflessness and died as a result of his actions, like the martyrs in Judeo-Christian tradition. His body was treated and then buried in a tomb. Every year on March 25, his followers would celebrate his death and resurrection. They would replay the death of the savior during the day, "but when night had fallen, the sorrow of the worshippers was turned to joy. For suddenly a light shone in the darkness: the tomb was opened: the god had risen from the dead; and as the priest touched the lips of the weeping mourners with balm, he softly whispered in their ears the glad tidings of salvation" (Frazer, 1961, p. 272). Worshippers took the resurrection of their god as evidence and assurance that they, too, would one day be resurrected. Their resurrections from the dead were only made possible because of the self-sacrifice demonstrated by their savior Attis.

The worship of Attis and celebrations of his death and resurrection were extremely popular in Rome. Emperor Claudius incorporated the Phrygian worship of the sacred tree—

under which Attis bled to death — as well as some other religious celebrations that centered around the worship of Attis. One particular ceremony was rather gruesome. It was thought that resurrection was only possible through the bloodshed of the savior — it was his sacrifice that opened the gates for all other humans. It was through his bloodshed that the remission of sins was also attained. Yearly, a bull was sacrificed in order to reenact the divine process of shedding blood for the resurrection of the body and for the forgiveness of sins. This sacrificial ceremony used to take place in the current location of the Vatican, where St. Peter's now stands. This is known because of a number of inscriptions that were found relating to these rites of Attis when the church was being enlarged and renovated in 1608. Such rites were extremely important in Rome, and their remnants can be found in later religious traditions in the same area.

33

Mithra: The Zoroastrian God of the Sun

Mithra was another predecessor of Jesus. A Persian god, he was incredibly popular in Rome, and monuments to him have been found all over the empire. There are many similarities between the cult of Mithra and the cult of Jesus, now known as Christianity. In the Vatican, where St. Peter's is today, pagan priests once celebrated mass with gifts of bread and wine to Mithra. This practice most likely came about because of something that Mithra had said to his followers. Before he sacrificed himself to save others, Mithra told his 12 disciples, "He who will not eat of my body and drink of my blood, so that he will be made one with me and I with him, the same shall not know salvation."[1]

Mithra, who was called the Son of God and the Good Shepherd, originated in the ancient Indian Vedic religion. Originally, the god was known as Mitra, but as the faith traveled, the god became known by different names: Mihr and Mithra. He was known as a sun deity, and various historians have pointed out the likelihood that he was associated with the Egyptian god Horus, who was identified with Ra in ancient times. Some of the traits of and stories about Mithra were likely picked up from other religions. It seems that it is human nature to take elements from older faiths and add them to new ones. What is liked is retained. What is not appreciated is discarded. So as Mithraism traveled, it changed. Most of the traditions and stories that we associate with Mithraism today come from the Romans' adaptation of the faith beginning c. 70 B.C.E.

The similarities between Mithraism and the later religion of Christianity are striking, and there is no doubt that many of the ideas that formed the basic structure of Christianity were taken from its Zoroastrian predecessor. The births of both saviors were on the same day, and they were both born in a cave. Both saviors were known as intermediaries between humans and God, and it was their blood that was shed for the remission of sins and for the salvation of humankind. They were both called traveling prophets, and they both had 12 disciples. The religious rituals that surrounded Mithra and Jesus included baptisms and communion meals, which both made use of bread and wine. Eschatological ideas were also similar. Both had ideas about the immortality of the soul residing in humans, as well as notions about the existence of both heaven and hell. Mithraism and Christianity held that souls would be judged after death, and adherents of both believed in the resurrection of the body.

Mithraism and Christianity were similar in almost every aspect, insofar as their religious beliefs and rituals went. But the two religions were politically at odds. In one respect, Mithraism, like Buddhism and some other major faiths, was open to new ideas. It was ever seeking the truth, and its adherents did not believe that they alone were keepers of it. Therefore, they were tolerant of other faiths. Christianity, on the other hand, was intolerant. "Its teachers were confident that they alone had the whole and only truth, that all else was error with which there could be no compromise. It would brook no rival; Mithraism, like all else pagan, was ruthlessly and completely crushed when the Empire became Christian" (Shaff, 1953, p. 419).

Mithraism was extremely popular in Rome, even after Christianity had begun, and there were Mithraic sanctuaries in many locations along Roman roads and waterways. It was a common faith in both urban and rural areas, and by the first century its teachings were widespread. The religion was made official and accepted by important individuals, including emperors. Commodus (ruling from 180 to 192) was initiated into the faith, Aurelian (ruling from 270 to 275) made the religion official, and by the third century the Roman emperors had a Mithraic chaplain with whom they communicated. They even dedicated a major temple to Mithra in the capital. Mithraism prospered in this period of religious freedom. However, all this changed when Christianity gained a stronghold. "Under Constantine, imperial favor was withdrawn, and Christianity demanded the repression of the cult. A Roman panegyric of the year 362 says that under Constantius no one dared to look at the rising or setting sun, and that farmers and sailors were afraid to observe the stars" (Shaff, 1953, p. 423).

Basically, one savior who was born on December 25 in a cave, who was visited by three shepherds, and who later died for our sins and was resurrected was snuffed out and replaced with a new one. Worship of other religions was outlawed, and the Christians destroyed many of the holy texts of religions like Mithraism, replacing them with their own. The early Church put together a text that was based on earlier sources, edited out anything that might have been contrary to their teachings, and then declared it to be the only truth. In order to explain away the similarities between Christianity and the other faiths that preceded it, they proposed one of the most bizarre explanations in the history of the world, and they called it diabolical mimicry. They claimed that the devil knew about the coming of Christianity and that he decided to put the other religious texts and traditions in place before the birth of Jesus in order to eventually discredit the teachings of the Church. The Church father Tertullian and Justin Martyr both claimed, "The observances of Mithraism were the cunning parodies devised by Satan to discredit the holy things of God and to seduce the souls of men from the true faith by a false and insidious imitation of it" (Shaff, 1953, p. 419). In other words, Christianity did not take anything from other traditions, but the other traditions took things from Christianity before Christianity came into existence! This type of reasoning could only be accepted by an ignorant or unintelligent population, which might be why scientific progress (and freedom of religious thought) was all but halted by the Church.

Once religions such as Mithraism were destroyed and outlawed, Christianity took over and the Dark Ages began. Freke and Gandy (1999) wrote:

> The ancients had built the pyramids and the Parthenon, but within a few hundred years of Christianity, people in many areas of Europe had forgotten how to make brick houses. In the first century B.C.E. Posidonius had created a beautiful revolving model of the solar system that faithfully represented the orbits of the planets. By the end of the fourth century C.E. it was sacrilegious not to believe that God placed the stars in the heavens each night. In the third

century B.C.E., the Alexandrian scholar Eratosthenes had correctly calculated the circumference of the Earth to within a few percent, but now it had become a heresy not to believe that the world was flat [pp. 250–251].

The knowledge of the ancients was forcefully cast out and discredited, and in time scientific and spiritual knowledge faded away, giving rise to a 1,000-year period that is called the Dark Ages. In many of the old pagan religions, there were two distinct elements called the Mysteries. There were the Outer Mysteries, which many interested people could become a part of. These included the various celebrations for gods or holy men and the rituals performed in their honor. However, the most important components were termed the Inner Mysteries, which were secret knowledge that was only conveyed to those initiated into the faith. Once this knowledge was understood, the true meaning of all of the rituals would be brought to light. The Inner Mysteries were the genuine sacred teachings, and they included knowledge about the world and the heavens. When the Church adopted pagan teachings and rituals for use in Christianity, however, they only took the Outer Mysteries, so the true knowledge found in these ancient faiths was lost (Freke and Gandy, 1999). However, the underlying ideas and practices of ancient faiths are still present in Christianity, including the seemingly contrary practices of preserving bodies and then desecrating them in order to provide relics.

34

Pythagoras and Dionysus

The son of God Pythagoras (581–497 B.C.E.) was thought to be the child of Apollo. Pythagoras's birth was miraculous. His father, on a trip to Delphi, was informed about the birth by the oracle there, which was obviously shocking, since his wife showed no signs whatsoever of being pregnant before he left. He was told that the child would surpass all those who had ever lived in beauty and wisdom, and he realized that Pythagoras must have been fathered by God. Iamblichus of Chalcis (c. 245–c. 325) wrote: "No one will deny that the soul of Pythagoras was sent to mankind from Apollo's domain, having either been one of his attendants, or more intimate associates, which may be inferred both from his [miraculous] birth and his versatile wisdom."

From an early age, Pythagoras was extremely interested in religion, and he learned everything that he could about the Phoenician mysteries. He learned, though, that the majority of Phoenician traditions and teachings actually came from Egypt. Therefore, he traveled to Egypt and learned from all of the priests there, traveling from temple to temple. "He visited all of the Egyptian priests, acquiring all the wisdom each possessed" (Iamblichus of Chalcis, n.d.). After many years in Egypt, he was captured by Cambyses's soldiers and taken to Babylon. This was not a bad situation for Pythagoras, however, who learned how to worship the gods correctly from some Magi. After a long period of study, he traveled around, teaching those who asked for instruction. He was a traveling prophet, instructing in Greece and in (the ancient city of) Crotona and amassing a number of followers. Then he traveled to Italy, where he taught love and friendship in a number of Italian cities that had previously oppressed their neighbors with slavery.[1] He continued to travel about, and many miracles were credited to him, some of which show up in the Bible as miracles that Jesus also performed. Either they performed similar miracles or elements of Pythagorean tradition were also incorporated into Christianity. He taught in Italy and he even established religious groups in the Greek colonies of southern Italy, so it is not inconceivable that his influence extended to the local religious beliefs.

Miracles are common in just about every religion in the world, and many of the historical saviors were also known to be miracle workers. When stories of miracles carried out by different gods are exactly the same, however, one must wonder if they are two distinct deities, as they appear, or if some of the historical accounts have been (inadvertently or intentionally) combined. This has occurred in many religions, and it is why it is now known that Tammuz and Adonis are the same god and why it is thought that "Osiris" and "Dionysus" might refer to the same original deity. Herodotus (c. 490–431 B.C.E.) discovered this fact early on and did not hesitate to equate Osiris with Dionysus, Demeter with Isis, and Horus with Apollo. Plutarch (c. 46–120) arrived at the same conclusions. "Osiris," he wrote, "is identical with Dionysus." There are other historians who believe Osiris is also Tammuz (Barton, 1915). This would suggest that many of the gods in various civilizations were nothing more than differing versions of the same original deity — a god who was so important in the distant past that his worship has continued throughout time, although under different names in various civilizations.

The miracles that both Jesus and Pythagoras share include calming the seas so that their disciples might pass over the water more safely and predicting the exact number of fish that would be caught by others. Jesus predicted that 153 fish would be caught (John 21:11). In the accounts of Pythagoras, the exact number of fish that he predicted would be caught is not recorded, but 153 is the sacred number in Pythagorean mathematics. It was a holy number known as "the measure of the fish," and it was utilized to create the "sign of the fish," which was used as a symbol of early Christianity.

Another sacred number of Pythagoras is 12. Twelve spheres surrounding one central sphere was a common image used by the Phythagoreans to represent God, whom they conceived as being spherical. "The ancients discovered that if a sphere is surrounded by others of exactly the same dimension so that all of the spheres are in contact with each other, the central sphere will be surrounded by exactly 12 others" (Freke and Gandy, 1999, p. 42). This could explain why the accounts written to describe the lives of saviors often mention that they were surrounded by 12 disciples. Jesus had 12 disciples, and so did Mithra. Almost all of the god-saviors who have ever existed had 12 disciples (Mangasarian, 2004). Other numbers that are important are the numbers 7, 3, and 40. They all are considered sacred in sun myths, and the same numbers are prominently featured in the Bible. This cannot be a coincidence. Some of the earlier knowledge and ideas were incorporated into Christianity, and they have not dissipated.

Other miracles that were credited to Pythagoras are similar to those performed by other Christian holy men. St. Francis was supposed to have had a special affinity for animals, and he functioned as an intermediary in order to negotiate a truce between a town and a hungry wolf. After he communicated with the wolf, it left the townspeople alone. Similarly, Pythagoras detained the Daunian bear, which had previously injured a number of inhabitants. Pythagoras fed it, and then made it swear an oath to stop harming living creatures. Another miracle involving Pythagoras and animals is the following:

> At Tarentum he saw an ox feeding in a pasture, where he ate green beans. He advised the herdsman to abstain from the food and to tell the ox to abstain from this food. The herdsman laughed at him, remarking that he did not know the language of oxen but that if Pythagoras did, he had better tell him so himself. Pythagoras approached the ox's ear and whispered into it for a long time. Hereafter the ox not only refrained from them, but never even tasted them [Iamblichus of Chalcis, n.d.].

Certainly, stories like these, involving Pythagoras, St. Francis, or other holy men, might be considered strange or silly, but the mere fact that they are found in many traditions signifies that they held some importance to human beings hundreds or even thousands of years ago. Other miracles credited to Pythagoras are similar to the miracles of Catholic saints, including bilocation. Padre Pio was often said to have miraculously appeared in two places simultaneously. Pythagoras, too, miraculously did the same. "All his biographies insist that during the same day he was present in Metapontum in Italy and at Tauromenium in Sicily discoursing with his disciples in both places" (Iamblichus of Chalcis, n.d.). He also predicted various natural calamities. In his teachings, he stressed the need for abstention from meat and alcohol, and the abhorrence of wealth and fame. His followers, who lived in colonies in southern Italy, had no possessions, and they were all vegetarians.

The Pythagoreans were careful when writing anything not to reveal the true substance of their philosophy. The inner secrets were maintained and not revealed to outsiders. "All Pythagoric discipline was symbolic, resembling riddles and puzzles, and consisting of maxims, in the style of the ancients" (Iamblichus of Chalcis, n.d.). In this manner, their true knowledge was protected. After the death of Pythagoras, the cult was prohibited by authorities and their teachings were not explicitly continued. Instead, some of the sacred numbers and metaphysical theories of the Pythagoreans were adopted by other traditions and continued on as part of the Inner Mysteries of other faiths.

Dionysus is another savior who predated Jesus and likely influenced Christian philosophy and historical accounts. He also is a son of God, as his father was thought to be Zeus. Zeus's divine wife, Hera, approached the mother of Dionysus, Semele, and explained to her that she was pregnant—that the child that she was carrying was the child of the King of Gods himself, who had found favor with her. Dionysus, like Jesus and Mithra, was miraculously born. He was a traveling prophet, and he performed various miracles, including turning water into wine (Diodorus 3:66.3). After his death, like other savior-gods, he was resurrected. It should be noted, though, that various historians have pointed out the likelihood that the Greek god Dionysus, called Bacchus in the Roman pantheon, is the same as the Egyptian god Osiris. The accounts of these two gods are therefore intertwined, and it is difficult to cleanly separate the two. The written myths of the god Dionysus are but one aspect of the god and his traditions and celebrations. How his worshippers thought of him and what they passed on as his history are equally important. In fact, talking about any deity as having but one truthful historical account is not only illogical but also harmful. The historical accounts of gods are embellished and edited over time. The elements that believers deem important are stressed, and the elements that are seemingly without significance are

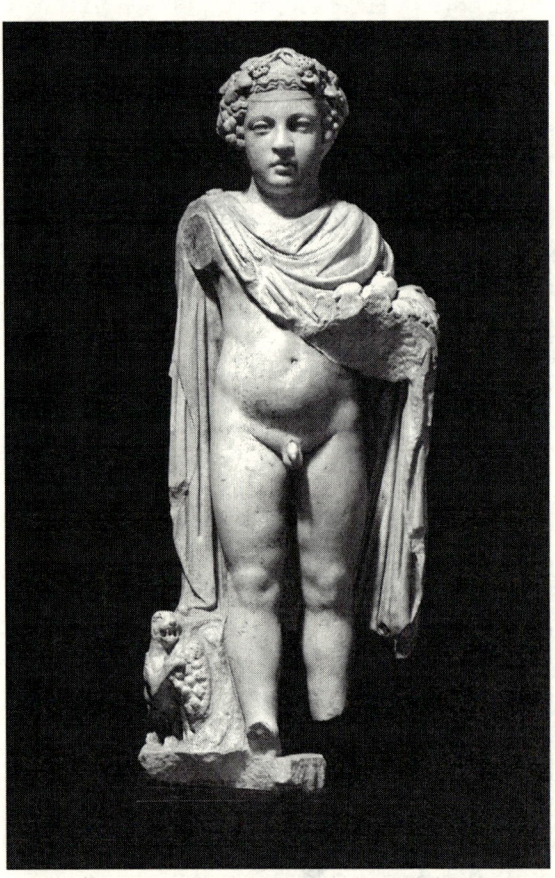

The child Dionysus (Roman, Imperial Period, 140–170 C.E.) (© 2012 Museum of Fine Arts, Boston).

Another representation of the child Dionysus found at the ruins of Pompeii, just outside of Naples, Italy.

discarded. Therefore, depending on the worshippers and their own preexisting notions about what constitutes divinity, the historical accounts of the gods will differ.

Sometimes, stories of one god will be applied to another. And sometimes, the legends of one god will be mistakenly separated into two distinct deities throughout the ages. Some believe that a number of gods, from various parts of the world, are simply different versions of the same ancient god. Osiris is one such example. Reade (1861) wrote that Osiris was worshipped under different names throughout the world. "He was the Mithra of the Persians, the Brahma of India, the Baal or Adonis of the Phoenicians, the Apollo of the Greeks, the Odin of Scandinavia, the Hu of the Britons, and the Baiwe of the Laplanders." Whether Reade was correct or not is irrelevant. It is enough to know that legends and myths combine throughout history. Although they may all hint at the existence of a single ancient God, this God cannot be known through a single religious tradition, as it provides but one small aspect of the original whole.

With this in mind, it is possible, if not probable, that the legends of Osiris and Dionysus both refer to the same deity. Many stories that originated in Egyptian beliefs about Osiris were applied to Dionysus. Plutarch and Herodotus may have been the earliest historians to have written that the myths and rituals of the two gods referred to the same deity, but this knowledge was definitely not confined to them alone. To properly understand the true nature of Dionysus, it is necessary to explore the same god from the Osirian perspective. Therefore, it is useful to understand the function and importance of Osiris as he relates to Christian beliefs and Italian practices.

35

The Cult of Osiris

"Herodotus found the similarity between the rites of Osiris and Dionysus so great, that he thought it impossible the latter could have arisen independently; they must, he supposed, have been recently borrowed, with slight alterations, by the Greeks from the Egyptians" (Frazer, 1961, p. 127). Plutarch also thought that the rites of both Osiris and Dionysus were so close that they must have been connected. It is for this reason that some scholars have suggested that the representations of the two actually refer to the same individual — an individual who was most likely an actual human and not just a mythical creation. Timothy Freke and Peter Gandy (1999) reasonably combined the two of them and referred to the single god whom they dubbed Osiris-Dionysus in their book. They were looking at this deity as being a precursor for the entire creation of the Christ myth, and it is easy to see the connections between this deity and the Christian savior.

There is ample evidence available with which to speculate that Tammuz and Osiris were the same god, which would mean that the myths surrounding Tammuz, Osiris and Dionysus might have all referred to the same god. (Others, however, equate Tammuz with the son of Osiris, Horus, whose cult and importance was similar to that of his father.) The cult of Tammuz may have been transferred to Egypt in the distant past, and it most likely initially originated from the Semitic peoples. The god was known as Dumuzi by the Babylonians, Tammuz in Hebrew, Dhu 'l Shara by the northern Arabians, and Eshmun and Adonis by the Phoenicians (Barton, 1915). Osiris most likely is these other gods, although he was called by different names. Even in Egypt, however, he was referred to by different names, including Dedu and Busiris.

Osiris, pronounced "wasir" in ancient Egyptian, is thought to have been an actual historical entity — a remnant of the distant past. Evidence supports the conclusion that he was a deified king. There are hymns and prayers to Osiris in hieroglyphs on the walls at five pyramids in Sakkara, the earliest written approximately 2625 B.C.E. However, it is thought that many of these inscriptions were based upon and copied from much older texts. Osiris might be one of the oldest gods still researched today. The notion that Osiris had been an actual person has existed for hundreds of years. Samuel Sharpe (1863) wrote that among all of the Egyptian gods, "Osiris and his family alone had any biography. They once lived upon earth." Osiris was born on Mount Sinai, which is called Nissa by the Egyptians. "Hence, according to Diodorus Siculus, was derived the god's Greek name Dionysus, which is the same as the Hebrew Jehovah-Nissi" (Sharpe, 1863).

The knowledge that he was a primeval king gained further momentum after his tomb was found. "The carved monument of Osiris which was found in the sepulchral chamber appears indeed to be a work of late Egyptian art, but it may have replaced an earlier sarcophagus" (Frazer, 1961, p. 198). In the same tomb was a human skull that was missing the lower jawbone, and an arm covered with expensive jewelry. This tomb was identified with the tomb of King Khent, who reigned during the First Dynasty, and it was thought that the head was the king's and the arm belonged to his queen. Frazer (1961) has suggested the possibility that Khent was Osiris (Osiris being a posthumous name) and that the body parts found in the Tomb of Osiris might therefore belong to Osiris and Isis. Worshipping dead kings was a custom of the ancient Egyptians, and sometimes pieces of the remains would be worshipped in different places. For example, a dead king in Uganda was worshipped at his temple, while his head was worshipped at another site and a leg bone was the object of veneration at another locale.

The worshippers wished to pray before the remains of their king, and the separation of body parts made this possible in numerous locations. The body itself was thought to possess some spiritual powers in

Painted wooden figure of Osiris (c. 1295–1186 B.C.E.), wearing a crown (London, England) (© The Trustees of the British Museum. All rights reserved).

Egypt, powers that were evidence of the eternal soul of the king. Therefore, it was not uncommon to have pieces of important bodies in multiple places. This is not unlike the Catholic practice of preserving relics and sending them to different locations. Another similarity between both Catholicism and Egyptian religious traditions is the mummification of bodies. This custom was based upon the shared belief in resurrection that necessitated the practice. In ancient Egypt, if a king was revered enough in time he could rise to godlike status. This custom of worshipping the dead was not just confined to royalty. In many parts of Africa, the living made sacrifices to the deceased in order to pacify their spirits. It was thought that the dead could influence the living for better or for worse and it was therefore important to appease them.

Osiris, during his life, brought civilization to the Egyptian people, and his importance did not remain with the Egyptians alone but extended into other cultures. Some believe that other gods are just different manifestations of Osiris and that gods like Dionysus and Attis were simply partial descriptions of the same original god-king. Certainly, his religion was extremely important and his influences are found in societies and in religious traditions all over the world. His wife, Isis, was also venerated, and she and her son, Horus, were the subject of countless works of art. The holy mother and her child, Horus, known as the

Lamb of God, also miraculously appeared to many believers in visions. Their worship was far-reaching and widespread, and their influence on different religious traditions cannot be overstated.

Although Osiris may have been an actual person, when he died his worship continued to expand. He became more important than even the sun god Ra. The story of Osiris's life, death, and resurrection was reenacted during the ceremonies of the Mysteries of Osiris, and he became the archetypal savior-god. "In the faith of the Egyptians the cruel death and blessed resurrection of Osiris occupied the same place as the death and resurrection of Christ hold in the faith of Christians" (Frazer, 1961, p. 159). In fact, in the entire history of religion it would not be a stretch to say that Osiris and Jesus have collectively inspired more personal devotion than any other gods. Diodorus Siculus (c. 90–21 B.C.E.) reported that Osiris was a flesh-and-blood human who was a traveling prophet. He traveled "over the entire inhabited world," performing miracles and doing amazing things. According to such historical accounts, Osiris conquered India and founded many cities. Where he traveled, the worship of Osiris was found. Whether this is, in fact, true or not is unknown, but the story does mimic the account found by Nicolas Notovitch that stated that Jesus had also traveled to India during the "missing years." After his travels Osiris returned to Egypt and was worshipped as a god-king, and after his death he was worshipped as a chief deity.

Over time, Osiris took on the attributes of the other gods. He became associated with the sun, and he became the god of the afterlife. According to Egyptian religious beliefs, after death individuals had to pass through a Hall of Judgment, before proceeding to the next existence. Here a person would be judged good or evil depending on his or her actions during life, and the decision made here would determine where the deceased would go — to heaven or to hell.[1]

When Osiris was born, a voice proclaimed, "The ruler of all the earth is born." According to Plutarch (46–120):

> In course of time he became king of Egypt, and devoted himself to civilizing his subjects and to teaching them the craft of the husbandman; he established a code of laws and bade men worship the gods. Having made Egypt peaceful and flourishing, he set out to instruct the other nations of the world. During his absence his wife Isis so well ruled the state that Typhon [Set], the evil one, could do no harm to the realm of Osiris. When Osiris came again, Typhon plotted with seventy-two comrades, and with Aso, the queen of Ethiopia, to slay him; and secretly got the measure of the body of Osiris, and made ready a fair chest, which was brought into his banqueting hall when Osiris was present together with other guests. By a ruse Osiris was induced to lie down in the chest, which was immediately closed by Typhon and his fellow conspirators, who conveyed it to the Tanaitic mouth of the Nile [Budge, 1895].

Osiris was killed by his brother Seth, who is also called Set and Typhon. He was once the equivalent of a Christian angel, but he was "thrown from his high estate" and he became the equivalent of the Christian Satan, who was also a fallen angel. It is probable that the Hebrew word *sheitan*, which meant "adversary," stemmed from the Egyptian name Seth. It is this word that became "Satan." According to legend, Seth killed his brother Osiris. Isis searched for and eventually found the body. With the help of Anubis, she restored it (to life) by treating the remains and then wrapping them in cloth. Then she laid him to rest. Seth, however, was not finished. He found the body and, wishing to disgrace Osiris further, dismembered it. Seth chopped his brother into 14 pieces and scattered them. Isis once again searched for his remains. Wherever the pieces were found, she built a temple and enshrined a portion of the god. For this reason, there were many tombs of Osiris, and it is unknown which one, if any of them, was the real one.

Osiris died in his 28th year. It is unknown whether this number refers to his age or the year of his reign. It is possible, too, that the entire story about how he died was just a myth, as the numbers utilized are important for other reasons. The numbers 14 and 28 were important because they referred to the cycle of the moon. It is interesting that in a lot of religious texts sacred numbers are prominently figured. There are many theories to explain this, but sometimes the simplest is the best. In ancient times, if people had access to knowledge that they considered to have been imparted by divine sources they would want to record such knowledge for future generations. This type of knowledge would not be meant to stay within one small community forever, though. It would likely be shared with others, who may have spoken different languages. The easiest way to communicate elaborate metaphysical ideas to others without regard to language barriers is through mathematics. However, this information would probably be safeguarded and only shared with those worthy to receive it. This is why most of the pagan religions had both Inner and Outer Mysteries. Most individuals could go their entire lives believing that they were serving the gods appropriately, even though they only knew the Outer Mysteries.

The Inner Mysteries were reserved for the select few — those individuals who devoted their lives to spiritual and religious pursuits. Once they understood the secret meanings of the celebrations and the mysteries, such rites became significant. Once they understood the secret codes in the holy texts, then, and only then, could they read the truth. It is possibly for this reason that sacred numbers feature prominently in the holy scriptures of many religions, including the Bible.

Whatever the historical occurrence that led to Osiris's death, it was what happened afterward that made him even more popular. Three days after his death, he was resurrected. Since he was restored to life, he could help others to be resurrected as well. "Osiris died and rose again from the dead, so all men hoped to arise like him from death to life eternal" (Budge, 1895). This is one of the reasons why he became known as a savior — a redeemer of souls and judge of the afterlife.

An observance commemorating his resurrection was celebrated for more than a thousand years, beginning in the Middle Kingdom (2055–1650 B.C.E.). At these ceremonies, those in attendance would be given beer and bread that symbolically came from the body of Osiris. This symbolism is also found in Catholicism, where wine and bread that issued from the body of Jesus are distributed. The wine is said to be the blood of Jesus, and the bread is considered to be his flesh. This symbolic and cannibalistic Christian rite most likely originated in the well-known sacraments of the savior Osiris. During these services, believers reenacted the death and resurrection of Osiris. They looked for his body until eventually it was declared that "Osiris has been found." Then, the body in an ark, worshippers followed the funerary procession to his tomb. His remains were placed inside, and prayers were said for the resurrection of the god. After this, followers mourned for three days, until his resurrection took place. On the day of his resurrection, his body miraculously gone, the Pillar of Osiris was erected in front of the temple and an image of the bearded god was prominently displayed. This ceremony was so widely practiced that it survived for thousands of years.

It was even practiced during the Roman times, and it had a strong influence on some Christian texts and customs.

After Osiris died and the pieces of his body were gathered together again, Isis had a son named Horus. He was immaculately conceived, and he was born on the Winter Solstice, December 25. It was Horus, the Lamb of God, who carried on his father's legacy. Known as Krst, the anointed one, Horus was the new savior, who died and was resurrected after three days, like God the father before him. When he was born, he said, "I am Horus, the Prince of Eternity."

VI. The Egyptian Influence

Out of Egypt I called my son. — Hosea 11:1

36

Egyptian Influences in Italy

The Egyptian civilization was extremely popular among the Romans. Egyptian architecture was found in some religious centers, and there are even pyramids located in Italy. One of them is in Rome, near the Porta San Paolo. It is called the Pyramid of Cestius, because it was created as a tomb for Caius Cestius. Built c. 12 B.C.E. from slabs of white marble, it is approximately 27 meters high and its base is 22 square meters. The burial chamber inside is about 6 meters long, 4 meters wide, and 5 meters in height. Although it was once considered important, by the 15th century the pyramid had been overgrown by vegetation. This was cleared away beginning in 1660. During the excavation, statue bases were found outside of it and frescoes were found inside.

Other pyramids have been found in Italy as well. There were three of them found in Montevecchia, although they are now all covered with vegetation and have not yet been excavated.[1] The highest pyramid is 500 feet tall, and due to the degree of their inclinations they align with the constellation of Orion, which is linked to the god Osiris. The Egyptian custom of mummifying the dead and burying them in elaborate burial chambers was not confined to Africa. As recent discoveries have illustrated, these customs also existed in Italy.

The pyramid of Cestius, in Rome, Italy. The presence of this pyramid suggests that there is a strong connection between Roman and Egyptian customs and beliefs.

In addition to some pyramids, there are a number of Egyptian obelisks in Rome. The first ones were taken from Egypt and brought to Italy, but some of them were actually made in Rome in the same style. Some were destroyed in wars and natural disasters, but many are still standing. Today, more than a dozen of them are still in the capital. The first obelisks were stolen from Egypt by the Roman emperor Augustus (63 B.C.E.–14 C.E.), who conquered Egypt in 30 B.C.E. He displayed these prominently within the capital, but after more than 1,500 years the majority of them were in pieces, mingling with other ancient ruins that are now tourist attractions in Rome. Pope Sixtus V (1520–1590) saved many of them. The obelisks were repaired and relocated to beautify some new roads and squares that were built. He converted some of the obelisks by placing a Christian cross on the top of them or by adorning them with papal insignias.

The obelisk that is currently located in the Piazza del Popolo was relocated to this location in 1589, but it initially was at the center of the Circus Maximus. It was first created by the pharaoh Rameses II (1279–1213 B.C.E.), and it was erected in Heliopolis. It was plundered in 30 B.C.E. by Augustus, and it has been in Italy ever since. This object is covered with hieroglyphs and Egyptian religious carvings, but since it was dedicated to Osiris, who was related to the sun, it had to be modified by the Church. Pope Sixtus V ordered that symbols of his reign and a cross be placed on the top of it. The symbols of his papacy are mountains and a star. These were symbols unique to this pope that appeared on his coat of arms. Each pope had a different coat of arms, and often the symbols of one pope that appeared on buildings were replaced with the coat of arms of the next pope when he made minor repairs or architectural adjustments, effectively getting rid of signs of the old papacy to make room for the new leader.

The Egyptian obelisk that is located in the Piazza del Popolo (Rome, Italy).

The obelisk that stands in the Piazza di Montecitorio was originally built by Psammetichus II in the seventh century B.C.E., and it was stolen, like the others, by Augustus. Upon its arrival in Rome, the emperor placed it in a city square called the Horologium Divi Augusti. Here it functioned as a sundial; its shadow indicated the time of day. At some point, however, it was destroyed, and it was found in multiple pieces in 1748. It was repaired, although some of the hieroglyphs and carvings were damaged, and the new leader put his coat of arms and a cross at its summit. Now, it is a standing monument to the papal reign of Pope Pius VI (1717–1799).

The tallest obelisk in Rome, and the last to have been taken from Egypt, is the Obelisk of Thothmes IV, which is currently located in the Piazza San Giovanni in Laterano. This obelisk was relocated to Rome by Emperor Constantius II in 357. He had a ship specially built solely in order to plunder this heavy monument. When it was first brought to Rome, it was erected in the Circus Maximus, but it was destroyed when Rome was sacked in the fifth century. In 1587, the obelisk was found in three pieces among the ruins of the Circus Maximus and Pope Sixtus V ordered that it be repaired. Upon its summit he placed his own personal heraldic symbols: three mountains, a star, and a lion holding pears, which referred to the town where sixtus grew up, called Peretti.

The Obelisk of Augustus was built and erected in Alexandria by the Romans, and it was modeled after the obelisks from Egypt. It was placed in the Vatican and relocated to its current location in the center of St. Peter's Square, right in front of the cathedral, in 1586. Other obelisks were built in Egyptian style by the Romans. Augustus had seen the tomb of Alexander the Great in Alexandria, which was adorned with obelisks. Apparently influenced by the reign of Alexander, who was mummified Osiris-like in the Egyptian fashion, Augustus had similar obelisks built around his own tomb. The monuments were erected at the Mausoleum of Augustus, and although they followed Egyptian style, hieroglyphs and Egyptian reliefs were not used to decorate the stone.

After the fall, the obelisks were in pieces and considered unimportant. The area flooded many times, and the obelisks slowly sank into the ground. They were not worth saving to the people in the area at the time. However, as archaeology consistently demonstrates, those things that were discarded and deemed unimportant are imbibed with significance once again in later centuries. In 1519, a road was built and one of the broken obelisks was uncovered. It was reassembled and placed at the end of a road that the pope ordered built that led directly to the Church of Santa Maria Maggiore, an important Church center.

The Obelisk of Domitian commemorates Emperor Domitian (51–96), the last emperor of the Flavian Dynasty. He built it after a large fire had destroyed much of Rome in the year 80, and it originally stood in a Roman temple complex that was dedicated to the Egyptian gods Isis, the virgin mother, and Serapis, who was a composite figure, representing Osiris and another deity. He was primarily worshipped in Alexandria. The creation of this obelisk, and its placement here at this center of worship, is indicative of the spiritual pursuits of the Romans during this period. Although the obelisk was initially erected and built by Domitian in order to commemorate his reign, after his death the obelisk was moved and renamed in order to commemorate the reign of another. Emperor Maxentius (d. 312) moved it to the center of a circus (i.e., a stadium for chariot racing) built to honor his son near Via Appia in 309. Approximately 200 years later, it fell and it was broken into multiple pieces. It was not found and repaired until the 17th century, but once it was, the treatment

This Egyptian obelisk stands in the Piazza San Giovanni in Laterano. It is the tallest obelisk in Rome.

This obelisk is found in St. Peter's Square, in the Vatican. This is one of the few obelisks that was not stolen from Egypt. Rather, it was created in Italy, following the model of the Egyptian obelisks (Rome, Italy).

The Obelisk of Domitian, which is currently located at the Piazza Navona (Rome, Italy).

36. Egyptian Influences in Italy

Another Egyptian obelisk that is located outside of the Pantheon (Rome, Italy).

of this obelisk was unique. It was actually placed on top of a fountain that was being built per the demands of Pope Innocentius X (1574–1655), who wanted it built in his honor. The fountain was built by Bernini. Initially, the pope did not want Bernini to build the monument because of his preexisting ties with Innocentius's predecessor and rival Pope Urbanus VIII, but Bernini wanted the money that he would be paid for this commission, so he contrived a way to have the pope see his model for the monument. Once Pope Innocentius X saw it, he wanted Bernini to carry out his plan. The pope paid him a sizeable amount from the Church treasury, and Bernini set to work creating a large and elaborate monument that would announce and commemorate the glory of the pope. The top of the obelisk is decorated with the coat of arms of Pope Innocentius X, symbolized by a dove.

The obelisks in Rome, and their use as monuments to the reigns of various popes, is strong evidence of an important relationship between Roman and Egyptian traditions. This exact same practice was carried out by pharaohs in Egypt. The worship of Egyptian gods in Rome, too, is evidence of the connections between Egyptian religious ideas and those found in Italy. The influence of Egypt on Roman development is extreme, and it likely began in 30 B.C.E., when Augustus conquered Egypt, thus making it a province of the empire. Approximately 200 years later, Egyptians were given citizenship, and many Egyptian customs were adopted by the Roman government. The emperor ruled with the title of Pharaoh, Lord of the Two Lands, and the divine aspects of the Egyptian kings were given to the Roman emperor. Augustus and subsequent emperors continued to build temples to the Egyptian gods following the architectural methods employed by the Egyptians, and over time Egyptian ideas of death and resurrection infiltrated Roman religious ideas and ultimately came to affect the new faith — Christianity.

37

Alexandria and Coptic Christianity

Before the Roman rule of Egypt began, its sovereignty was in the hands of the Greek Ptolemies, and through them Alexandria became a melting pot of the ancient world. The city was divided into different sections. The Jewish people lived in two of the sections, while the native Egyptians occupied the western side of the city. Greeks lived in the remaining areas, and there was an assortment of faiths and ideas commingling. Various philosophers and scientists were there, and remarkable advancements were made during this period. The ancient religious beliefs of Egypt were present, but they were modified to fit an emerging model of the cosmos — a new religion for the future. The governing bodies also modified the religions in order to deal with some minor problems that had arisen due to the number of inhabitants who had different beliefs and different cultural backgrounds. At the time, religions served multiple functions. One was obviously to explain the world and the nature of divine beings. Another was to direct ethical behavior and to provide meaning to life. The other function of religions, however, was seen as more important by the governing bodies. The purpose of a faith was to unite people under one leader. If individuals were believers in the same god(s), they could be more easily controlled, as their beliefs and customs would be the same in their most important aspects.

In order to bring the diverse people of Alexandria together, the government decided that a mutual religion was necessary. This was not as overwhelming of a task as it might seem now. The citizens of Alexandria were all familiar with other ideas and different faiths. In addition, most religious beliefs at the time were not intolerant; this meant that certain aspects of their faiths could be modified without causing any undue distress. The government decided that the creation of a mutually respected deity was in order (Riad, n.d.). If the citizens of Alexandria worshipped the same gods, problems due to their cultural and religious backgrounds would be eliminated, or at least lessened. The government hoped that tension between the Egyptians and the Greeks especially would be eliminated, so they set about creating a new god.

Some of the gods of Egyptian beliefs were already present in the Greek pantheon, only they were represented in different ways and they were called by different names. However, the stories were the same, especially with regard to the important elements of a miraculous Virgin Birth, the death and resurrection of a savior-god, and the shedding of divine blood for the benefit of humankind. A god that both cultural groups could worship was created. They combined the Egyptian god Osiris with Apis, who was worshipped in Memphis. They joined these two names to create Serapis, and he was represented as an old man with a beard. His wife was the Egyptian goddess Isis, and their son was the Egyptian savior Horus.

The creation and worship of this deity and the transference of the goddess Isis to Alexandria in a new, modified myth served to unite the people. These deities became widely respected and praised. "The worship of the ancient gods, Isis and Serapis, became separated from the traditional mythology in which they had borne a part, broke through all barriers of place and nationality, and went forth to conquer over the whole Mediterranean world" (Emerton, 1910, p. 187).

In the first century, Christianity began, and it spread to Alexandria. Like other philosophical ideas and religious traditions, it was accepted at Alexandria, and it later spread to other parts of Egypt. The fact that it was so similar to other preexisting faiths allowed it to easily assimilate into the existing culture. The first Christian church was established in Alexandria c. 40, and the faith spread to Upper Egypt by the second century. Initially, the Egyptian priesthood had no apparent problems with Christianity and the two faiths coexisted in relative peace. In fact, there was a commingling of the two religious traditions. People in Alexandria had no problem with the introduction of a new deity. They were open to new ideas, and they believed that all depictions of gods referred to the same overarching deity. The Egyptians in particular did not think of each god as separate and distinct but simply as a different reflection of the same divine essence (Mojsov, 2005). Therefore, it was not heretical to embrace a new image and representation of the same god.

The citizens of Alexandria worshipped both Serapis and Jesus as though they were an identical god. Emperor Hadrian (117–138) wrote the following, referring to the indistinguishability of the rites and traditions performed by followers of Serapis and supporters of Jesus alike: "Those who worship Serapis are Christians, and those who call themselves bishops of Christ are devoted to Serapis" (Meinardus, 1977, p. 30). The two faiths blended together, and therefore, there was no religiously motivated violence.[1]

However, things changed during the reign of Marcus Aurelius (161–180), when a revolt broke out among the Egyptian priests in the Delta. The exact reasons behind this revolt are unknown, but this led to the suppression of the Egyptian priests by the rising Christian powers. Eventually, it smothered some of the old faiths and increased its political strength. Christianity gained a stronghold in Alexandria and began one of its most important religious centers there.

Egyptian Christianity is known as Coptic Christianity, and in this faith the assimilation of the two religious traditions (Egyptian and Christian) is obvious. The church in Alexandria rose in importance as the Christian Church of Rome became increasingly more powerful, and at the Council of Nicea in 324 the Coptic Church was declared to be the most important governing body other than the one found in Rome. For this reason, the early Coptic Church had a direct role in implementing religious traditions and ideas and in the formulation of Christian religious dogmas. If it were not for the input supplied by Coptic Church officials, Christianity today would be a much different tradition.

Due to its input in the creation of dogma and its assistance in increasing political power, the size of the Coptic Church continued to expand. By the year 333, there were approximately 100 bishops in Alexandria. However, something that occurred at a church council forever changed the relationship of the Coptic and Catholic Churches. In 451, the Council of Chalcedon was initiated so that the ideas of the nature of Jesus could be clarified. The way Jesus was portrayed in the Bible suggested that he was both God and man. He had both attributes. He had human doubts and emotions, which were displayed at the end when he uttered, "My God! Why have you forsaken me?" but he also had divine attributes, evidenced by the recorded miracles and god-like knowledge. The purpose of this Church council was to determine the nature of Jesus. Did he have two natures?

Some individuals had already been declared heretics for ignoring the divinity of Jesus. At this early stage of Christianity, the charge of heresy did not mean death, but it did mean a sentence of an eternity in hell by the ruling Church body.

> Long before Constantine, the Christian Church had employed all its resources against heretics. It possessed no power of punishing them by fines, torture or death, but it threatened them with hell in the next world and excommunicated them in this. "Heretics," says Dr. Gieseler, "were universally hated as men wholly corrupt and lost," and the Church pronounced against them her sharpest penalties. These were indeed merely spiritual, but they were transformed into temporal punishments as soon as Christianity was able to effect the change [Foote and Wheeler, 1887].

The other extreme, at the opposite end of denying his divinity, was to state that Jesus was not a man at all but that he only had divine attributes. The purpose of the Council of Chalcedon, held in 451, was to come to a decision regarding whether Jesus was all God or part God. The Coptic Church had an interesting interpretation. They thought that Jesus had one nature, but that there were two different aspects of that nature. However, the Catholic counterpart eventually reached the conclusion that he did not have one nature but two distinct natures. They ordered the Coptic Church to adopt the same dogma, but the Coptic Church did not agree. This initiated a schism between the two organizations, and it led to the forcible closure of Coptic churches, along with the torture, exile, and killing of Coptic Christians (Chapin Metz, 1990).

All military support was taken away from the Copts, which meant that they had no protection. They were therefore an easy target for attacking Muslims and were unable to repel the invaders. Many of the Copts, in an effort to save their lives, converted to Islam. However, the Coptic Church is still extant. They have a pope, and they have bishops and other priests. Their dogma is slightly different from the dogma of the Catholic Church, but they have similar practices of mummification. They also venerate saints, although there are some different saints in the Coptic tradition.

With regard to their dogmatical differences, one of them is significant, and it is also the point that caused the Coptic Church's schism with the Catholic organization. The Coptic religion is thought to be monotheistic, but they emphasize that there are three different aspects of God, in a belief system called the Trinitarian Faith. In other words, there are various essences. All of them reflect some aspect of God, and all of them together are his total essence, which cannot be understood by mere mortals. This is considered a mystery of the Coptic faith. This, in a sense, is related to the major theological difference between the Catholic and the Coptic religions, which centers on the divine and human nature(s) of Jesus.

The Catholic idea held that Jesus had two distinct natures. He was not divine and mortal at the same time, but he had a divine essence and he also had a human essence. The Copts thought that he had one essence that was both human and divine. This is similar to some Buddhist ideas that suggest that to find God one must look inward. Such an idea signifies that divine attributes are found within human beings. For example, since humans were created by God, and in his image, it stands to reason that humans have been infused with the essence of God himself. If this truly were the case, then human beings could attain what Jesus attained if they were subjected to the same training and influences. This is a very complicated phenomenon. The ancient Egyptian religion delineated the various different essences that human beings had on a spiritual level. It is likely that such concepts influenced the Christian ideas, in the same way that Egyptian monuments, mummification and burial practices also influenced Christianity.

38

Early Egyptian Religious Beliefs

The problem with the study of ancient civilizations is that only part of their understanding is transferred to the present. In other words, it is impossible to determine exact metaphysical ideas because they were not represented in writing and in diagrams alone. Beliefs are a product of external cultural influences, group brainwashing, and a myriad of other factors. When the religious views of an ancient civilization are researched, an in-depth understanding might always be elusive. It is possible, however, to get a general idea of their beliefs and to then determine how they influenced subsequent religious traditions and practices.[1] With this in mind, it is necessary to explore the ancient Egyptian idea of the soul, as it was their idea that had a profound influence on the Christian perception.

According to Egyptian religious beliefs, a human being was composed of at least nine different parts. Eight of these parts were spiritual in nature, while the ninth was the physical body itself. However, the body, too, was thought to have been spiritual in a way. Therefore, to gain even a basic understanding of the complex interplay of all of these parts, it is better to think of the physical form as one of them, equal to the others. This physical structure was called Khat or Kha. If it was not protected and preserved, it could eventually decay and therefore cease to exist. In this perspective, the Kha is the least permanent aspect of an individual.

Among the strictly spiritual aspects, the Ka and the Ba are the most commonly discussed essences. The Ka is often translated as "shadow," and it typically refers to the vital energy that a person has during life. It continues to survive after death and into the afterlife. In a sense, this corresponds to the Christian concept of the soul, but it is a bit different. The Ka is a type of shadow that is the person, yet at the same time it is simply coexisting with the person. After death, this spiritual essence can linger with the body. It can also be found in statues of the deceased or in anything else that is a representation of him or her. Therefore, it does not just linger with the physical body. It is more autonomous, and it can function on its own, independently of the body, throughout both life and death. In addition, the Ka is sustained by means of funerary offerings, and it might have even been thought that without such offerings the Ka would cease to exist (Thomas, 1920). As if this is not confusing enough, it seems that there were two different essences that both made up the Ka. One was a higher Ka, which might be compared to the Catholic idea of a guardian angel: a higher spirit that was inextricably bound to an individual person and yet was not the person. It looked out for the person and it was connected to the person, but it was distinct. The lower Ka was influenced by knowledge gained here in this plane of existence during life. Spiritual knowledge gained throughout life changed the nature of the Ka. So it was possible to alter one's spirituality through learning.

This might correspond to ideas about the usefulness of meditation found in various spiritual traditions. Through meditation, practitioners hope to gain spiritual and practical knowledge, as well as gaining control of the emotions. Through such practices, individuals become more spiritual, and it is believed (by practitioners) that they can elevate their spirit to higher levels. Eventually, having increasingly elevated their spirituality, they can become something more than human. In Buddhism, they might attain enlightenment and become a Buddha or a Bodhisattva (Shiba, 2003). In Christianity, they might develop the attributes of their savior and become saints (Hoever, 1955). Of course, the ideas in all of these faiths are slightly different. They are offered here only to demonstrate that comparable ideas are found in other modern religions today.

The aspect of the spirit that is frequently treated alongside the Ka is the Ba. This unusual phenomenon is often represented in papyri by a bird with a human head. During the day, it is thought, this "bird" sustained the deceased by bringing it food and water. To put this into more workable and understandable language, this is an element of the spirit that continues to remain in the body, possibly helping to maintain the continuity of the individual into the afterlife. On one hand, the Ba seems to be similar to the idea of merit found in East Asian religious traditions. Some of these traditions believe that although the soul itself leaves the body after death, there is a spiritual essence (called merit) that stays behind in the physical remains. This energy is responsible for the granting of miracles. It is power that is infused in the physical remains, but it does not remain forever. Again, the Egyptian idea of the Ba is different from the East Asian ideas; this comparison is just being made in an attempt to simplify and elucidate these unusual concepts. On the other hand, the Ba is not the same as merit, because it was known as the "breath of life" and flew away from the body like a bird. It existed into the afterlife. It could exist independently from the Ka, but it was the goal of Egyptians to reunite the Ba and the Ka in the afterlife. Only by this union could the person actually continue to exist into the next life. Mummification was necessary in order to permit this union.

The khaibit was another strange component of the soul. It was a shadow-like entity that could separate from the body at will. It was thought to remain near the Ba, so there is likely an interrelationship that exists between these two aspects. Actually, all of the essences are connected and related; some of these connections are simply stronger than others. The khaibit "was supposed to have an entirely independent existence and to be able to separate itself from the body; it was free to move wherever it pleased, and, like the Ka and Ba, it partook of the funeral offerings in the tomb, which it visited at will ... in later times at least the shadow was always associated with the soul and was believed to be always near it" (Budge, 1895).

The sahu was basically the equivalent of the physical body and the person who inhabited it in all aspects. It appeared after the judgment of the dead took place. A strange thing is that there was another spiritual portion that resided in this essence. Like the soul that resides in the physical body in Catholic beliefs, there was a spiritual aspect called the khu that resided in the sahu. The khu was an aspect of the soul that might be comparable, in a sense, to the idea of a spiritual aura. Also known as an *akh*, *akhu*, or *ikhu*, it only came into being after a person died and after his or her judgment. It only appeared when the Ba and Ka were reunited. It was represented by the mummy, and it has been translated as "intelligence," "glorious," or "shining one," but it has also been simplified as just "spirit." It also had the attributes of being an invisible casing that surrounded the physical body, and for this reason (at the risk of oversimplification) it is something like an aura that surrounds a body.

As if this were not comprehensive enough, the ancient Egyptians conceived of even more spiritual aspects. The sekhem was a personification of the life force, conceived of as the vitality of a human being that animated the physical body. The ren, too, which can be translated as a person's name alone, also had a spiritual attribute, which could live on separately from the body. It was thought to have been able to continue to live in heavenly realms among the gods. In this way, it is more than a name — it is the entirety of who and what a person is.

The *ib* is another metaphysical idea that is not easily understood. Also called the *yb* or the *ab*, it was a person's heart. Considering it from this definition alone, it is seemingly a simple phenomenon. However, the meaning of this term goes beyond the physical organ. It was the source of good or evil, and it was weighed against the feather of Maat at the judgment of souls. It could leave the body in its spiritual form, and it could lead an independent existence in the afterlife. If the heart did not weigh up against the feather of Maat, the person was deemed immoral and the heart was eaten. In this event, the *ib* would be eaten by Ammut, the Devourer, and it would therefore cease to exist.

The nature of the soul in Egyptian religious beliefs was multifaceted. Each person was a composite of various spiritual essences, and if these spiritual essences stayed together, the individuality of the deceased would continue and be perpetuated throughout eternity. However, this was not easy. Each aspect had its own specific and individual attributes, and most of them could split from the body and continue to exist separately. If any of these parts did separate, though, it would mean the end of the person who once inhabited the physical body. Therefore, it was of primary importance to the Egyptians to preserve these souls.

Some of the aspects could be maintained and preserved by means of ethical conduct in life. The *ib*, for example, would only pass the test and not be devoured if the person whom it belonged to was moral. In addition, the Ka had to be fed after death. The living provided offerings to the deceased, and these offerings included incense, essences from food, and even essences drawn from tomb paintings. Sepulchral offerings were needed in order to preserve the existence of the Ka. If a person was mean and despised during life, the living would not care for him or her after death. If this occurred, the Ka could dissipate and the individuality of the deceased would therefore not continue to exist. In order to effect the perpetuation of the individual after death, all of these spiritual aspects had to be considered. Every aspect had to be preserved and the continuity between them had to be maintained. Some of this was accomplished by the individual while he or she was still alive. Other aspects had to be carried out by others after death. The dead relied on the living, as the living believed the dead could influence life. There was a mutual coexistence, in which the living and the dead alike relied upon each other.

In order to encourage the ongoing existence of an individual through the transition of death, magical incantations (i.e., prayers) were used, as was the mummification of the body. Priests said prayers over dead bodies that eased their transition and called upon the gods of the netherworld, namely Osiris, for assistance. Similar ceremonies that include prayers for the deceased are also found in Catholic Christianity. Before burial, a body is placed in a casket that is covered with a cloth embossed with a large cross. The director of ceremonies then blesses the deceased with offerings of incense, and he[2] then makes incantations over the body in order to invoke divine assistance, which is required for a Catholic to be permitted access to heavenly realms. In the Christian tradition, bodies are typically mummified before such ceremonies, as they were in ancient Egypt. Just as the multiple aspects of the spirit had to be preserved, the body also has to be conserved.

The body, called the *Khat*, had spiritual attributes; most important was its role in helping the Ka and the Ba to remain united, or at least to reunite after death. For the individual to continue into the afterlife, these two aspects needed to remain together. For this reason, the body had to be mummified. Although the practices of mummification were altered and refined throughout the centuries in Egypt, the first forms of bodily preservation were simple, making use of natural phenomena to effect conservation.

39

Burial Practices

Mummification in ancient Egypt began with a simple practice of Class II preservation. Bodies were deliberately buried in the warm, dry sand in order to dry them out. Pits were dug in the sand, into which bodies were placed. They were not embalmed or treated in any way but simply put into a contracted position and lowered into the grave. Sometimes, the bodies were wrapped in some types of reed matting, animal skins or linen (Peck, 1998). The practice of wrapping remains in linen continued throughout Egyptian history, and it was transferred to other cultures, including Judeo-Christian traditions. Other useful objects were placed alongside the body in the desert graves, such as pottery and other valuables. The grave was then covered and left alone under the hot desert sun. The effects of the sun, combined with the drying elements of the sand, naturally led to bodily preservation. These two elements combined to desiccate the remains, and the result was natural mummification.

Over time, steps were taken to improve upon this natural method of preservation. An early account by Herodotus (1910) related that an Ethiopian stone was used to cut open the body. Then, all of the internal organs were taken out by hand. As the entrails were removed, they were treated with palm wine and incense, so that they smelled sweet. Most of the organs were removed. In some later Egyptian forms of mummification, the brain was also removed by using a small instrument that resembled a whisk. The ethmoid bone was punctured through one of the nostrils, and the brain was then liquefied by turning the instrument (David and Archbold, 2000). After this, the brain was poured out of the skull. In a rare variation, sometimes the brain was removed through a small hole that had been made in the skull (Harris and Weeks, 1973). Once the internal organs had been removed, the internal cavity was treated with an embalming solution made of palm wine and other fragrant herbs. The body was then stuffed with various fragrant substances, including myrrh[1] and cassia, and then the cavities were stitched together.

After this, the corpse was placed in natrum for 70 days. This is a salt-like substance found in Egypt that was held in high esteem for its preserving qualities. After 70 days, the body was removed, washed and anointed, and then wrapped in fine linen. The linen was generally cut into strips, and a gum was applied to it so that the strips would stick together. After this was carried out, the preservation of the body was complete. It was then put into a wooden casket that was carved in the shape of the deceased. The body, at this point, was placed in a safe location, where it would remain for as long as possible. The Egyptians wanted their bodies to remain untouched forever, so that the personality and attributes of the individual would be perpetuated after death. However, there were tomb robbers who stole bodies and there were other occurrences like natural disasters or battles that also damaged or destroyed some mummies.

Not all people in ancient Egypt were mummified in this manner. There was another method that is similar to a preservative technique utilized by the Catholic Church. According to Harris and Weeks (1973), "Instead of making an incision in the abdomen to remove the internal organs, a strong solution of an oleo-resin, not unlike turpentine, was injected into the body through the rectum and was left to soak for several days. When it was removed, it brought with it the dissolved organs — a grotesque but effective method, which greatly enhanced the chances of preservation" (p. 85).

Other techniques were also used. The bodies were generally all treated with an embalming solution that consisted of such substances as cedar oil and wax (Harris and Weeks, 1973). This technique continued to be carried out in Catholicism, as many of the bodies of saints on display in Italy have also been coated with wax. In Egypt, bodies were also treated with resins, which made the bodies fragrant. This method also continued to be used by the Catholic Church. In order to make the faces appear lifelike, the Egyptians padded the cheeks with linen. Variations of such methods were most likely used by the Church as well.

Not all individuals in Egypt were mummified with such care. In fact, some poor individuals were simply buried in the ground. The process of mummification was generally reserved for important people, although sometimes servants were preserved alongside their kings and queens, so that they could continue to function as servants in the next existence. People who were more important were generally treated with more expensive and more elaborate mummifications and burials. This is similar to the Church's policies regarding mummification. Bodily preservation was not permitted for everyone. It was a privilege reserved for high-ranking members of the Church and saints alone (Bingenheimer, 2005). In Egypt, kings and queens were especially revered, like popes and bishops are in Catholicism.

The tombs of kings and queens were elaborate, stocked with items that could be used in the afterlife. Often, individuals began stocking their burial chambers long before their actual death and the objects included useful items that were utilized in life and ritualistic instruments for use after death, such as magical papyri and protective amulets. Among these amulets, sometimes the ankh is found — the Egyptian version of the crucifix. Like Egyptian kings and queens, Catholic popes and other members of the clergy are often buried with crucifixes around their necks, which also function as protective amulets.

The coffins of Egyptian royalty also differed from the coffins that most citizens utilized. They were more elaborate, and there were typically more of them. Kings were buried in multiple coffins that were placed one inside the other. Often, there were three of them, the same as Catholic popes. Then the body, surrounded by these three protective coffins, was placed into a stone sarcophagus, which was elaborately decorated and surrounded by expensive items. The mummy of the king was adorned with a mask modeled after his actual appearance so that God would recognize him in the afterlife. This is similar to the Catholic custom of covering the faces of saints and clerics with wax or silver masks. The burial chambers, which have been extensively explained in many other publications, were huge. Pyramids were created to house the bodies of important figures, and other monuments were often raised in their honor.

The burial practices of Catholic popes are very similar to those of Egyptian kings. Like the kings, popes were mummified and buried in multiple caskets, which were adorned with gold, silver, and other valuables. Often, monuments were built for them after their deaths as well. In some cases, the monuments were huge statues made from marble or other expensive materials. In other cases, Egyptian obelisks were erected with symbols of the popes' reigns on top or giant fountains were created. In addition, the sarcophagi into which the bodies were placed were huge and ornate and the tombs where they rested were likewise exceedingly large, expensive, and overelaborate. The Catholic popes adopted a number of the attributes of the Egyptian pharaohs. This is not unusual, since Egyptian culture and history have had a profound influence on many cultures. In Alexandria, especially, people from various different countries were exposed to the religious principles and traditions of ancient Egypt.

Alexandria was a melting pot of religious ideas and cultural practices. These included burial practices, which differed throughout the city. Although many pagans chose to be cremated rather than buried, Egyptian and Jewish ideas influenced Alexandrian culture and many people were actually preserved and then buried. During the first three centuries of the Roman period, the individuals buried in the eastern cemeteries were mostly Greeks and foreigners, while those in the western cemeteries were Egyptians. Just about all of the bodies found in the western cemeteries were mummified. As time progressed, the custom of mummification, which was initially performed only on the bodies on the western side, began to be practiced on the eastern side. The Greeks had adopted the Egyptian custom of mummification (Riad, n.d.).

This might have happened because they adopted some of their religious ideas, namely the resurrection. It may have occurred because the idea of bodily preservation seemed less drastic than cremation. When a body is cremated, it is reduced to ashes. Cremation seems to be the complete and utter destruction of the individual. However, when a body lies in state for a number of years and it appears as though it were still alive, the individual does not seem to be forever gone. It seems that the person is only sleeping, which therefore helps the living to deal with the uncertainty of death. However it happened, the Greeks picked up this Egyptian custom of mummification. Through the Greeks, it was transferred to Catholic Christianity in Italy. This form of preservation was also adopted by the Coptic Christians, and it is likely that it also affected the Catholic tradition through early Coptic influences. (In other words, the practice of mummification was likely transferred to Catholicism by multiple independent sources. The idea came directly from the Copts, the Greeks, and the Egyptians themselves.) In this way, Egyptian-style mummification continues to be performed by the Catholic Church.[2]

40

The Holy Trinity: Isis, Horus and Osiris

The Virgin Birth in Catholicism was a late addition. Like many other Catholic religious ideas, there was no mention of this in early Christian texts, even though it was declared genuine in 1897 by the Vatican. There was also no mention of it in the early versions of the gospels. This idea and passages used to support it were added to the Bible in the third or fourth century (Wells, 1971). In 692, the concept evolved further. The Church decided at this point that Mary was "ever-virgin" (Gadalla, 2008). However, the notion of the Virgin Birth was still not thought of as a historical fact. It is an idea that is not historical. It is a product of myth, and is therefore not a legitimate topic for historical investigation (Mangasarian, 2004). The Virgin Birth was a spiritual concept that was found in earlier Egyptian traditions. It was not until the 13th century, due to the writings of Thomas Aquinas, that this idea became thought of as historical in nature. After more than 1,000 years, the Church decided that the Virgin Birth was a historical fact (Gadalla, 2008). They disregarded earlier notions, and they updated their teachings to reflect this new dogmatic addition.

The idea of the Virgin Birth likely came from Egyptian religious ideas. In Egypt, the gods Osiris and Horus were both born of virgin mothers and Egyptian kings were also said to have been born of virgins who were impregnated by God. This was not held as a historical fact, but it was a spiritual concept used in order to connect the kings to Osiris, who was born of a virgin mother. Osiris was the Son of God, who was present at the judgment of souls. It is through Osiris that Egyptians hoped to be resurrected, thus conquering death itself. The Egyptian king was fulfilling the role of Osiris in this world, and therefore, he spiritually took on the role of Osiris. In the Heb Sed festival, the statue of the king was painted black, the color of Osiris as depicted in art, and a crook and flail were put into his hands. These are also symbolic of Osiris, who is always artistically rendered with these items in hand. The statue, thus adorned, was buried. This was symbolic of the self-sacrifice performed by Osiris (Mojsov, 2005).

The Egyptian king was divine, taking on the role of Osiris in this existence. It was said that the father of an Egyptian king was God and that he would one day be resurrected as well, following in the footsteps of Osiris. In sum, Egyptian leaders were kings of men but sons of God. Similarly, it used to be thought that popes were the vicars of Christ on Earth. This is where the idea of papal infallibility stems from. Since God cannot err and the pope is the voice of God on earth, he therefore cannot make mistakes. This concept came directly from Egyptian religious and political concepts. Roman emperors were even depicted iconically with the same pose and regalia as Egyptian pharaohs. When Alexander conquered Egypt, he was

A statue of the Virgin Mother and Child, found at the Pantheon, in Rome. Once the concept of the Virgin Birth was introduced to Christianity, this is how Mary and Jesus were frequently represented. This is exactly how Isis and Horus, the Egyptian virgin mother and divine child, were represented.

Another representation of Mary and Jesus that is similar to the iconography used to represent the Egyptian pair. This is found in the Cathedral of San Giuseppe dei Teatini, in Palermo, Sicily.

The headdresses worn by Church leaders, called miters, are very similar to the crown worn by Osiris and the kings of northern Egypt (Palermo, Italy).

thought of by the Egyptian people as a liberator. He became king and pharaoh, and since he was a pharaoh, according to Egyptian custom he was therefore divine. Later on, when Ptolemy became king, he also became divine (Riad, n.d.). This idea of divinity represented by political leaders transferred to Christianity and in some ways is still present today. Once Church leaders took political control, the pope took on the pharaoh's role. Like the Egyptian pharaohs, it was thought that the pope was representative of God here on earth. The outfits that continue to be worn by popes and bishops today are very similar to those worn by the Egyptian leaders, especially with regard to their pointed headdresses, called miters.

The Christian concept of the Holy Trinity likewise finds its origins in Egypt. Osiris is God the father, Isis the virgin mother, and Horus the savior child — the Son of God. Mojsov (2005) wrote, "The worship of Osiris explicitly encompassed the doctrine of One in Three: the Resurrected Redeemer, the Holy Mother, and the Savior-Child" (p. 91). There is only one difference between the concept of the Holy Trinity in Egypt and the concept in Christianity. In Egypt, this idea was a spiritual one put into place in order to demonstrate a metaphysical concept alone. In Christianity, the Egyptian idea of the Holy Trinity was interpreted as actually being three deities in one (Emerton, 1910). Therefore, the nature of the three was discussed among theologians, as was the interrelationship between the three aspects of the same Godhead. There were varying schools of thought regarding this point, and even today the concept is not clearly elucidated through Catholic dogma. Some of the religious ideas were incorporated into the new Christian faith without complete understanding of their natures. They were simply assumed to be true, since many people accepted the ideas as historical facts, and they therefore were perpetuated in a new form.

There are other Egyptian philosophies and dogma that were also adopted by the Christians. The notion of the savior child was one of them. Horus, the savior, can be related to Jesus, as the two of them were similarly regarded by followers and because their hagiographies are alike. When Horus arrived in this plane of existence, he said:

> I am Horus the Falcon who is over the ramparts of the mansion of the Hidden-In-Name. My flight has reached the horizon, I having surpassed the gods of the sky, so that I have elevated

my place more than the Ancients. The aggressor cannot reach my first flight, so my place is far from Seth, the enemy of my father Osiris. I have traversed the roads of eternity to the dawn after having ascended in my flight. There is no god who can equal me, so I may show vengeance against the enemy of my father Osiris [Wsr], who will have been set under my sandal, by this my name of Avenger. I am Horus [Hrw] born of Isis [Ist], whose perfection was within the ovary. I cannot be attacked by the fiery blast of your mouth, nor can what you say against me reach me. I am Horus, far distant from people and from gods. I am Horus, son of Isis [O'Connell, 1983, p. 75].

The symbol of Horus was a lamb. An early Christian symbol was also a lamb. It was an actual lamb (that had been slain) that St. John saw opening the seals in his Book of Revelation. "And between the throne and the four living creatures and among the elders I saw a lamb standing, as though it had been slain, with seven horns and seven eyes, which are [symbolic of] the seven spirits of God sent out into all the earth. And [the lamb] went and took the scroll from the right hand of him who was seated on the throne" (5:6–7).

Sometimes in early Christianity, the image of the lamb appeared with a cross or even on a cross, and a lamb is entombed in the "holy sepulcher." Once Jesus became known as a real person rather than a myth, he started to take the place of the lamb in iconographical depictions. A letter from the Bishop of Mende, c. 800, reads: "Because the darkness has disappeared, and because also Christ is [now considered] a real man, Pope Adrian commands us to paint him under the form of a man. The Lamb of God must no longer be painted on a cross, but after a human form has been placed on the cross, there is no objection to have a lamb also represented with it, either at the foot of the cross or on the opposite side."[1]

Artists did not easily give up this long-standing idea of a savior being represented by a lamb, so in early depictions of Jesus and the cross he was fully clothed, with his arms outstretched. The cross was set back behind him, and a lamb was resting near his feet. Today, depicting a lamb on a cross would be considered blasphemous by the Church, but this is exactly what the earliest Christians did. This change demonstrates how religious ideas and values change over time and how earlier teachings can evolve in time. Concepts were borrowed from ancient Egyptian religious traditions, including this idea of the savior-god being represented by the lamb. Horus, the savior-god who was born of the Virgin Isis, was called the Lamb of God. He was an important figure in Egypt and even in Rome, where he was worshipped as Apollo.[2] Old ideas are not easily discarded by human beings, as they do not generally like change.

Imagine the introduction of a new religion today that was meant to displace the existing Christian faith. No believer would wish to give up his or her previously held ideas. In fact, he or she would likely be unable to do so, as a person's beliefs shape who he or she actually is. For another faith to take the place of a preexisting religion entirely, the tactics used by the early Church might be necessary. Government infiltration would be necessary, as the new church would need to enforce its teachings and the imposed requirements of the people through legal and military means. Other religions would be banned, and the worship of another deity would be considered a blasphemy, punishable by death. In addition, questioning the governing body, which tells people what is true and what is not, also would be considered blasphemous. In this way, people can be forcefully made to embrace a new religion. However, using these evil tactics, as the Church once did, will not eliminate earlier traditions and deeply embedded beliefs. For this reason, the religious concepts that were introduced by the Egyptians early on were not discarded but integrated into the new religion: Christianity.

The savior-god Horus therefore lives on in the historical accounts of Jesus. Just as Herodotus connected the gods Horus and Apollo, it is not far-fetched to equate Horus to Jesus. Horus was born of a virgin named Isis, who is also called Meri. The written form of Meri was "Mr," and it meant "the beloved." An angel informed her that she was pregnant, and she later gave birth to Horus in a cave. There were shepherds there who witnessed the birth. During his infancy, there was danger. Just as Herod wished to have the baby Jesus killed, Herut wanted Horus killed. A heavenly being appeared before Isis and Joseph and told them both to hide their children. "Come, thou goddess Isis, hide thyself with thy child" is the Egyptian version, while "Arise and take the young child and his mother and flee to Egypt" is the biblical version. At the age of 12, both Horus and Jesus attended a ritual rite of passage.

Unfortunately, there is no information available about Jesus between the ages of 12 and 30. Likewise, there is no information about Horus between the ages of 12 and 30. Both of them were baptized at the age of 30—Horus in the river Eridannus and Jesus in the river Jordan. This was not a good thing for the individuals who baptized them, though, since both of their baptizers were later beheaded.

Horus was taken from the desert and led to a mountain by his rival Set, while Jesus was led there by Satan. Upon arrival, both gods were tempted, but they resisted and were therefore victorious. During their lives, both performed various miracles. They walked on water, performed exorcisms, and restored sight to the blind. They also raised people from the grave. Horus and Jesus were both transfigured on a mountain, where they later addressed people. In both traditions, this is called the Sermon on the Mount. The two gods met their ends in the same way as well. They were both crucified alongside two thieves and then later buried in tombs (Murdock and Acharya, 2011). They both descended into hell and were resurrected after three days. Both of them were known as "the anointed one," "Krst" in Egyptian and "Christ" in Greek. They were also both known as the Lamb of God, the Good Shepherd, and the Bread of Life (Murdock and Acharya, 2011).

It is undeniable that their histories are similar. The belief in Horus and in his powers of restoring life has not dissipated. It has simply been transferred to Christianity, as it was transferred to Greek and Roman religious traditions. The influence that Horus had on the development of early Christianity cannot be underestimated. There are even depictions of Horus with his virgin mother in the catacombs in Rome! Later, the images of Horus were replaced with pictures of Jesus and Isis was replaced by Mary, but the iconography was the same. In the Egyptian Museum of Turin, there is a statue of the Virgin Isis with her child, Horus, that was created in the sixth century B.C.E. This statue inspired the 15th-century painter Masaccio, who used its imagery when painting the *Virgin and Child*. After this, many other artists followed suit, representing Mary and the baby Jesus in the same iconographical pose displayed by Egyptian sculptures of Isis and Horus (Gadalla, 2008). Christianity adopted not only the ideas of the Egyptians regarding the holy trinity but also the iconography that they had used to explain it.

41

Religious Rituals and Practices

Many Egyptian customs were transferred to the new faith. Many of their beliefs were likewise repackaged and then transferred to Christianity as well. These obviously included such metaphysical concepts as the Holy Trinity, the death and resurrection of a savior-god, and the promise of eternal life, but they also included more corporeal facets. These included the practice of mummification and the use of magical incantations and symbolic images for religious purposes.

The practice of mummification is a major component of ancient Egyptian religious faith that lives on in Christianity. The purpose of mummification in Egypt, as previously discussed, was to help the different aspects of the soul to stay together, therefore preventing the true death of the individual. Terms like "life" and "death" when dealing with religious beliefs are misnomers, and they limit the things that can be discussed with ease. True death in Egypt was not when the physical body died but when the individual ceased to exist, which might not ever happen as long as the body were preserved and the proper rituals were carried out. The Egyptians sought eternal life, and it is for this reason that they mummified the deceased.

The Christians also believed in the possibility of eternal life, and it is for this reason that they, too, needed to mummify the bodies of the dead. St. Augustine wrote: "The Egyptians alone believe in the resurrection, as they carefully preserve their bodies. They have a custom of drying up their bodies and making them as durable as brass" (Mojsov, 2005, p. 17).

This is an important statement, as it provides deep insight into one of the true reasons behind Christian mummification. From his viewpoint, St. Augustine knew that the Egyptians had to have believed in the resurrection of bodies, because otherwise they would not have mummified them. This can be summed up succinctly: Mummification was necessary in religions that believed in the resurrection. Of course, the ideas behind this resurrection might have been somewhat different. Just because one culture influences another does not mean that all of the ideas are the same. Ideas taken from one tradition are modified to fit new traditions. Therefore, although the influences from other faiths might be present, they sometimes do not continue in their original form. Rather, they are changed.

In Egypt, they mummified bodies because they did believe in the resurrection, but the practice of preserving bodies had more to do with helping the spiritual essences to remain connected. Since some of the essences were connected to the body, even after death, the only way to effect this was through the preservation of the deceased. In the Christian tradition, this idea changed slightly. They, too, believed in the resurrection, but it was the actually resurrection of the physical body, which would be reanimated at the end of time. When the apocalypse was carried out, the dead would be restored to life. For this reason, bodies had to be preserved.

Some of them in Christianity were preserved just like the Egyptians. The organs were removed, the body cavities were stuffed, and then the bodies were treated with embalming solutions. After this, they were wrapped in fine linens, buried in three distinct coffins, and then laid to rest in sarcophagi. In other cases, bodies were simply embalmed and then buried in protective caskets. However it was carried out, the aim was to make the body endure, so that it could be reanimated when God returned to take vengeance on the people of the earth. Of course, ideas about the resurrection of the body changed over time. Many Catholics still believe that the bodies of the faithful will be reanimated, but today some do not believe that the actual physical body will be brought back to life. This modified belief runs contrary to the description of events as recorded in the Bible, but the beliefs and practices of Catholic Christianity are not all from the book. Ideas have a tendency to change throughout time, and there is little that anyone can do to prevent this metamorphosis. Although metaphysical conceptions might change, the practices performed in the past continue. They are thought of as tradition, and even though some individuals might not know the reason behind their actions, they still carry them out. Resurrection required mummification. The practice, as perfected by the Egyptians, was adopted by the Roman Catholic Church, which made even more advancements in the process. Such advancements included the injection of embalming solutions that maintained a rosy skin color, and other solutions that did not have to be injected, solutions that could be absorbed via osmosis.

Another concept that was adopted from Egyptian faith into Christianity was the use of magical charms and amulets. Bodies of the dead were adorned with various symbols and pieces of jewelry that had religious purposes. They were utilized to help the deceased through the trials of the afterlife so that he or she could be blessed with eternal life. The Egyptians also made use of such protective amulets during life. Catholic Christians today do the exact same thing. They believe that the bones of a saint are especially powerful. Second in power to this are secondary relics, which could be pieces of cloth that had touched the body of a saint. Such items are held in high esteem, and are used for magical purposes. Those who hold them might ask for favors or might simply keep them as items that will protect them from misfortune. When neither primary nor secondary relics are available, Catholics make use of crucifixes or brown scapulars.

One Christian website explains that although prayer can be helpful for overcoming problems, there are other ritual items that can be used for protection or for effecting change. One item that this organization believes is especially efficacious is the rosary. They state:

> We should pray the Rosary for many reasons. The first reason you may consider is the first class miracles associated with the Rosary throughout the centuries. The Rosary has repeatedly proven its great power to overcome every problem, small and large, personal, national and international. For example, the Rosary is associated with the Miracle at Fatima in 1917, witnessed by some 70,000 people. The Rosary is also associated with the winning of several popular battles throughout history as well as having saved a Church near where an atomic bomb was dropped in Japan during Word War II.[1]

For protection purposes, this Christian organization suggests wearing a brown scapular. They state that it can protect individuals in many different situations, including those who are in the armed forces, those who work in dangerous careers, and those who are about to have an operation. This item is considered by Christians to be a talisman of protection, and therefore, by definition, it is a magical item. However, as is often the case in religions that make use of magic, they explicitly state that it is not magic. This website states:

> Some may initially have doubts about a garment such as the Brown Scapular having such powers. How could a piece of cloth offer such protection, and how can it be attributed to so many miracles throughout history? To explain, first, the brown scapular is not magic, or a good luck charm. Its benefits and protection are given to those who wear it and believe that it was given to us from heaven and have faith that protection will be granted from heaven to those who wear it. There is nothing else to it![2]

This is not rational thinking. Whether they know it or not, this is a practice of magic (Stark, 2001). Anytime logic takes a backseat, and there is no rational explanation for so-called miracles, other than the fact that an object was present, it can be referred to as magic. Magic is never separated from religion, and it is not a condescending term. Some individuals who make use of magical-religious charms or incantations believe that the description of their actions by scholars as magic is disdainful. Wax and Wax (1963) explained why this might be the case: "During the Middle Ages, the Roman Catholic Church attached the label of magic to a variety of deviant religious practices, ranging from the remnants of heathen, pre–Christian rites to sophisticated perversions of the Catholic Mass. Rather than characterizing magic as an empirically inaccurate or logically fallacious system of philosophy, the Christian saw it as an impious, evil, and blasphemous perversion of religiosity" (p. 497).

However, this is not the case. Magical elements can be found in many traditions. There have been some scholars who have tried to equate the terms "religion" and "magic" so that they were one and the same (Goody, 1961). However, doing such a thing would eliminate the possibility of discussing such practices within a religious context. When divine powers are thought to infuse a physical object — be it a piece of cloth or a necklace — that is a belief in magic. Many religions in the world utilized magical practices in the past, and many of them still do. The fact that this concept existed in Egyptian religion and that it exists in Catholicism today does nothing to link the two of these faiths together in this aspect. However, the similarity of some of the magical items and some of the religious ceremonies does provide a definite connection between the two traditions. The notion of holy water, for example, has origins in Egypt. In Christianity, a spell is recited over the water and the water changes. Believers think that it is now sacred and that it can be used to protect those who anoint themselves with it. This practice stemmed from the Egyptian practices of baptism and of sprinkling people with sacred water from the Nile as part of their religious rituals (Mojsov, 2005). The Egyptians also made use of various talismans and magical symbols that were utilized in early Christianity as well, some of which continue to be used in altered forms even today.

The Egyptians made use of a symbol called an ankh. It was essentially a cross with a ring at the top, and was a symbol of eternal life. With regard to the theology of Paul on the function and true purpose of the symbol of the cross for Christians, it had little to do with the death and suffering of Jesus. Rather, it had to do with his resurrection and, therefore, his eternal life (Gadalla, 2008). The same philosophy was maintained in the Gospels of both St. Thomas and St. Mark: that the cross was symbolic of resurrection and of eternal existence.

The accounts of the death of Jesus are not uniform. Some of the texts mention that he was crucified, while others describe that he had been hanged, like other savior-deities such as Dionysus. Many of the savior-gods from other traditions were connected to a (sacred) tree in one way or another. Since the Bible states that Jesus also was hanged from a tree (Acts 5:30), it is more evidence of the connection between the Christian savior and the saviors from earlier traditions. It is possible that Jesus was actually hanged and the image of the crucifixion was only adopted due to its significance, which had begun in Egypt and was transferred from the old religions into the new one. According to Gadalla (2008), hanging was most likely the true means of death, but crucifixion was recorded in some accounts because of the spiritual idea that it represented. Crucifixion and the sign of the cross referred to eternal life, and it is for this reason that there is a common tendency in some religious traditions to use both terms. In some accounts Dionysus was hanged, and in others he was crucified. The same is true of Horus. The fact that the same incontinuities are found in Christian texts indicates the figurative significance of crucifixion, and references to Jesus being hanged connect him more closely to previous gods who influenced his historical accounts.

The ankh: an Egyptian symbol of eternal life. This one is found on the obelisk in the Piazza Navona (Rome, Italy).

An interesting symbolism is revealed in the shape of the ankh itself, which is basically a round, circular form on top of a T. The cross that Jesus would have been crucified on, according to drawings of crucifixions created about the same time period, was not a cross at all but a T-shaped structure. The ankh appears as a noose, which would have been used in a hanging, on top of this T shape, which is indicative of a crucifixion. Gods in earlier civilizations had multiple accounts of their deaths: some accounts stated that they had been crucified, while others stated that they had been hanged. (Similarly, the accounts of Jesus also point to both conclusions: that he could have been hanged or crucified.) The symbol of the ankh joins both of these methods of death together. The shape combines hanging and crucifixion.

The connection between the ankh and the cross is strong, and it should not be underestimated. Philosophically, they mean the same thing, but there is even more concrete proof that the notion of the ankh had a direct influence on the use of the Christian cross in rituals and practices. In early Christian burials, two talismans were used to assist the deceased into the next life and to assist in his or her resurrection. Bodies were buried with both ankhs and crosses. Sometimes, both symbols, the Egyptian and the Christian, appeared on tombs and in catacombs beside each other (Mojsov, 2005).

The existence of these two symbols side-by-side is indicative of the early acceptance that Christianity expressed toward Egyptian religious elements. In addition, it lets us know that the two faiths, although tolerant of each other, were distinct. Otherwise, one symbol alone would have been used, modified from the original Egyptian in order to represent the new nature of Christianity. However, the two images are next to each other, each equal in importance. Christianity is not simply the Egyptian religion restated, as some historians have posited. There are many elements of Egyptian metaphysical concepts and religious practices that were absorbed into Christianity, but such elements were only absorbed in order to enhance the structure and depth of the new religion.

42

Integration and Assimilation

Many of the ideas that are considered fundamental to Christianity today had their origins in Egypt. Egyptian stories aspired early Christian writers. However, there was one difference when the Egyptians wrote about their deities. When they wrote about the death and resurrection of a god, for example, they did not necessarily take the story as historical fact. Rather, it was allegorical and used only to convey spiritual dogma. Massey (2000) believed that the early Christian writers were simply ignorant of this fact. They thought that the Egyptian stories of their savior-god were actually historical accounts and rewrote them as such in Christian texts.

At the beginning, the origins of Christianity were known, but this changed over the next 300 years. In the third and fourth centuries, the Church explicitly began to state that the stories had not been taken from other sources (Gadalla, 2008). This was not believed by most people, as they were still familiar with the Egyptian ideas. The Church realized that this was not working, so they created the idea of diabolical mimicry. They told people that they had not taken ideas from the Egyptian tradition, but that the same stories were created in the Egyptian religion by the devil in order to discredit the future religion of Christianity. Why the Church had a problem stating that some ideas were absorbed from other traditions is unknown. Perhaps they believed that if the same concepts were found elsewhere, it would make Christianity less unique. But then again, perhaps it was for political reasons alone.

When the explanation of diabolical mimicry did not convince people, the Church banned other faiths and they became "extremely violent, which led to murder, destruction, and terrorizing the masses" (Gadalla, 2008). Religion was used as a means of binding people and forcing allegiance. Once the Church took political control, it did all it could to wipe out its connections to the earlier religions that influenced its development. Otherwise, their statement that they were the one and only true faith could not be maintained (without the use of force). Politically, the actions of the Church were smart. They put a religion in place that abounded with familiar ideas, taken from other traditions, in order to entice individuals to join them. The ideas were so similar to preexisting traditions that many did not think twice about joining. Christianity was simply a different path to the same God. Then, once they grew in power and in numbers, the Church claimed that theirs was the only true religion and that believers in other faiths would burn in hellfire for all eternity. The Church then began to use force to keep followers in line. The Church could not be questioned, for a question could result in a charge of heresy, punishable by death (Foote and Wheeler, 1887). After enough time had passed, the Church stopped executing people. Followers believed the Church entirely, because they were no longer able to think critically. The majority of them chose not to read any historical account that ran counter to Church statements, and they regarded religious doctrines from earlier traditions as heretical and idolatrous. This is editing history to match a belief and not changing a viewpoint due to uncovered historical truths. In this way, some people became ignorant and they lost their ability to reason.

All of this was done to stop individuals from realizing that the precepts of Christianity had roots in other traditions, especially Egyptian religious concepts. However, there is nothing wrong with a tradition being influenced by those that preceded it. In fact, that is probably impossible to avoid. Humans beings are more likely to have the same religious beliefs as their parents, only because they grow up surrounded by them. The children simply accept these beliefs as truth, because they do not know anything else. After enough time has passed, they are unable to rationally consider other faiths or to even question their own. Due to their parents' beliefs, children lose the ability to think critically in such areas. This is why many children do not explore different faiths but simply adhere to their parents' religious beliefs. In a similar manner, it is impossible for one religion that emerges in the midst of others to emerge completely independently. There must be influences from other traditions. This is not a bad thing, and the majority of great faiths have borrowed traditions and religious practices from earlier civilizations. Christianity likewise borrowed many concepts from other religions. Many of the things that it absorbed came from Egypt.

Although some individuals do not know anymore where their practices originated from, there are statements made by many early Christian writers and even Church fathers that suggest that they did know where such practices originated. The concepts that were utilized that have origins in earlier traditions, however, had to be modified to fit the changing philosophies and dogmatic truths of the new faith. In this way, concepts from Egypt, and from other traditions, appeared in a different form in early Christianity.

The Holy Trinity, which was originally represented by Osiris, Isis, and Horus, changed. The Egyptian images of the virgin mother holding the savior child continued on, but the three of them together was no longer considered the Holy Trinity in the Catholic tradition. The woman was eliminated in Christianity, and they replaced her with the Holy Spirit. Thus, the Trinity is the Father, the Son, and the Holy Spirit. This may have been because the Church, even today, does not regard men and women as being equal. Even today, a woman cannot hold any high-ranking position within the Church. She cannot be priest, cardinal, bishop, or pope. Some have suggested that this is due to the story in Genesis in which God made man in his image but made woman from one of man's ribs. However, there were various other Adam and Eve stories and some of them portrayed men and women on equal footing. When the Bible was first put together at one of the earliest Church councils, they specifically chose this version for inclusion. It could be that this dogmatic change, as well as the previous choice in editing, was done for political and not religious purposes. In any case, the Egyptian idea was corrupted and the Christian idea was born.

Another Egyptian concept that was modified was the sacrament of the Eucharist. In a custom stemming directly from the cult of Osiris, believers engaged in a symbolic meal that consisted of beer and bread, which were metaphors for the flesh and blood of Osiris, the god who died and was resurrected. This symbolic yet cannibalistic process actually joined the faithful to their God. Upon eating and drinking those things that were symbolic of his body, they had the very essence of God within them. Therefore, symbolically they had become one with God. The same practice is carried out in Catholicism. In this altered cannibalistic practice, they drink wine instead of beer. Other than that minor change, the practice and its significance remain relatively unchanged.

There are many other practices in Catholicism that originated in Egypt. Many of them stemmed from the city of Alexandria, when everyone was surrounded by the intriguing customs. When Christianity first arrived in the city, the Egyptian faith was so deeply embedded in the hearts and minds of the citizens that it had no choice but to be absorbed into the new tradition. Mojsov (2005) wrote:

> The partaking of Osiris as the food of life, the judgment of the soul in the next world, and the resurrection of Osiris as the risen sun had sunk deeply into the minds of the people. So had baptism in the sacred river, wearing black as a sign of mourning god's sacrifice, and sprinkling the faithful with Nile water. Isis had been called the "mother of God" centuries before Mary. The birth of the savior-child is still celebrated by the entire Christian world [p. 116].

If bodily resurrection were an actual thing and one of the great kings of Egypt's past were reanimated, he would of course be overwhelmed by the various changes that have taken place on this planet. When learning about Christianity, however, he would likely feel right at home. It would be familiar to him. The great god Osiris had been called by many names, so referring to him by a different name would not be shocking. Based on the recorded history of the god alone, the king would recognize him. For this reason, upon hearing the history of Jesus, the king would likely recognize the god as either Osiris or Horus, just

After the destruction of the Egyptian faith, the popes became the new pharaohs. They used religion to bring people together under one ruler. This is a statue of Pope Pius VII, found in St. Peter's Basilica.

called by a different name — a common practice in different lands. Many of the stories would be the same, with many references to his homeland, Egypt. The notion of the Virgin Birth and a savior child would be familiar, as would be the exact hagiography of the savior, as the major events in the lives of both Jesus and Horus matched up almost perfectly.

The king would recognize the religious rites performed in Christianity as being the same as or at least similar to the rites performed in his own ancient faith. These rites included baptisms, the performance of Mass, the partaking of the Holy Eucharist, and the use of holy water, sacred talismans and magical symbols. Also very familiar would be the practice of mummification and the interment of important individuals in elaborate burial chambers. Such practices are carried out in Christianity because of their certainty in the resurrection, a belief that the king would also share. When he met the highest-ranking members of the Church, the king would likely feel as though he were speaking with his own brethren, as their robes and miters resembled the long, pointed crowns and robes worn by Egyptian kings. The pope, like the Egyptian kings, wears gold jewelry, and he has servants who cook for him, clean for him, and arrange everything for him. He does not need to work, for he has access to as much wealth as he could possibly desire. He is the new pharaoh, symbolic of Christ on Earth, as the Egyptian kings were portrayed. Christianity has taken much from the religious traditions of ancient Egypt. As the Greek proverb says, "Every new world springs from an older one."

VII. The Reasons Behind Christian Mummification

Jesus said, "The dead are not alive, and the living will not die." — Gospel of St. Thomas

43

The Bodily Preservation of Jesus

At first glance, it seems that the practice of mummification in Christianity runs contrary to the precepts of the faith. For outsiders, the practice might defy explanation. Bodies are intentionally preserved after death and then they are buried. Years later, the bodies are unearthed. If any are found preserved, the mummification is marveled over and the body is prominently displayed for others to see. Then, another seemingly bizarre custom is initiated: the taking of relics. In the view of outsiders, the bodies are desecrated. The remains are treated initially as though they were important. Members of the clergy attempt to preserve them and then bury the bodies in multiple caskets for protection. Later, the remains are unearthed, redressed and displayed. At this point, it is a common Catholic practice to remove pieces of the bodies. Sometimes the fingers or toes are cut off. Occasionally, pieces of the spine or ribs are taken. And then sometimes, internal organs like the heart are taken and enshrined. In the case of several saints, their heads were removed and taken to diverse locations. For outsiders, these are indeed strange practices.

These practices reflect contrary yet equally important ideas within the faith. There are non-biblical influences that have had a great influence on the development of Christianity and on the Christian practice of mummification. However, there are also reasons for such mummification found in the Bible, namely the preservation of Jesus Christ. According to the Old Testament, Joseph had asked his servants to embalm the body of his dead father, and this tradition of embalming remained in the Middle East for many years.[1] It was a Jewish tradition to preserve the bodies of the deceased. The bodies were typically embalmed and then entombed. Since he was Jewish, the body of Jesus also had to be preserved, as was the custom. The New Testament briefly describes how he was embalmed: After his death, mourners treated his body with natural plant-based preservatives. Joseph of Arimathea asked Pontius Pilate for Jesus' body, and the request was granted. He took the body away, and Nicodemus joined him.

Nicodemus brought 75 pounds of aloe and myrrh. Both materials were used for embalming, and myrrh was favored by the Egyptians. According to the Gospel of John: "They took the body of Jesus and bound it in linen cloths with the spices, as is the burial custom of the Jews" (19:40). It is thought by some theologians that the body was wrapped in strips of linen and anointed with the myrrh and aloe. However, due to the fact that Nicodemus had 75 pounds of aloe and myrrh with him, it is safe to speculate that Jesus may have actually been eviscerated and embalmed. Evisceration was not a custom of the Jews, but it was a custom of the Egyptians, who performed this procedure so that the physical bodies of important people would be preserved forever. There is no evidence that this is what happened, and some would say that this possibility is highly unlikely. However, this is too large an amount of aloe and myrrh to be used on the skin alone. The exact manner of mummification is unknown, but it is known that Jesus was, in fact, embalmed.

It was the duty of early Christians to follow Jesus as much as possible. It is for this reason that the earliest saints were martyrs, who followed him into death. At the beginning, to be a saint a person did not just have to die for Jesus, but he or she had to die like Jesus (Woodward, 1996). In other words, he or she had to imitate Jesus as closely as possible in order to be recognized for canonization. Once Christianity became legal and the age of the martyrs had ended, the meaning of the term "saint" was modified. One no longer had to die like Jesus, but he or she still had to follow him as much as possible. Later saints demonstrated some of the virtues displayed by Jesus of Nazareth, and every saint was thought to demonstrate, to varying degrees, the qualities that Jesus himself had displayed (Hoever, 1955). If the duty of Christians was to follow in the footsteps of their lord and if Jesus was embalmed, it is logical that they would also want to be preserved after death. For this reason, individuals were buried in multiple caskets, kept in protective tombs, and maintained in dry environments. They were treated with embalming solutions, which were either applied to the skin, injected, or absorbed into the bodies through osmosis. In other cases, the internal organs were removed before the remains were treated. Various methods were used to effect bodily preservation, so that Christian believers could follow, in some small measure, Jesus Christ himself.

44

The Rapture

Roman Catholics believe the Rapture is an actual event that will occur. According to their religious beliefs, eventually Jesus will break seven seals, unleashing pain and calamity on living creatures. St. John is credited with writing the Book of Revelation, which he directed toward the "seven churches in Asia" (1:4). According to his revelation, which supposedly came to him in a vision, he saw a scroll in the right hand of God that had seven seals, which only the Lamb could open. St. John saw a lamb in the midst of 24 elders. It had been slain, and it had seven horns and seven eyes. These were the "seven Spirits of God" (5:6). The Lamb took the scroll from God's hand and began opening the seals.

Once the first seal was broken, a man who held a bow and wore a crown appeared on a white horse. He rode forth to conquer.

The second seal permitted another man into existence, this one on a red horse, wielding a large sword. He would take peace away from the people on earth and make them kill each other.

The third seal materialized a black horse, upon which was seated a man with a scale in his hand.[1] The rider who came into being upon the breaking of the fourth seal was on a pale horse. His name was Death, and Hades was with him. "And they were given authority over a fourth of the earth, to kill with the sword and with famine and with pestilence and by wild beasts of the earth" (6:8).

The fifth seal brought into being an image of the martyrs who had died for God, and they were asking for retribution. "Oh Sovereign Lord," they called out, "how long before you will judge and avenge our blood on those who dwell on earth?" Even in their heavenly abode, they could not turn away from the past. They wanted revenge. They were each given white robes and told to wait — to wait until their brethren were killed just as they had been killed.

Then the Lamb opened the sixth seal, and devastation occurred. There were great earthquakes, the moon turned red, and all of the stars in the sky fell to earth like "the fig tree sheds its winter fruit when shaken by a gale" (6:13). The sky vanished, and every mountain and island was removed from the earth and suspended in the sky.[2] Everyone, in an effort to save themselves, hid in caves and called to the mountains, begging the mountains to fall on top of them in order to hide them from the face of the one seated on the throne of heaven and to hide them from the wrath of Jesus (the Lamb).

Then, in St. John's revelation, he saw four angels standing guard on the four corners of the earth (which was still thought of as being flat) and they were holding back the wind. They were delaying the destruction of everything until the servants of God were saved. All of those who were deemed worthy were permitted into heaven, and they stood in front of the throne and near the Lamb in white robes, holding palm branches, an important substance in Egyptian rituals. They had washed their robes white in the "blood of the Lamb" (7:14). This most likely meant that they were all believers in the divinity of Jesus, so they were saved.

Once all of the believers were gathered together in heaven, Jesus destroyed the non-believers. He opened the seventh seal, and seven angels took their places with seven trumpets. Another angel took a censer, filled it with incense and prayers, and then added fire from the altar. It threw the censer to the earth, which turned into thunder, flashes of lightning, and an earthquake. Then the angels who held the trumpets began performing their roles. The first one blew into its trumpet, and hail and fire, mixed with blood, hit the earth. A third of the earth was burned, along with a third of the trees and a third of the grass.

When the second trumpet sounded, a giant mountain, covered with fire, was thrown into the sea and a third of the oceans became blood. A third of the ships were destroyed and a third of the sea creatures were also killed.

The third trumpet sounding brought a star down, which fell on a third of the rivers and springs and polluted the water. People who tried to drink from such waters were poisoned and died, unable to escape the wrath of the Lamb.

The fourth angel blew its trumpet, and the sun, the moon, and the stars lost a third of their light.

When the fifth trumpet sounded, a star fell to earth and it was given a key.[3] The star took the key and opened the shaft of the bottomless pit. Smoke bellowed from the pit, and locusts issued from within the smoke. The locusts had specific instructions. They were not to kill anyone or to harm any green plant or tree. Instead, Jesus wanted them to torture all non-believers for five months. The actual text follows:

> They were told not to harm the grasses of the earth or any green plant or any tree, but only those people who do not have the seal of God on their foreheads. They were allowed to torment them for five months, but not to kill them, and their torment was like the torment of the scorpion when it stings someone. And in those days people will seek death and will not find it. They will long to die, but death will flee from them [9:4–6].

The sixth trumpet was blown, and God released four murderous angels who killed a third of humankind. Those who were not killed did not stop worshipping other gods. This displeased the Christian God and made him jealous. In Deuteronomy, God says, "I the Lord your God am a jealous God" (5:9). He alone could be worshipped. Those who were left alive did not stop praying in front of statues of their god either, which was anathema in early Judeo-Christian tradition. Having a statue of any deity was considered heresy, since one of the Ten Commandments reads: "You shall not make for yourself a carved image, or any likeness of anything that is in heaven above, or that is on the earth beneath, or that is in the water under the earth. You shall not bow down to them and serve them" (Deuteronomy 5:8–9).

Then authority was given to two witnesses to prophesize for 1,260 days in a city that was symbolically called Sodom and Egypt, the same location where "their Lord was crucified" (Revelation 11:3–9). Once this time period was over, they were killed, but their bodies were not buried. They remained in the street. After three and a half days, they were resurrected, carried to heaven upon a cloud. Once they were in heaven, the citizens left behind suffered.

There was an earthquake, and a tenth of the city fell. Seven thousand people were killed, and the rest of them decided to embrace Christianity out of fear. "The rest were terrified and gave glory to the God of heaven" (Revelation 9:13).

The elders who were in front of the throne of heaven then explained that the time had come for the dead to be judged and for the servants of God to be rewarded. Those who feared God would also be rewarded. God then opened his temple, which housed his covenant. From this temple there was a sign. A woman would give birth to a child who would rule all the nations with a "rod of iron."

Then a war broke out in heaven. Michael and his warrior angels fought a dragon that had appeared in heaven, and they cast him down onto the earth. Furious, he called another beast into existence that had sacrilegious names on its head. It was charged with saying blasphemous things against Jesus and waging war against the saints. The second beast that was unleashed had its eyes on commerce: No one could buy or sell unless he or she had a mark, which was either the "name of the beast or the number of its name" (13:17).[4]

Finally, the end of the wrath of God neared. There were seven angels with seven plagues. These were given to the angels in golden bowls "full of the wrath of God" (15:7). The angels went into the sanctuary, and they began to pour these out onto the earth. The first one emptied led to painful sores on all non-believers. The second one turned the water of the sea to blood, and every creature within it was killed. The third angel poured out its bowl, and the rivers and springs also became bloody. The fourth angel did not empty its bowl on the earth. It was poured onto the sun instead, which began to scorch people. The fifth angel poured a bowl (of wrath) onto the throne of the beast, and the world was plunged into darkness. When the sixth bowl was emptied into the river Euphrates, the water dried up. The last bowl ended the destruction. There were storms and earthquakes, and the cities of the world fell. Islands were washed away and no mountains at all were found on the earth. Hail pounded the earth, and each hailstone was about 100 pounds. All things were destroyed. All non-believers were made to suffer, and then they were killed. The only individuals who were saved from this torment and death were those who gave their allegiance to the Christian God.

This is why many Christians think that all non-believers will end up in hell. From a purely Christian perspective, if a person is not a believer then he or she cannot enter heaven, no matter what he or she might do in life. The Reverend Raymond Barber (n.d.) wrote: "Jesus Christ is coming again. Are you ready? Have you been saved? Are you born again? Is your name written, not on the church roll, but in the Lamb's book of life? 'Whosoever was not found written in the book of life was cast into the lake of fire' [Revelation 20:15]."[5] From the perspective of many Christians, non-believers are destined to spend an eternity in hell.

From a traditional Catholic perspective, the requirements are even more narrow: A person cannot get to heaven without the intervention of the Church.[6] (Someone like Gandhi, considered a saint by many individuals throughout the world, is in hell, according to Roman Catholic dogma.) Belief in the Christian God is necessary in order to get into heaven; so is membership in the political organization, as without its help people will suffer and die. They will be punished by Jesus. This might sound bizarre to outsiders and even to some Christians. However, this is precisely what was taught by the Church. Once the Church took political power, it was a crime to have different beliefs. This policy was not confined to religion alone, but it extended into the sciences and into every other field of scholarship. Mangasarian (2004) wrote:

> To build up their churches and maintain their creeds, the priests pulled down and destroyed the magnificent civilization of Greece and Rome, plunging Europe into the dark and sterile ages which lasted over a thousand years. When Galileo waved his hands for joy because he believed he had enriched humanity with a new truth and extended the sphere of knowledge, what did the Church do to him? It conspired to destroy him. It shut him up in a dungeon! Clapping truth into jail; gagging the mouth of the student — is that building up or tearing down? When Bruno lighted a new torch to increase the light of the world, what was his reward? The stake! During all the ages that the Church had the power to police the world, every time a thinker raised his head he was clubbed to death.

Incredible models of the universe were built before the Church established its power. In the first century there was a working, accurate model of the solar system, reflecting spherical planets circling the sun. The Church made belief in this model a heresy. It was blasphemous to believe that God did not place the stars in the sky. In the third century B.C.E., a scientist had accurately calculated the circumference of the planet, but this information was buried when the Church took over. They made it a heresy to believe that the Earth was not flat. Thinking was a problem for the Church, as many of their teachings would not stand up to logic. In order to protect themselves, they banned thinking.

People who could no longer think believed anything that they were told by the Church. They believed in the Rapture, and they believed in the resurrection of the body that would occur at the end. Even today, there are many Christians who believe this story word for word. One religious organization explains:

> All previously saved Christians, totaling perhaps 5 to 10 percent of the world's population, will suddenly have their bodies converted into a different form that they will wear for all eternity in Heaven. They will rise vertically into the air. Many believe that they will pass right through ceilings, roofs of cars, etc. to meet Jesus Christ in the sky. The vast majority of humans will be left behind. There will be extensive devastation on planes, trains and automobiles as their pilots, engineers and drivers suddenly disappear and the vehicles crash. The bodies of Christian believers who have died during the previous two millennia will be reconstituted into their original bodies which will then also be converted to spirit bodies. They will rise out of their graves and ascend to meet Jesus.[7]

A common belief among Christians is expressed in the preceding explanation: The original bodies will be reconstituted, and then these actual physical bodies will be converted into spiritual bodies. The physical body is still necessary! In order to be prepared for the resurrection, the bodies of those faithful to Christ still had to be in existence. It is for this reason that Catholics, even today, seek to preserve the bodies of the dead. This need to preserve the physical remains because of the resurrection was explicitly explained by St. Augustine, when he was commenting on the Egyptian religion. Since the Egyptians practiced mummification, he wrote, they must have believed in the resurrection (Mojsov, 2005).

This statement is important. It indicates an early teaching of the Church that has continued. Since the Egyptians believed in the resurrection, they mummified the deceased. Similarly, the physical remains were necessary to be saved (by Jesus) in early Christian philosophy. The physical bodies would be reanimated, temporarily turning them into something like zombies. Then those physical bodies would be converted into spiritual bodies, which would abide forever in heaven. In order to exist forever, bodies had to be mummified.

Galileo Galilei was imprisoned because some of his ideas ran contrary to the ideas of the Church. He died while confined. This statue is found near the Uffizi Gallery, in Florence, Italy.

Statue of the philosopher Giordano Bruno. He was burned alive because the Church did not like his ideas (Rome, Italy).

According to Christian teachings about this phenomenon, which are explicitly found in the Bible, if corpses were not preserved, they would not be resurrected (Bertholet, 1916). This is exactly the case in the Egyptian eschatology as well. In order for the individuality of a person to exist forever, the body had to be preserved. Therefore, the Church utilized various methods to protect the physical remains of the people whom they deemed important, such as members of the clergy and saints. The Church eviscerated and embalmed their members, treating the bodies with fragrant solutions that would help them to endure. Worried that even this might not be enough, they buried many of the bodies in three distinct coffins, including one made from lead, which was soldered shut. This is an elaborate procedure carried out in order to protect the deceased from a fate worse than death.

45

Early Concepts of the Soul

The nature of the soul was not known in early Christianity, and there were various different theories to explain the phenomenon. Some believed that it was one singular essence and, upon death, it immediately separated and moved away from the body. However, this thought was not common. It was more commonly believed that the spirit remained in close proximity to the corpse for an extended period of time. In the Egyptian tradition, this time period lasted 40 days. This period of time is significant in Christianity as well, which still continues to celebrate Ascension Day 40 days after Easter. On this day, Jesus's ascension into heaven is celebrated. This is evidence that the early Christians believed that the spirits of the deceased remained near or in their physical remains.

The singular nature of the soul was a concept that did not exist in early Christianity. It was not believed by Church fathers, by other members of the clergy, or by Roman Catholic laypersons. Instead, they believed that the soul had multiple aspects. There was an early Christian practice of sleeping in the tombs of saints. Believers thought that this was a particularly efficacious practice in order to become more spiritual and to become closer to God. Others wished to be buried next to the bodies of saints, because they thought that they would have a better chance of getting into heaven. They thought that the spirits of the saints were near their graves and that the saints would assist others in the same geographical area to get to heaven.

Augustine had stated "men who had shown themselves, as martyrs, to be true servants of God could bind their fellow men closer to God than could the angels."[1] For this reason, an incredible number of people wished to be buried next to saints or at least in tombs and catacombs that were affiliated with a church. Thousands were taken in and preserved by the Capuchins in Rome and in Palermo, and others were preserved by friars in Comiso and in other parts of Italy, but there was not enough space in Rome and in other major cities for individuals to be buried next to saints. It was such a problem that Augustine eventually had to tell people that they did not have to be buried next to a saint or a martyr in order to be saved. However, although he stated this publicly, he may not have believed it himself. The stories of visions and unusual phenomena observed at or near the graves of martyrs and other saints made him wonder, as did the numerous miracles that were said to have occurred in the vicinity of their physical remains (Kaufman, 1994).

The Church, during Augustine's life, began to profess the singular nature of the soul, but earlier beliefs were still present. Sometimes, people cannot give up a previously held belief too easily, and therefore, the notion that there were multiple aspects of the soul continued. Obviously, teachings of the Church were adopted from many other traditions, including the Pythagorean school, which was located in Italy. Iamblichus of Chalcis (n.d.) stated: "The Pythagorean school filled Italy with philosophers," and the Pythagorean concept of the soul held that it was composed of multiple parts. Timaeus Locrius (480–450 B.C.E.) also wrote that it was composed of two distinct parts, and the Egyptians, who had a huge influence on the development of Christianity, held that it had eight distinct yet interconnected aspects. Christians, too, believed that the soul was a composite. They believed, for example, that the soul of the deceased could be in heaven next to God yet simultaneously near the physical body. What is interesting is not that they thought that parts of the soul were in different places, but that they believed the entire being was simultaneously in different locations. They thought that the saints were in their physical remains, yet at the same time they were also in heaven (Bynum, 1995).

Many miracles that were credited to saints actually occurred while in the proximity of their physical remains — either their entire bodies or just a bone. Other miracles were reported to have occurred in the presence of secondary relics, near a shirt that a saint had worn, for example. Any discussion on the subject of miracles has to be tempered, however, since the true nature of the phenomenon is unknown. Just because something inexplicable has occurred does not constitute proof of any particular god. Miracles happen in just about every religious tradition on this planet. If a miracle were evidence of the existence of each god, then there would be a number of gods who have been proven to exist. It would force a worldwide polytheistic faith, since evidence of the existence of all of them would be present. Obviously, this cannot be the case. There are other possible causes of miracles that must be considered before thinking about the possibility that they were caused by the physical remains themselves. A logical one is the power of the human mind.

The Church no longer accepts evidence of stigmata as a miracle in the process of canonization. This is because the power of the mind is not yet fully understood and it is possible that deep meditation on the crucified form of Jesus might actually result in the wounds that the practitioner developed. The majority of individuals who had developed stigmata spent a great amount of time thinking about the Passion and stared intently at a statue or painting of Jesus crucified. The artistic renderings of the Passion, however, did not reflect any kind of historicity. Yet, in every case, the wounds that people developed on their hands and sides matched perfectly the wounds displayed in the artistic image upon which they meditated. So it is not unlikely that many miracles actually come into being because of the power of the mind. There are some Christians who utilize faith healing and who believe in miracles occurring whenever they are asked for. However, such occurrences will only happen if someone believes intently that they will. If the occurrence was initiated by something outside of the mind, then belief would not be a requirement. Belief would only be necessary if the process originated from within the mind itself. This is why Jesus does not appear to Hindus when they pray and why Krishna does not appear to Christians when they pray. The mind controls what is seen. The mind, therefore, might create miracles.

However, if this was not the case — if the mind was not responsible for the existence of such phenomena — maybe the cause is found in the physical remains themselves. The Buddhist concept of merit is useful in understanding this. According to some Buddhist sects, individuals who engage in ascetic practices develop a spiritual power known as merit. This is a power that can be used for various purposes, including curing individuals of diseases and performing various other so-called miracles. Just being around people that have a lot of merit is thought to be uplifting. Once a person dies, his or her soul may leave the body, but the spiritual essence called merit stays behind. Therefore, the spirit has not completely left the body. It is still found in the remains. Something similar to this concept is found in Christianity as well.

If the spirit completely left the body upon death, then miracles and other strange occurrences at or near graves of holy individuals could not be explained. In other words, if the remains were but decaying flesh alone, devoid of spiritual essence, there is nothing there that could cause inexplicable phenomena. However, if there was still a powerful, unseen essence that remained with the body, then miraculous healing, visions, and other unusual occurrences could then be explained. If this spiritual essence did remain with the cadaver, mummification would be necessary. The decomposition of the body would be an awful thing, as the decay of the flesh could mean the dissolution of the spirit that infused it. For this reason, the bodies had to be preserved. Because early Christians believed that the spirits of the dead remained close to their physical bodies, they wanted the bodies to endure. For this reason, they were mummified.

Early Christians thought that the soul was connected to the physical body, even after death. This is why they wished to be buried next to holy remains and why they prayed near the bodies of pious individuals. This has not ceased even today, as pilgrims go out of their way to travel to holy locations, just to pray in front of the deceased. If the corpse were only a physical object, would they do this? Original ideas shared by humans are difficult to eradicate. They linger throughout centuries, despite efforts to eradicate the beliefs. They fester just outside of the consciousness, so that people feel the importance of such mummies, but they cannot justify or explain their feelings. Kneeling in front of the remains of pious and holy individuals, who are on display in churches and cathedrals in Italy, believers sense that the saints are still present in their bodies. They are still a source of wonderment and awe.

46

The Power Inherent in Bodily Remains

The spiritual essence that remains in the bodies of holy individuals was a source of miracles, and villages needed these bodies in their proximity so that they would be protected from misfortune. This need that Christians felt led to the theft of whole bodies and of bodily relics in Italy. Sometimes, a priest from one location would steal portions of a body from another church and then transfer the body parts to his own church. When this happened, members of the community would actually rejoice, because now they were protected by the saint whose body part they had stolen. The need for these relics led to a number of individuals making a lot of money. Merchants would obtain bits of saints and then sell them to churches, who would usually pay big money for slivers of bone or fingers and toes.

Part of this had to do with a canonical law imposed by the Vatican. At the Council of Nicea (767), it was declared that every church had to have the remains of a saint. But such remains were not always easy to come by. Churches had a problem. If they did not have parts of such dead bodies, their buildings would not be consecrated. Therefore, they paid lots of money to buy pieces of corpses. Merchants hungry for more profit would sometimes steal the bodies of saints in order to turn a profit. In other cases, merchants would take some random corpse, cut pieces from it, and then state that they came from the body of a holy and famous saint. For this reason, it is possible that the body parts enshrined in some churches are not pieces of saints as might be believed.

The Church officially condemned the sale of relics, but there was a problem. Church members needed pieces of these bodies for protection from the devil and for the possibility of miracles. Although they did not like people stealing the bodies and then selling them, the Church did not want the sale of these body parts to cease. Therefore, they updated the canonical law to state that it was wrong to sell relics, but it was acceptable for members of the clergy to buy them (Geary, 1978). The Church was caught in a conundrum: The theft and sale of these important items was wrong, but if the sale of them were banned, the Church might not have access to them. In Christianity during the Renaissance, patrons of the Church would not attend Mass in a location that did not house the remains of a saint when there were other places nearby that did have such good-luck items. The presence of relics was important to believers. St. John Damascene said, "Christ gives us the relics of saints as health-giving springs through which flow blessings and healing."

When the bodies of many saints were unearthed for identification purposes during the processes of either their beatifications or their canonizations, relics were taken. Bodies were

During the Renaissance, many people would not attend Mass in a location that did not house the remains of a saint. In Italy, this practice has not dissipated and the bodies of saints, beati, and venerables are still found in many locations, often right under the altars. The body of St. Clare is underneath this altar (Naples, Italy).

unearthed; pieces of them were cut off and then given to those in attendance, who either took them home or took them to different religious centers for enshrinement. Sometimes, the hagiographies report that the bodies had not been treated in any way. Think about how this would occur today. Pieces of bodies that had not been treated in any way would not simply be wrapped in cloth and taken home. They would be placed in a biohazard container, as they could be a source of disease. In addition, who would want a finger or a hand that would decay while on display? If such an item were placed in a church, patrons could each day marvel as they watched the flesh turn green and then black. They could pray in front of it, thinking about the saint whom it belonged to, while decay set it and it began to fester and reek. Then, when the black and smelly flesh dripped off the hand, would it be left in the reliquary for believers to enjoy or would it be removed by clergy members so that no one became sick to their stomachs? Certainly, the natural processes of decay are not pleasant to behold. No matter how great the individual was in life, decomposition is a dreadful occurrence and no one wishes to behold the spectacle firsthand.

However, we know that many individuals deemed saints were actually embalmed before their entombment. When the bodies were preserved and the natural processes of decay were halted, the removal and taking of relics would then no longer be as much of a problem. In other words, if the relics were prone to decay, then the relics themselves would be a source of disease and (possibly) disgust — not the traits that accord with the Christian concept of the saint. But if the bodies were embalmed before the collection of relics, the transport and translation of these objects would then be less vile. For this reason, bodies had to be preserved after death. No one in their right mind would take relics from a decaying body and then just hope that they did not become ill. Bodies were mummified for the safe removal of relics, but they were also preserved so that the relics themselves would endure. Since they were a source of miraculous powers, the Church wanted them to endure forever.

47

Foreign Influences

Early Christianity was influenced by a number of other religions outside of the Judeo-Christian tradition. The Pythagorean school was popular in Italy, and there is evidence of its influence in the Bible, where its sacred numbers are prominently featured. Likewise, myths and legends surrounding the gods and goddesses of Greece, Rome, and Egypt influenced Christian practices and historical accounts. So much has been absorbed from other traditions, in fact, that many historians have theorized that Jesus did not even exist — that he was a compiled myth with origins in earlier traditions. Historically, nothing was known about the individual, and the time period in which he lived is still debated. Therefore, it is not surprising that historical data were taken from other traditions and applied to this savior-god. Just because some ideas were borrowed and adapted to fit the ideas of Christianity, however, does not mean that Jesus did not exist. In fact, there is just as much evidence to support the existence of Jesus as there is of Osiris, Tammuz, and other resurrected deities. In other words, if Osiris is likely to have existed, there is no reason to suppose that Jesus did not exist, since the amount of evidence supporting both claims is comparable. The early Christian scholar Origen (c. 185–254), to whom the arrangement of the New Testament was largely credited, explained this. He noted that stories of miracles and the like that were told of Jesus were also told of many pagan gods. The stories attributed to the pagan gods were thought to have been true. Therefore, since they were considered historically accurate with reference to older gods, they could also be true when talking about Jesus (Mangasarian, 2004).

Ideas about the birth, resurrection, and miracles of Jesus are found in earlier traditions, and therefore, the story of Jesus is nothing new. The Christian historian and Church father Justin Martyr (103–165) clearly explained this to worshippers of other gods: "When we say also that the Word, which is the first birth of God, was produced without sexual union, and that he, Jesus Christ, our teacher, was crucified, died, and rose again, and ascended into heaven, we propound nothing different from what you believe regarding those who you esteem sons of Jupiter" (Apology 1:11). He explicitly stated that the Jesus story is not different from the religious myths of other (pagan) traditions. Therefore, pagan believers should not have a problem believing the new Christian myths or even joining the faith.

Once Christianity gained a foothold, it banned other religions. Constantine, the first Christian emperor, who murdered his father-in-law; eldest son, Crispus; and wife, Fausta, wished to consolidate and expand his reign (Schaff, 1890). He did so under the banner of Christianity, a faith that fulfilled his sanguine desires. "He eventually decided to impose it upon all his subjects and to extirpate every other faith" (Foote and Wheeler, 1887). He

Obelisks, like this one in front of the Church of Saint Mary over Minerva, provide evidence of the influence that other cultures had on the development of Italian religion (Florence, Italy).

made heresy a crime punishable by death, and anyone who spoke out against Christianity was burned to death. "The Church in subsequent ages took ample advantage of the opportunity that Constantine created, and remorselessly burnt heretics at the stake for the glory and honor of God" (Foote and Wheeler, 1887). These penalties were first put into place after the Church Council of Nicea, when the Nicene Creed was ratified to encourage the burning of books about other faiths or against Christianity and the burning of heretics or those who failed to burn such books. Constantine said the following about one non-believer named Arius who spoke out against Christianity:

> If any book composed by Arius shall be found, it shall be delivered to the fire, that not only his evil doctrine may be destroyed, but that there may not be the least remembrance of it left. This also I enjoin, that if anyone shall be found to have concealed any writing composed by Arius, and shall not immediately bring it and consume it in the fire, death shall be his punishment: for as soon as ever he is taken in this crime, he shall suffer capital punishment. God preserve you [Chandler, 1813].

Using such tactics, Christianity flourished. It took ideas from other faiths, including the ideas of the Holy Trinity, the Virgin Birth, and the savior-god, and then stamped out the other religions from which they originated. It might seem that the study of such ancient traditions and beliefs is a sad thing, as ancient gods who once were esteemed are now forgotten. However, the story of Jesus is a compilation of stories of previous gods, who were likewise born of virgin mothers on December 25 in caves and who similarly died and were resurrected after three days. Gods like Osiris were worshipped in many countries, and they were referred to by many different names. It is probable, however, that all of these names

Another obelisk located at the top of the Spanish Steps, a popular place for young people to relax, drink, and play music (Rome, Italy).

were used to refer to the same original deity who existed in the ancient past. Other gods were simply different incarnations of the ancient god. Perhaps the newest incarnation is Jesus. The ancient gods are not dead; they live on through Christianity. Similarly, traditions found in Christianity have origins in other religions, and thus they continue. They do not die.

The custom of preserving the bodies of the dead is found in Jewish traditions, as it is found in Egyptian religious traditions, both of which had strong influences on the shaping of early Christian beliefs and practices. For this reason, the practice of mummification is still found in Christianity. It is a tradition that has carried on. Traditions are handed down and continued without thought. People might not be able to explain why they do the things that they do, but it makes them feel better to do them. When it comes to bodily preservation, very few people could actually explain why they want it done, but the behavior of individuals suggests that it is extremely important. There are soldiers who risk their lives and the lives of many others only to retrieve the dead bodies of their fallen comrades. The importance of the physical remains cannot be doubted.

Grieving parents wish to look upon their dead children one last time before burial, and they want the bodies to appear as they did in life. Important individuals, like politicians and religious figures, are often mummified. Followers want the bodies preserved. They want to be able to look at the remains for years, decades, or even centuries. However, if they were asked why, they may not be able to answer. They do not know. It just is.

Such ideas have been absorbed from earlier traditions, and they are so infused in the minds and hearts of followers that there is no thought necessary. Thought might not even be possible. It is just so familiar of a custom that continuing to do it makes believers feel more at ease. In this way, practices from other faiths are absorbed into new ones and continued. All individuals are influenced and shaped by their past experiences. The same holds true in the development of religions. No religion is developed in a vacuum. There are cultural elements, folklore, and traditions from other religions that are typically adopted. The custom of mummification was adopted from Jewish and Egyptian traditions alike and modified to meet the needs of the new Christian religion. It still exists in modern Catholicism today.

48

Enduring Virtuosity

The purpose of hagiographies is not to create an accurate historical account. It is more important to create a perfect exemplar — a model that others can follow. Catholics deemed great often lived virtuous lives, and they were highly respected and admired by those who knew them. Sometimes, their kind exploits and deeds of charity were well known even outside of their own towns and countries and they came to be admired by countless individuals. However, everything is temporary. Life is short, and death is something that affects all. Saints and other holy people are admired through generations, but eventually time stops lengthy consideration and ultimately erases all memories. Historical accounts can help to preserve such knowledge of the past, but humans by nature need something more than written words in order to establish a true connection. When the bodies of important individuals are still in existence, they become a constant reminder of the attributes that such individuals possessed. Reading about the life of a saint, who has no image, can provide background historical information, but viewing the body, while learning about him or her, makes the experience more powerful. The bodies of the dead become symbols — living symbols, for although they themselves are dead, they continue to influence the living. They become relic-bodies of an ideal that others still hold high, one that is still valued and considered important.

Important individuals in many countries have been embalmed or mummified in other ways to fulfill such roles. They include important heads of state, like Mao Zedong and Vladimir Lenin, and religious leaders like the Dalai Lamas and popes. Heads of state are sometimes preserved when they are considered important enough. When their impact in life continued to affect the masses after death, the bodies were conserved. Vladimir Lenin, for example, did not want to be mummified. He specifically asked not to be preserved, and he thought that honoring the physical bodies of revolutionaries was not only improper but also unnecessary. It was better, he believed, for individuals to bury and to forget about the physical bodies and to concentrate on the revolutionaries' ideas instead. However, "when the body can be made to serve a higher purpose, such as symbolizing a country's ideology, it is put to use despite the wishes of its former occupant or his or her next of kin" (Quigley, 1998, p. 27).

Against his wishes, his body was preserved after his death by a panel of experts, and a special mausoleum was created in order to house the remains. It is temperature and moisture controlled, so that the body stays mummified for as long as possible, and the body continues to be cared for today. Every 18 months, the body is undressed, examined for signs of decay, which are treated, and then immersed for an entire month in a bath of glycerin and potassium

The relics of Beata Umiliana dei Cerchi. An artistic rendering of her head appears on the altar, while her bones are enshrined beneath. They are visible so that believers can feel closer to her. Her remains are located at Santa Croce, in Florence, Italy.

The body of St. Joachim, at the Church of St. Ignacio de Loyola (Florence, Italy).

acetate (Quigley, 1998). This procedure continues to be carried out regularly to protect a body that is considered important to a nation.

What are the psychological reasons behind the veneration of a corpse? This is a difficult question to answer. Something deep within the nature of human beings makes them unwilling to give up the physical remains of those who they love and honor. It may seem to many that the destruction of the body makes things more final. If the body was not gone but still present among the living for years after death, however, then the person who once utilized it is also nearby. He or she can still influence the living. This might not be a metaphysical concept but a mere psychological one. When followers of an important religious individual kneel in front of his or her remains, meditating on his or her virtues and teachings, it does not seem like the deceased is far away. He or she might seem nearby, because the physical remains are still extant. These bodies are like living statues. They are representations of the people, yet they actually are them on a physical level. This is a strange concept, because although followers know that the individuals have died, it is not like they are really gone. The bodies are still present, and their stories are still told. In this way, they live on. Although their souls may have departed long ago, since their physical bodies linger, they still exist in this life. For followers, they are not gone, even though they have moved on.

Saints, priests, bishops, popes, and others are lying in state all over Italy. In some cases, the skin is perfectly preserved, along with the bodies. In other cases, the skin has darkened substantially or even decayed, but the bodies are still dressed as though they were alive. They wear religious robes or habits and jewelry or other expensive items that are indicative of either the position they held in life or the honor that others showed them after death. Many of the individuals are looked upon as holy people close to God. They remind people that death cannot be avoided. However, they also serve as a constant reminder that even though life is short, it is significant.

49

Symbols of Life and Death

Life is short, and time does not stop. It rages on, relentless, and sweeps human beings along with it. Some of them do not try to fight the flow. They live their lives moment by moment, without looking back. These are people who find true happiness. They are not bound by the past, and the future is without limit. There are other people, however, who find themselves in unhappy circumstances. They do not recognize the true nature of life and death, of growth and decay, and they look at them in terms of good and bad. These people cannot see them for what they really are: simply different facets of the same phenomenon.

These people cannot let go of the past, and for them the future is uncertain. They may believe that they cannot change their own fate and that their life circumstances are given to them by outside sources and cannot be altered. They cannot take initiative in modifying their own circumstances, because they do not recognize that their circumstances are theirs to change.

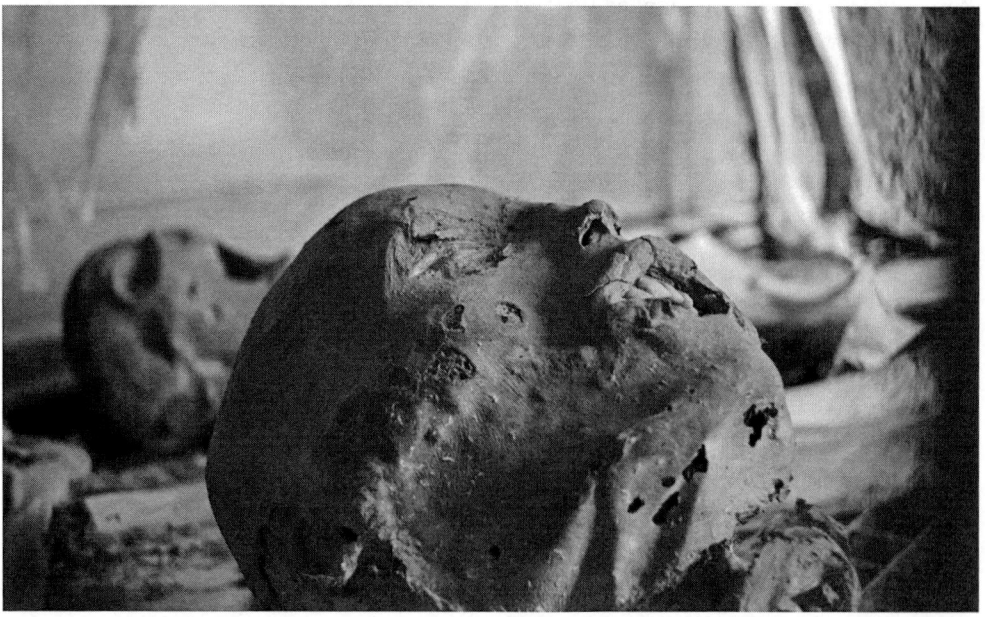

Death will affect all. Mummies, whether they were created naturally or artificially, are a constant reminder of this fact (Ferentillo, Italy).

A possible description of this distinction is "internal responsibility" versus "external responsibility," and it is a topic that is worthy of scholarly inquiry. People who have internal responsibility blame themselves when something goes wrong. If they did not get a job that they wanted, they look at their résumé. Perhaps they do not have adequate experience or education, or perhaps they were not model employees in their previous jobs. They hold themselves responsible, and they make changes within themselves to effect changes in their lives.

People who hold on to external responsibility, however, do not see such occurrences as being caused by themselves. The responsibility and the blame for life's occurrences are directed outward. If they did not have the educational background to obtain a high-paying job, they might blame a divine source for not giving them adequate intelligence or they might blame their parents for not stressing the importance of an education for future success. If they get fired from a job, rather than looking at their productivity or the number of times they called in sick, they will look outside themselves and think that perhaps their boss simply did not like them or that God was punishing them for something.

The nature of the world does not change. It is the same, but depending upon a person's viewpoint, it will seem different. An angry person who walks into a room of people might see others as also being angry, while a happy person will perhaps believe that everyone else is happy. In a sense, a person's perception of the world actually influences reality. For example, people who are surrounded by Christianity their entire lives will likely believe that it provides an accurate depiction of the cosmos. People who have been surrounded by Islam or Hinduism, on the other hand, will most likely believe that their teachings are the true

Consider the true purpose of religions worldwide. The crucifix is a symbol of both life and death, resurrection and redemption (Florence, Italy).

metaphysical explanations. For all of these people, the world did not change, but since their perceptions are different, their notions of the universe are diverse. It appears different to them. However, the truth is right in front of everyone. It is in plain sight, yet no one can see it clearly. This is because they are too caught up in form and appearance.

It should be remembered that the original purpose of all religions was not political. It was not to incite violence. Rather, it was to explain the cosmos and the world that we all inhabit. All religions had this same original charge, and yet unfortunately, many have strayed from this. Reade (1861) wrote: "There is no study so saddening and none so sublime as that of the early religions of mankind. To trace back the worship of God to its simple origin, and to mark the gradual process of those degrading superstitions, and unhallowed rites which darkened, and finally extinguished His presence in the ancient world." Whatever a person's beliefs, the original purpose of all faiths was the same. They did not cast people out. Neither did they kill nor give in to ego. There was no idea that they alone had access to the truth, and that all other beliefs were wrong. This misguided belief, which has been the source of death and destruction for years, stems from the arrogance of human beings. Its nature is not divine. Perhaps, the only thing necessary for the salvation of all, is to recognize the similarities in faiths, and not the differences.

Mummification is a similarity found in many religious traditions. Maybe by exploring the reasons behind it we can better understand the true nature of humankind. In the Christian tradition, there are various reasons why mummification was utilized. Jesus himself was embalmed, so it is natural that his followers emulate him in this manner. There are scriptural reasons why mummification was necessary, since the physical remains were needed at the end of time. They would be reconstituted before becoming spiritual bodies. Another need for bodily preservation stems from the uncertain nature of the human soul. An early belief

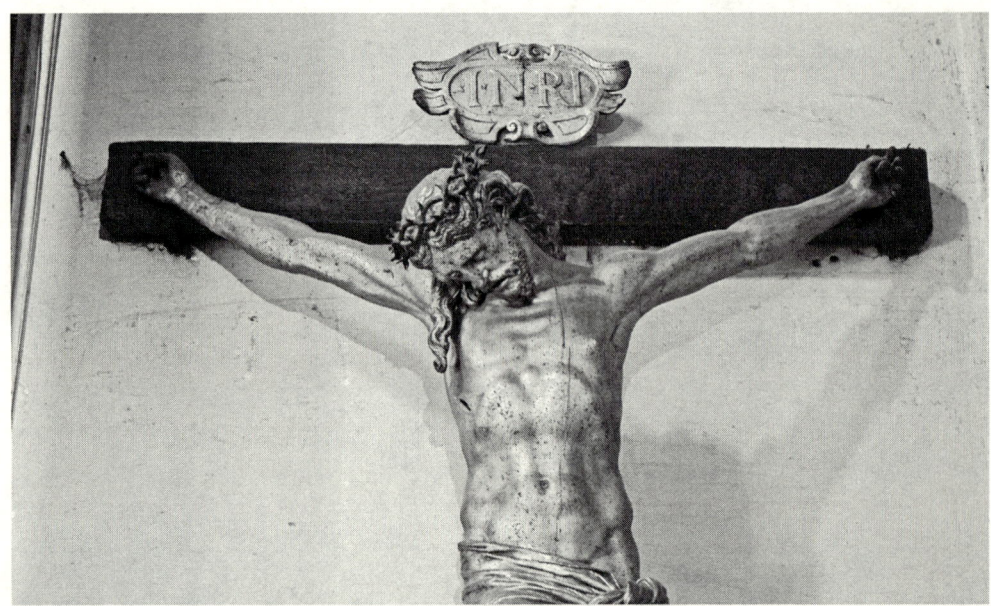

The Crucifixion (Florence, Italy). This image helps believers to recall the virtues that Jesus had. The mummified bodies of saints, beati, and venerables help to do the same.

that has not completely dissipated held that the soul was composed of multiple aspects. Part of it left the body after death, while part of it remained in the physical remains. Therefore, mummification was needed to maintain the existence of this spiritual essence in the world. Since the remains were infused with this spiritual essence, which could cause miracles, parts of the bodies were removed and sent to other locations for the protection and benefit of all living people. In order to safely transfer and enshrine these relics, they had to be preserved. For this reason, the bodies were embalmed before the relics were taken.

Other reasons why bodies were mummified in Christianity are found in other religious traditions that influenced the development of the faith. Mummification was performed in the Jewish and Egyptian traditions, and both of these religions had a strong influence on Christianity. Perhaps the most important reason behind the practice of mummification in Christianity, however, is the significance of such bodies for the living. The remains serve as a constant reminder of the virtues that the individuals had — virtues that are admired and that others aspire toward. The mummies also are reminders of the transitory nature of life. Everyone will die, so it is important to live life to the fullest, and to do nothing that will later be regretted. These two final explanations for the practice of mummification are found in religions all over the world and are significant. The bodies continue to speak to the living long after death. They remind us all that although human life is short, what we do in that small window of time can have far-reaching effects.

Appendix: Locations of Select Mummies or Bodily Relics in Italy

Amandola
Antonio da Amandola (1355–1450), Church of St. Agostino

Ancona
Gabriele Ferretti (1385–1456), San Giovanni Battista
Silvestro Guzzolini (1177–1267), Monastery of Montefalco (Marche)

Arezzo
Margaret of Cortona (1247–1297), Sanctuary of Saint Margaret in Cortona
Giustina Bezzoli (c. 1257–1319), Santa Maria del Fiore
Ugolino da Cortona (c. 1320–1367), Church of St. Agostino
Veronica Laparelli (1537–1620), Santissima Trinità

Assisi
Clare of Assisi (c. 1193–1253), Basilica of Santa Chiara of Assisi
Francis of Assisi (1181–1226), Basilica of Santa Chiara of Assisi

Avellino
Giulio da Nardò (?–1601), Sanctuary of Montevergine
Guglielmo da Vercelli (1085–1142), Montevergine

Bari
Ambrogio Grittani (1907–1951), Molfetta
Girolamo Pallantieri (1533–1619), Catthedrale of Bitonto
Maria Chiara (1909–1948), Clarisse Mon. at Albano Laziale

Bologna
Caterina da Bologna (1413–1463), Church of Corpus Domini
Domenico da Guzman (1170–1221), unknown
Elena Duglioli dall'Olio (1472–1520), San Giovanni in Monte
Prudenziana Zagnoni (1583–1608), Church of Santi Bartolomeo e Gaetano

Brescia
Angela Merici (1474–1540), Casa S. Angela

Bucchianico
Camillo De Lellis (1550–1614), Sanctuary of Bucchianico

Cagliari
Salvatore da Horta (1520–1567), Church of Saint Rosalia

Cagnore
Lorenza Mantovani della Cagnore, Church of Cagnore

Camerino
Battista Varano (1458–1524), Church of Clarisse

Capri
Serafina (Prudenza Pisa) di Dio, Ex Cattedrale di Santo Stefano

Castello
Margherita da Città (1287–1320), Church of San Domenico

Corato
Luisa Piccareta (1865–1947), Santa Maria Greca

Cosenza
Giovanni da Castrovillari (c. 1480–1530), Parish of Saint Francis of Assisi

Enna
Angelo Lo Musico (1540–1610), Church of Santa Maria di Gesù

Florence
Alessio Strozzi (1349–1383), Santa Maria Novella
Andrea Corsini (1301–1373), Basilica del Carmine
Antonio da Firenza (1389–1459), Basilica of St. Marco
Domenica del Paradiso (1473–1555), Monastery of Crocetta
Filippo Benizi (1233–1285), Santa Maria del Fiore
Giuliana Falconieri (1270–1341), Basilica of Santa Annunziata
Giustina Bezzoli (c. 1257–1319), Santa Maria del Fiore
Mary Magdalen de' Pazzi (1566–1607), Carmelite Church, Careggi
Mary Bagnesi (1514–1577), Carmelite Church, Careggi
Teresa Margaret (1747–1770), Monastery of St. Teresa

Foggia
Maria Celeste Costarosa (1966–1755), Monastero Redenturista
Padre Pio (1887–1968), San Giovanni Rotondo

Genoa
Catherine of Genoa (1447–1510), St. Catherine (Annunziata) of Genoa
Ilario Cales (1573–1636), Church of Santa Croce

Sebastiano Maggi (1414–1496), Santa Maria di Castello
Virginia Centurione Bracelli (1587–1651), Monte Calvario

Laurenzana

Egidio da Laurenzana (1443–1518), Santa Maria Assunta

Lucca

Zita (1218–?), Cattedrale di San Frediano

Macerata

Damiano da Cingoli (1875–1936)

Mantova

Anselmo da Baggio (c. 1040–1086), Cathedral of Mantova
Arcangela Girlani (1460–1495), Cathedral of Mantova
Bartolomeo Fanti (c. 1428–1495), Cathedral of Mantova
Giacomo di Mantova (d. 1332), Cathedral of Mantova
Osanna of Mantua (1449–1505), Cathedral of Mantova

Messina

Antonio Franco (1585–1626), S. Lucia del Mela
Nicolo Politi (1117–1167), unknown

Milan

Anthony Maria Zaccaria (1502–1539), Church of St. Barnabas
Charles Borromeo (1538–1584), Cathedral of Milan
Giovannangelo Porro (1451–1505), Convent of St. Carlo
Maria Catterina Brugora (1489–1529), Monastery of Saint Margherita

Montecerignone

Domenicoda Randazzo (1450–1521), Church of Santa Maria in Recluso

Montefiascone

Lucy Filippini (1672–1732), St. Margaret's Cathedral

Monza

Gerardo Tintori (c. 1135–1207), Church of Monza

Naples

Andrea Avellino (1521–1608), Church of San Paolo Maggiore
Angela Iacobellis (1948–1961), San Giovanni Battista
Egidio Maria di San Giuseppe (1729–1812), Convent of San Pasquale a Chiaia
Francesco Caracciolo (1563–1608), Church of Santa Maria Maggiore
Francesco di Sant'Antonio (1680–1764), Mon. di Santa Lucia al Monte
Francis of Naples (1763–1841), Basilica of Saint Peter
Giacomo della Marca (1394–1476), Sanctuary of the Madonna delle Grazie

Maria Cristina di Savoia (1812–1836), Basilica of Santa Chiara
Maria Giuseppina (1894–1948)
Maria Lorenza Longo (1463–1539)
Nunzio Sulprizion (1817–1836), Chiesa di Santa Domenico Soriano
Orsola Benincasa (1547–1618), Church of Immaculate Conception

Narni

Lucy of Narni (1476–1544), Cathedral of Narni

Onda

Vincent Pallotti (1795–1850), Church of St. Salvadore

Padua

Antonio da Padova (c. 1195–1231, Basilica of Padova
Beatrice da Calaone (1215–1239), Monastery of Gemmola
Beatrice da Gemmola (1206–1226), Monastery of Gemmola
Elena Enselmini (1207–1241), Sanctuary of Arcella
Eustochio Bellini (1444–1469), Church of St. Peter
Gregorio Giovanni Barbarigo (1625–1697), Duomo di Padova
Leopoldo Mandic (1866–1942), Cappuccini Ordini

Palermo

Benedetto Manasseri (1526–1589), Church of Santa Maria di Gesù
Benedict the Moor (1526–1589), Church of Santa Maria di Gesù
Bernardo da Corleone (1605–1667), Chiesa dei Cappuccini
Giorgio Guzzetta (1682–1756), Cattedrale dell'Eparchia
Nicolo Sciortino (1705–1772), Chiesa dei Cappuccini

Perugia

Arcangelo Canetoli (1460–1513), Monastery of St. Ambrogio
Chiara da Montefalco (1268–1308), Monastery of Santa Chiara (Montefalco)
Giovanni da Lodi (c. 1025–1105), Cathedral of Gubbio
Leopoldo da Gaiche (1732–1815), Monteluco di Spoleto
Maria Teresa (1881–1947), Cascia Basilica
Pietro da Gubbio (c. 1211–c. 1306), Chiesa degli Agostinani
Rita da Cascia (c. 1381–1457), Cascia Basilica
Ubaldo da Gubbio (c. 1084–1160), Basilica of Saint Ubaldo sul Monte Ingino

Pisa

Ranieri da Pisa (1118–1161), Cathedral of Pisa

Potenza

Domenico Lentini (1770–1828), Chiesa di San Nicola di Lauria
Giovanni da Chiaromonte (c. 1280–1338), Church of Chiaromonte

Prato

Catherine dei Ricci (1522–1590), Basilica of Prato

Ragusa
Maria Candida (1884–1949), Albano

Reggio Calabria
Gaetao Catanoso (1879–1963), Volto Santo

Rieti
Filippa Mareri (c. 1195–1236), Monastery of Santa Chiara
Massimo Rinaldi (1869–1941), Cattedrale di Santa Maria

Rome
Anna Maria Taigi (1769–1837), Basilica of St. Chrysogono
Antonietta Meo (1930–1937), Church of Santa Croce in Gerusalemme
Catherine of Siena (1347–1380), Church of Santi Giovanni e Paolo
Elisabetta Canori Mora (1774–1825), Chiesa di San Carlino
Felice da Cantalice (1513–1587), Church of the Immaculate Conception
Filippo Neri (1515–1595), Chiesa Nuova
Francesca Romana (1384–1440), Church of Santa Maria Nova
Francesco Antonio Placidi (1655–1729), Ritiro di Bellegra
Francesco Saverio (1506–1552), Church of Jesus
Giancarlo Marchionne (1613–1670), Convento di San Francesco a Ripa
Giuseppe Labre (1748–1783), Santa Maria de Monti
Giuseppe Maria Tomasi (1649–1713), Chiesa dei Teatini, Rome
Josaphat (1580–1623), St. Peter's Basilica
Leonardo da Porto Maurizio (1676–1751), Chiesa di San Bonaventura al Palatino
Maria Gabriella Sagheddu (1914–1939), Grottaferrata
Philip Neri (1515–1595), Chiesa Nuova
Pietro della Madre di Dio (1565–1608), Convent of Santa Maria della Scala
Pietro Fioretti (1668–1750), Church of the Immaculate Conception
Stanislao Kostka (1550–1568), Church of Saint Andrea at Quirinale
Stefano Bellesini (1774–1840), Santuario del Buon Consiglio (Genazzano)

Salerno
Donato da Ripacandida (1179–1198), Church of San Nicola

Sanremo
Giorgio Baldassarre Oppezzi (1503–1525), Parish of St. Mary of the Angels

Siena
Agnese da Montepulciano (1268–1317), Sanctuary of Saint Agnese at Montepulciano
Francesco da Siena (1266–1328), Basilica dei Servi

Taranto
Francesco de Geronimo (1642–1716), Chiesa dei Gesuiti di Gottaglie

Trento
Maria Domenica Lazzeri (1815–1848), Capriana

Trino Vercellese
Arcangela Girlani (1460–1495), Church of St. Lorenzo

Turin
Alessandro da Ceva (1538–1612), Church of Pecetto
Luigi Comollo (1817–1839)
Maria degli Angeli (1661–1717), Mon. di Moncalieir

Vengono
Alfredo Ildefonso Schuster (1880–1954), Vengono, Varese

Venice
Agostino di Biella (1430–1493), Parish of San Giacomo (Biella)
Giordano Forzate (1158–1248), Parish of San Benedetto
Giovanni Olini (d. 1300), Duomo di San Biagio (Istria)
Giuliana da Collalto (1186–1262), Church of St. Eufemia
Lorenzo Giustiniani (1381–1456), Church of St. Peter

Verona
Maddalena di Canossa (1774–1835), San Giuseppe Convent
Maria Domenica Mantovani (1862–1934), Castelletto di Brenzone

Chapter Notes

Part I

Chapter 1
1. Except for those religious traditions that develop separately from other religions and ideas due to geographical barriers. For example, if a small village is cut off from surrounding people and is completely isolated, it may be considered that their religious traditions developed independently from other traditions. It would still be necessary, however, to rule out possible influences made in the distant past.

Chapter 2
1. Interestingly, the archaic meaning of the term "embalm" is "to give a pleasant fragrance to."

Chapter 3
1. A chancel is the part of a church near the altar that is reserved for the choir or clergy members.

Chapter 4
1. However, the Church and the Vatican are not subject to Italian laws.

Chapter 5
1. Quoted in Bingenheimer, 2005.
2. See my book *Living Buddhas: The Self-Mummified Monks of Yamagata, Japan* (2010) for more information about these individuals.

Chapter 6
1. Many of the monks in China, Japan, and other East Asian countries were unearthed after three years. The number three is significant in Buddhism, as it is in Christianity, and it refers to the three treasures: the Buddha, the Dharma, and the Sangha. In addition, in Shingon Buddhism there are the three mysteries, which are the mysteries of the Dharmakaya's body, speech, and mind. These can be unlocked and revealed by means of the three secret techniques: *mudras* (finger positions), *dharani* (secret verses), and *yoga* (meditative discipline).

Chapter 7
1. Some might argue against the resurrection of the body in Buddhism. Of course, reincarnation is a dogmatic element of Buddhism, so the soul lives on forever. It is inexhaustible. However, the body is seen as nothing more than a shell. So, the body is not considered to be resurrected. Physical remains, though, decay and are eventually reduced to dust. They become one with everything else, and therefore, even though the original form is not maintained, the elements of the body do continue on. They continue in a different form, just as the soul does not perpetuate the existence of the individual from incarnation to incarnation, but they do endure.

Part II

Chapter 8

1. There are many books available that explore the scientific capabilities and spiritual knowledge of ancient civilizations, and such books provide evidence that such civilizations had an incredible amount of knowledge, the origin of which is not easily explained. Some individuals have taken the evidence of such capabilities as proof that aliens had visited this planet in the distant past, conveying knowledge to humankind. It is beyond the scope of this book to get into the technological advancements of ancient civilizations in great detail, but it might suffice to say that some authors have determined that various ancient civilizations have recorded the following capabilities: superior astronomical knowledge, lightbulbs, aircraft and nuclear weapons, and unusual communication devices. Any book that explores the existence of ancient aliens can point interested readers in the correct direction. One very interesting book is *There Were Giants upon the Earth: Gods, Demigods, and Human Ancestry: The Evidence of Alien DNA*, by Zecharia Sitchin (2010), but there are many more like it.

2. Quoted in Amdur, 2009.

3. It is human nature to try to fill in the gaps, because people do not like mysteries left unanswered. This causes a potential problem. It is quite possible that some of the things that we know about the history of life on this planet are wrong—completely wrong—and yet the majority of people might never consider alternatives that are different from the current understanding of history. Instead of trying to fit new information into the existing structure of history and then casting it out as something unexplainable if it doesn't fit, it is far better to rethink and rework history based on new information. The following is an example that will be explored in more detail later: The majority of people in the Western world believe that Jesus of Nazareth did not have brothers or sisters. However, there is no historical evidence to support this. In fact, there is historical documentation to support the claim that he had brothers and sisters. Such evidence is found in the writings of Josaphat and in the biblical Gospel of St. Matthew.

4. There are many chambers in Egyptian pyramids in which sunlight cannot enter, but there are some that are so deep and far away from fresh air that even torches cannot be lit. If researchers enter with torches in their hands, by the time they reach certain chambers the fires will have been extinguished. Yet these chambers contain elaborate paintings, one of which looks very much like a lightbulb. This has led some researchers to suggest that the ancient Egyptians actually had lightbulbs. This is one of the only theories that explain the phenomenon. Otherwise, how could the rooms have been lit? However, there are many people out there who would likely dismiss this theory as nonsense only because it does not fit the mold of what they think they know about this civilization. They do not have open minds, and therefore (to borrow the words of the ancients), the truth will never be revealed to them.

5. The official Web site for the catacombs is http://www.catacombe.roma.it. Tour information and hours of operation can be found at this site.

Chapter 9

1. Burying bodies or storing them in other places was a health concern for early Romans, and so cremation was the preferred method of disposing of the deceased. Early Christian beliefs, however, required the preservation of bodies, which was not healthy. This was one cause for concern that authorities had regarding early Christians.

Chapter 10

1. The definition of the term "martyr" will be loosely confined to the Catholic Church's definition and interpretation in this study.

2. Quoted in Kaufman, 1994, p. 7.

3. Martyr Polycarpi, xviii.

Chapter 11

1. This quote was taken from the City of Palermo Web site: http://www.palermoweb.com/sottopalermo/catacombe/cappuccini1.htm.

2. Why they did not want their bodies to decay is a question that will be explored in later chapters, as will the practice of artificial mummification by Christian monks.

Chapter 12

1. He is also referred to in some accounts as Antonio Pezzulla.
2. There is an unusual account of an occurrence that supposedly took place during the beheadings that is recorded in the *Compendiosa istoria degli ottocento martiri otrantini* (The brief history of the eight hundred martyrs of Otranto), written by Saverio de Marco. It involves the beheading of the tailor. According to this account, once his head was cut off, the body stood upright and was immovable. Some of the Ottoman soldiers thought that this was a miracle, a sign from the Christian God, and they converted on the spot. Those soldiers were immediately killed by their brethren, and the beheadings then continued. This account is of dubious historical accuracy.

Chapter 13

1. The Church officially issued certificates for relics up until 1952.

Chapter 14

1. Personal communication, October 2009.
2. Why this text and others like it were excluded from the Bible will be dealt with in subsequent chapters.
3. The linguistic problem that comes up is the connotation of the term "God" as defined by different cultures. In Christianity the term "God" is generally used to describe the creator of all things, but in other religious traditions a god does not have to be a creator.
4. Obviously, the relationships between all of these archetypal figures cannot be delineated in as simple a manner as I just presented it. This was done solely in order to facilitate understanding.
5. This will be explained more fully in the next part of this book.

Part III

Chapter 15

1. Saints are revered because the Church tells Catholics that they should be.

Chapter 16

1. At the onset of Christianity, however, all believers who had been baptized were considered saints (*hagioi* in Greek) and the denomination referred to the community of believers as a whole and not individual members of the faith.
2. Why Hoever used the Greek term "Christ" after the name Jesus is a subject to be discussed in later chapters.
3. An example of a magical practice in Roman Catholicism is the creation of holy water. A priest will perform a specific physical action with his hands and voice an incantation over the water, after which it allegedly becomes infused with magic powers. It ceases to be normal water and becomes holy water.
4. Here angels can be either good or evil. It should be remembered, too, that Satan was, in fact, an angel in heaven before he was cast out. This impending and ongoing war that exists between the two powers is of great importance in Catholic dogma, and it must be understood in order to properly comprehend the beliefs that underlie the practices of the faith. This struggle for dominance will be explored more fully in later chapters.

Chapter 17

1. In early Christianity, historical accuracy was not all that important when determining who was a saint. In the modern process, however, historical accuracy is important.
2. This would also explain why visions of different deities are reported in religions all over the world. Maybe there are not hundreds of different gods that appear before people of different faiths all across the globe. Maybe the images stem from the individuals' own minds and not from an outside source.

Chapter 18

1. It was also delayed due to some political reasons. There was a scandal that involved his brother. In addition, some Vatican officials suspected that Padre Pio's stigmatic wounds were actually self-inflicted or caused by psychological means, such as prolonged meditation on an image of the Passion of Christ.

2. For more information on his canonization, see http://www.vatican.va/news_services/liturgy/saints/ns_lit_doc_20020616_index_padre-pio_en.html.

Chapter 19

1. St. Teresa of Avila was another individual who inspired Padre Pio.

Chapter 21

1. Quoted in Brown, 1981.
2. According to canon law, it was acceptable to buy relics in order to save them from potential disgrace or destruction.

Part IV

Chapter 22

1. All of the ideas proposed in this part of the book by non-believers to discredit the notion of miraculous preservation come from Giuseppe Fallica's book on the Incorruptibles entitled *Il miracolo dei corpi incorrotti in 2000 anni di storia della Chiesa* [The miracle of incorruptible bodies in 2000 years of Church history] (2009).
2. Adipocere is also called mortuary wax or grave wax. Grayish-white or tan in color, it is a substance resembling wax that forms over the body as a result of the natural processes of decay. It is formed by the anaerobic bacterial hydrosis of fat cells found in the body.

Chapter 23

1. However, the body of St. Clare (c. 1193–1253), located in Assisi, was also seemingly covered with a silver mask and silver gloves. When the body was examined by Professor Fulcheri and three colleagues, they were shocked to discover there was no body there. It had decayed, but since she was an important person her bones had been put in a silver mannequin and face mask and then the mannequin had been dressed in her clothing, thus passing the display off as an Incorruptible (Pringle, 2001).

Chapter 25

1. Quoted in Fallica, 2009, p. 396.

Chapter 26

1. This has been paraphrased from the accounts found in hagiographies.

Chapter 28

1. It must always be remembered that the Church is a political organization, so it is not surprising that many of its motives are political.
6. This will be explained in detail in subsequent chapters.

Part V

Chapter 30

1. The Old Testament was written over a span of approximately 850 years, the earliest parts written c. 1313 B.C.E. and the newest parts approximately 450 B.C.E.
2. Enki is another name for Ea.
3. It seems as though God might not have had the power to call it off. This would not make sense unless we were actually talking about multiple deities.
4. There are some historians who have suggested that these individuals were not deities at all but were only interpreted as being gods because of their superior powers (Sitchen, 2010).

Chapter 31

1. The Chinese text is called the "Glass Mirror." There are 21 Muslim historical documents that refer to Jesus. In such texts, they call him Issa or Yuz Asaph. The Persian text is the *Kamul u-Din* by Said-

us-Saddiq, and the Kashmiri Hindu text is the *Bhavishya Maha Purana*, which relates an account of the Son of God. See Hassnain and Levi, 2006, for more information.

Chapter 32

1. However, some historians do not think that these stories are myths. Some believe that the characters thought of as being mythological may have been actual humans thought to have been close to God who existed in ancient times. One example is Osiris; many writers have posited that he was likely an actual person who lived and died and who was deified after his death.

2. Phyrgia was located in the area of modern-day Turkey.

Chapter 33

1. Mithraic inscription quoted in Freke and Gandy, 1999.

Chapter 34

1. This was paraphrased from Iamblichus of Chalcis's *Life of Pythagoras* (n.d.).

Chapter 35

1. Although Osiris is referred to as the judge of the dead, he did not judge the dead. He was merely present when a person's heart was placed on a scale and measured against the feather of Maat. Maat was a goddess of truth and justice.

Part VI

Chapter 36

1. Information found at http://www.crystalinks.com/pyramiditaly.html.

Chapter 37

1. The relationship has not completely dissipated today, as some Egyptian customs are found in Christianity.

Chapter 38

1. Another problem inherent in the study of Egyptian metaphysical ideas is the nature of hieroglyphs and the amount of time that passed before they could actually be translated and understood. Egyptian civilization was known by the Greeks and Romans from ancient times, but it was not until the nineteenth century that the written records of the Egyptians were actually translated and understood. The understanding that many historians had about the ancient Egyptian religious tradition was therefore formulated without consulting the Egyptian funerary papyri or any other document that explained their metaphysical views. For this reason, the information that we have from well-known historians is limited.

2 . A woman cannot perform this or any other ceremony in Catholic Christianity. The Church is a chauvinistic organization.

Chapter 39

1. It is interesting to note that the word "myrrh" is actually used as the word for mummy in some languages. In Japanese, for example, the Portuguese word for myrrh was adopted by the Japanese in order to classify preserved bodies. This word, *miira* in Japanese, indicates the worldwide knowledge that myrrh was used to effect bodily preservation. It is likely that the practice of using this herb in mummifications originated in Egypt.

2. The Egyptian practices of mummification were continued along with other methods of bodily preservation that are found in Jewish tradition. Beyond these two influences, there were unique forms of mummification utilized in Catholicism as well.

Chapter 40

1. Quoted from Mangasarian, 2004.

2. Herodotus (c. 490–431 B.C.E.) was possibly the first historian to have pointed out that these names

referred to the same deity, and he made the connection between Isis and Demeter, and Osiris and Dionysus.

Chapter 41

1. Quoted from http://overcomeproblems.com/about_the_rosary.htm.
2. Quoted from http://overcomeproblems.com/about_the_scapular.htm.

Part VII

Chapter 43

1. Joseph was also governor of Egypt.

Chapter 44

1. The actual text from the Book of Revelation reports that the man on the black horse had a pair of balances in his hand. I interpreted this as a scale, similar to the scale used by the Egyptian deity Maat to judge the morality of humankind.
2. The actual statement "suspended in the sky" is not in the Book of Revelation. However, it states that the mountains were removed from the earth and then the people in hiding called to the mountains, asking them to fall on top of the people in order to save them from the wrath of Jesus.
3. Athough the biblical translation is "star," it is unknown what this really is. It could be a type of angel or another creature that came from the heavens to earth, but the concept of a star here does not make sense. Earlier in his revelation, John mentions that the stars would fall from the sky to earth like figs from a fig tree. Perhaps, had he not understood the true nature of stars, he would have referred to small lights falling to the earth as stars. The true significance of this choice of words is not understood.
4. This is where the infamous number of 666 comes about, which is the number of the beast. What is interesting, however, is that in the Greek languages numbers were represented by letters. This statement might have been utilized to actually refer to a person who was alive at the time that this book was written. It could have been a political reference, just like those made by Dante Alighieri in his *Divine Comedy*.
5. Found at http://www.jesus-is-savior.com.
6. See http://www.catholicculture.org/culture/library/catechism/index.cfm?recnum=4663.
7. Quoted from http://www.religioustolerance.org/rapture3.htm.

Chapter 45

1. Quoted in Kaufman, 1994, p. 7.

Bibliography

Agnoli, F., M. Lucia, and A. Pertosa. 2008. *Santi e rivoluzionari* [Saints and revolutionaries]. Rome: Sugar & Company.
Ahern, E. 1973. *The Cult of the Dead in a Chinese Village*. Stanford: Stanford University Press.
Allegro, J. 1956. *The Dead Sea Scrolls*. New York: Penguin.
Amdur, E. 2009. *Hidden in Plain Sight: Tracing the Roots of Ueshiba Morihei's Power*. Shoreline, WA: Edgework.
Andō, K. 1963. "La mummia in Estremo Oriente [Mummies in the Far East]." *Il Giappone*, 3, 135–140.
———. 1968. "Des momies au Japon et de leur culte [On mummies in Japan and their cult]." *L'Homme*, 8, 5–18.
Aquinas, T. 1947. *Summa Theologica*. New York: Benzinger Brothers. Retrieved from http://www.ccel.org/ccel/aquinas/summa.i.html?highlight=summa,theologica#highlight.
Arriaza, B. 2010. "Momias Chinchorro: Patrimonio de Todos." Retrieved from http://www.momiaschinchorro.cl.
Arriaza, B., F. Cardenas-Arroyo, E. Kleiss, and J. Verano. 1998. "South American Mummies: Culture and Disease." In A. Cockburn, E. Cockburn, and T. Reyman (eds.), *Mummies, Disease and Ancient Cultures* (pp. 190–234). Cambridge: Cambridge University Press.
Arriaza, B., R. Hapke, and V. Standen. 1998. "Making the Dead Beautiful: Mummies as Art." *Archaeology*. Retrieved from http://www.archaeology.org/online/features/chinchorro.
Ascenzi, A., and P. Bianco. 1998. "The Roman Mummy of Grottarossa." In A. Cockburn, E. Cockburn, and T. Reyman (eds.), *Mummies, Disease and Ancient Cultures* (pp. 263–288). Cambridge: Cambridge University Press.
Ascenzi, A., P. Bianco, G. Fornaciari, and C. Rodriguez Martin. 1998. "Mummies from Italy, North Africa, and the Canary Islands." In A. Cockburn, E. Cockburn, and T. Reyman (eds.), *Mummies, Disease and Ancient Cultures* (pp. 263–288). Cambridge: Cambridge University Press.
Atkinson, J. 2010. "Essenes." *The Latter Rain Page*. Retrieved from http://latter-rain.com/Israel/essenes.htm.
Aufderheide, A., and M. Aufderheide. 1991. "Taphonomy of Spontaneous (Natural) Mummification with Applications to the Mummies of Venzone, Italy." In D. Ortner and A. Aufderheide (eds.), *Human Paleopathology, Current Syntheses and Future Options* (pp. 79–86). Washington, DC: Smithsonian Institution Press.
Bahn, P., and C. Renfrew. 1996. *Archaeology: Theories, Methods and Practice*. New York: Thames and Hudson.
Barber, R. n.d. "What Will Happen at the Rapture?" *Jesus-Is-Savior*. Retrieved from http://www.jesus-is-savior.com/Books,%20Tracts%20&%20Preaching/Printed%20Sermons/Dr%20Raymond%20Barber/what_will_happen_at_rapture.htm.
Barton, G. 1915. "Tammuz and Osiris." *Journal of the American Oriental Society*, 35, 213–223.
Baudrillard, J. 1979. *Lo scambio simbolico e la morte* [Symbolic exchange and death]. Milan: Feltrinelli.
Bertholet, A. 1916. "The Pre-Christian Belief in the Resurrection of the Body." *The American Journal of Theology*, 20(1), 1–31.
Beyer, B. 2008. "How to Teach Thinking Skills in Social Studies and History." *The Social Studies*, September/October, 196–201.
Bharati, A. 1971. "Anthropological Approaches to the Study of Religion: Ritual and Belief Systems." *Biennial Review of Anthropology*, 7, 230–282.

Bingenheimer, M. 2005. "Roushen Pusa and Corpus Integrum — Whole Body Relics in Buddhism and Christianity." In *Proceedings of the Contribution of Buddhism to World Culture*. Mumbai: Somaiya.
Boresky, T. 1955. *Life of St. Josaphat: Martyr of the Union*. New York: Comet Press.
Boyer, O. 1958. *She Wears a Crown of Thorns*. NJ: Rev. O. A. Boyer.
Bradbury, R. 1978. *The Mummies of Guanajuato*. New York: Harry N. Abrams.
Brookfield, S. 1987. *Developing Critical Thinkers*. San Francisco: Jossey-Bass.
Brown, P. 1981. *The Cult of the Saints: Its Rise and Function in Latin Christianity*. Chicago: University of Chicago Press.
Budge, E. 1895. *The Book of the Dead: The Paprys of Ani*. "Sacred Texts." Retrieved from: http://www.sacred-texts.com/egy/ebod/.
Bunson, M. n.d. *How the 800 Martyrs of Otranto Saved Rome*. "Catholic Answers." Retrieved from http://www.catholic.com/thisrock/2008/0807fea2.asp.
Bynum, C. 1995. "Why All the Fuss About the Body? A Medievalist's Perspective." *Critical Inquiry*, 22(1), 1–33.
_____. 1996. *The Resurrection of the Body in Western Christianity*. New York: Columbia University Press.
Canetti, L. 2002. *Frammenti di eternità: Corpi e reliquie tra antichità e medioevo*. Rome: Viella.
Canonici, L. 1961. *Antonio Vici: Principe Conteso*. Assisi: Edizioni Porziuncola.
Capasso, L., and G. DiTota. 1991. "The Human Mummies of Navelli: Natural Mummification at a New Site in Central Italy." *Paleopathology Newsletter*, 75, 7–8.
Carrothers, B. (director). 1999. *Pillars of Faith: Martyrs to Christianity* [DVD]. Caledonian Pictures.
Catholic Apologetics. 2010. "Saints and Beati." Retrieved from http://www.catholicapologetics.info.
Centini, M. 2006. *Misteri d'Italia* [Mysteries of Italy]. Rome: Newton and Compton.
Chandler, S. 1813. *History of Persecution*. London: Longman. Retrieved at http://www.archive.org/details/historyofpersecu00chanuoft.
Chapin Metz, H. 1990. *Egypt: A Country Study*. Washington, DC: GPO for the Library of Congress. Retrieved from: http://countrystudies.us/egypt/.
Chesterton, G. 1924. St. Francis of Assisi. New York: Image.
Coles, R. 1987. *Dorothy Day: A Radical Devotion*. Reading, MA: Addison-Wesley.
Comte, D. 1919. "Saint Bernadette Soubirous Body Examination Testimony." Retrieved from http://overcomeproblems.com/bernadette_exam.htm.
_____. 1928. "Saint Bernadette Soubirous Body Examination Testimony." Retrieved from http://overcomeproblems.com/bernadette_exam.htm.
Conybeare, F. 1899. "The History of Christmas." *The American Journal of Theology*, 3(1), 1–21.
Cornell, T., R. Ellsberg, and J. Forest (eds.). 1995. *A Penny a Copy: Writings from the Catholic Worker*. New York: Orbis.
Cornwell, J. 1989. *A Thief in the Night: The Mysterious Death of Pope John Paul I*. New York: Simon & Schuster.
Craig, S. 1956. *Jesus of Yesterday and Today*. Philadelphia: The Presbyterian and Reformed Publishing Company.
Crapez, E. 1933. *Blessed Catherine Laboure: Daughter of Charity of Saint Vincent de Paul*. Emmitsburg, MD: St. Joseph's Provincial House.
Cruz, J. 1977. *The Incorruptibles: A Study of the Incorruption of Bodies of Various Catholic Saints and Beati*. Rockford, IL: Tan.
David, C., and D. Jourdan. 1909. "Saint Bernadette Soubirous Body Examination Testimony." Retrieved from http://overcomeproblems.com/bernadette_exam.htm.
David, R., and R. Archbold. 2000. *Conversations with Mummies*. New York: William Morrow.
Day, D. 1993. *The Long Loneliness*. Chicago: St. Thomas More Press.
Demiéville, P. 1965. "Momies d'Extrême-Orient [Mummies of the Far East]." *Journal des Savants*, 144–170.
Diodorus Siculus. 1935. *Library of History*, vol. 2, books 2.35–4.58. (Translated by C. H. Oldfather.) Loeb Classical Library no. 303, v. 2. Cambridge, MA: Harvard University Press.
Eberl, J. 2004. "Aquinas on the Nature of Human Beings." *The Review of Metaphysics*, 58(2), 333–365.
Eisenman, R. 1997. *James: The Brother of Jesus*. New York: Penguin.
Ellsberg, R. (ed.). 1992. *Dorothy Day: Selected Writings*. New York: Orbis.
Emerton, E. 1910. "The Religious Environment of Early Christianity." *The Harvard Theological Review*, 3(2), 181–208.

Eunapius of Sardis. 1921. *Lives of Philosophers and Sophists.* Retrieved from http://www.tertullian.org/fathers/eunapius_02_text.htm.

Fallica, G. 2009. *Il miracolo dei corpi incorrotti in 2000 anni di storia della Chiesa* [The miracle of incorruptible bodies in 2000 years of Church history]. Tavagnacco, Italy: Edizioni Segno.

Farnedi, G. 1996. *Guida ai santuari d'Italia* [Guide to the sanctuaries of Italy]. Casale Monferrato, Italy: Piemme.

Feuillet, A. 1983. "Flavius Josèphe, témoin des origins chrétiennes, a-t-il parlé du Christ?" *Téqui,* 93, 532–539.

_____. 1995. *En prière avec la Bible: Approfondissement scripturaire de quelques aspects fondamentaux de la vie chrétienne: Retraite de vie chrétienne.* Paris: Téqui.

_____. 1997. *Le sacerdoce du Christ et de ses ministres: D'après la prière sacerdotale du quatrième Évangile et plusieurs données parallèles du Nouveau Testament.* Paris: Téqui.

Filliozat, J. 1963. "La mort voluntaire par le feu et la tradition bouddhique indienne [Voluntary death based upon faith and Indian Buddhist tradition]." *Journal Asiatique,* 251(1), 21–51.

Fischer, C. 1998. "Bog Bodies of Denmark and Northwestern Europe." In A. Cockburn, E. Cockburn, and T. Reyman (eds.), *Mummies, Disease and Ancient Cultures* (pp. 237–262). Cambridge: Cambridge University Press.

Foote, G., and J. Wheeler. 1887. *Crimes of Christianity.* London: Progressive Publishing Company. Retrieved from http://www.ftarchives.net/foote/crimes/contents.htm.

Forest, J. n.d. *A Biography of Dorothy Day.* "The Catholic Worker Movement." Retrieved from http://www.catholicworker.org.

Fornaciari, G. 1984a. "The Mummies of the Abbey of Saint Domenico Maggiore in Naples." *Paleopathology Newsletter,* 45, 13–14.

_____. 1984b. "The Mummies of the Abbey of Saint Domenico Maggiore in Naples." *Paleopathology Newsletter,* 47, 10–14.

_____. 1997. "The Mummies of the Basilica of San Francesco in Arezzo (Tuscany, Central Italy)." *Paleopathology Newsletter,* 97, 13–14.

_____. 1998. "Italian Mummies." In A. Cockburn, E. Cockburn, and T. Reyman (eds.), *Mummies, Disease and Ancient Cultures* (pp. 266–281). Cambridge: Cambridge University Press.

Fornaciari, G., and S. Gamba. 1993. "The Mummies of the Church of S. Maria della Grazia in Comiso, Sicily (18th-19th Century)." *Paleopathology Newsletter,* 81, 7–10.

Foxe, J. 1563. *History of the Acts and Monuments of the Church.* Retrieved from http://www.ccel.org/f/foxe/martyrs/home.html.

Frankfurter, D. 1994. "The Cult of the Martyrs in Egypt Before Constantine: The Evidence of the Coptic 'Apocalypse of Elijah.'" *Vigiliae Christianae,* 48(1), 25–47.

Frazee, C. 1988. "The Origins of Clerical Celibacy in the Western Church." *Church History,* 57, 108–126.

Frazer, J. 1961. *Adonis, Attis, Osiris: Studies in the History of Oriental Religion.* New York: University Books.

Freke, T., and P. Gandy. 1999. *The Jesus Mysteries: Was the Original Jesus a Pagan God?* New York: Three Rivers Press.

Fulcheri, E. 1996. "Mummies of Saints." In Konrad Spindler, Harald Wilfing, Elisabeth Rastbichler-Zissernig, Dieter zur Nedden, and Hans Nothdurfer (eds.), *Human Mummies: A Global Survey of Their Status and the Techniques of Conservation.* New York: Springer-Verlag/Wien.

Gadalla, M. 2008. *The Ancient Egyptian Roots of Christianity.* (Kindle Edition.) Greensboro, NC: Tehuti Research Foundation.

Gagliardi, I. 2002. *Santi frati e corpi santi: Il Beato Antonio (Patrizi) da Monticiano.* Siena, Italy: Cantagalli.

Geary, P. 1978. *Furta Sacra: Thefts of Relics in the Central Middle Ages.* Princeton: Princeton University Press.

George, K., and C. George. 1955. "Roman Catholic Sainthood and Social Status: A Statistical and Analytical Study." *The Journal of Religion,* 35(2), 85–98.

Gibbon, E. 1909. *The Decline and Fall of the Roman Empire.* London: Methuen.

_____. 1960. *The Decline and Fall of the Roman Empire.* London: Everyman Editions (6 volumes).

Gilbert, E. 2007. *Eat, Pray, Love: One Woman's Search for Everything Across Italy, India, and Indonesia.* New York: Penguin.

Gilsenan, M. 1973. *Saint and Sufi in Modern Egypt.* Oxford: Clarenden Press.
Giusti, M. 1990. *Trenta santi più uno: C'è un posto anche per te* [Thirty saints plus one: There's a place for you, too]. Rome: San Paolo Edizioni.
Gladden, W. 2004. *Who Wrote the Bible?* (Kindle Edition.) Charleston, SC: Nabu Press.
Goguel, M. 1926. *Jesus the Nazarene: Myth or History?* London: Prometheus.
Goody, J. 1961. "Religion and Ritual: The Definitional Problem." *British Journal of Sociology,* 12, 142–164.
Gordon, C. 1971. *Before Columbus.* New York: Crown.
Greyson, B. 2007. "Consistency of Near-Death Experience Accounts over Two Decades: Are Reports Embellished over Time?" *Resuscitation,* 73(3), 407–411.
Gruber, E., and H. Kersten. 1995. *The Original Jesus: The Buddhist Sources of Christianity.* Rockport, MA: Element.
Guitton, J., and J. Antier, J. 1994. *Poteri misteriosi della fede* [Mysterious powers of faith]. Casale Monferrato, Italy: Piemme.
Habig, M. 1973. *St. Francis of Assisi: Writings and Early Biography.* Chicago: Franciscan Press.
Hancock, G. 1995. *Fingerprints of the Gods.* New York: Three Rivers Press.
Hansen, H. 1998. "Bodies from Cold Regions." In A. Cockburn, E. Cockburn, and T. Reyman (eds.). *Mummies, Disease and Ancient Cultures* (pp. 336–350). Cambridge: Cambridge University Press.
Hanson, J. 2005. "Was Jesus a Buddhist?" *Buddhist-Christian Studies,* 25, 75–89.
Harney, M. 1941. *The Jesuits in History: The Society of Jesus Through Four Centuries.* New York: The America Press.
Harris, J., and K. Weeks. 1973. *X-Raying the Pharaohs.* New York: Charles Scribner's Sons.
Hassnain, F., and D. Levi. 2006. *The Fifth Gospel: New Evidence from the Tibetan, Sanskrit, Arabic, Persian and Urdu Sources About the Historical Life of Jesus Christ After the Crucifixion.* New York: Blue Dolphin.
Hatch, E. 1890. *The Influence of Greek Ideas and Usages Upon the Christian Church.* London: Books LLC.
Herbermann, C.G., Pace, E.A., Pallen, C.B., Shahan, T.J., & Wynne, J.J. (Eds.) 1914. *The Catholic Encyclopedia: An International Work of Reference on the Constitution, Doctrine, Discipline, and History of the Catholic Church.* New York: Robert Appleton Co.
Heriz, P. 1919. *St. John of the Cross.* Washington, DC: College of Our Lady of Mount Carmel.
Herodotus. 1910. *History.* (Translated by G. Rawlinson.) London: Dent.
Hinson, G. 1996. *The Early Church.* Nashville: Abingdon Press.
Hoever, H. (ed.). 1955. *Lives of the Saints.* New York: Catholic Book Publishing.
Hofer, J. 1943. *St. John Capistran, Reformer.* St. Louis, MO: B. Herder.
Hoffman, Y. (ed). 1986. *Japanese Death Poems.* Tokyo: Tuttle.
Hufford, D. 2008. "Teacher Education, Transformation, and an Education for Discontent." *Journal of Philosophy and History of Education,* 58, 83–91.
Hume, D. 1875. *The Natural History of Religion.* Retrieved from http://stoa.usp.br/briannaloch/files/2564/16389/The+Natural+History+of+Religion+-+David+Hume.pdf.
Huskinson, J. 1974. "Some Pagan Mythological Figures and Their Significance in Early Christian Art." *Papers of the British School at Rome,* 42, 68–97.
Iamblichus of Chalcis. n.d. *Life of Pythagoras.* Retrieved from http://www.completepythagoras.net/mainframeset.html.
Jeremiah, K. 2007. "Asceticism and the Pursuit of Death by Warriors and Monks." *Journal of Asian Martial Arts,* 16(2), 18–33.
_____. 2010. "Buried Alive: The Forgotten Practice of Self-Mummification." *The Virginia Review of Asian Studies,* 195–209.
_____. 2010. *Living Buddhas: The Self-Mummified Monks of Yamagata, Japan.* Jefferson, NC: McFarland.
John of Damascus. 1898. *Expositions of the Orthodox Faith.* Retrieved from http://www.ccel.org/ccel/schaff/npnf209.iii.ii.html.
John Paul II, Pope. 1996. Speech given to the Pontifical Commission for Sacred Archaeology. Retrieved from http://www.catacombe.roma.it.
_____. 1998. Speech given to the Pontifical Commission for Sacred Archaeology. Retrieved from *http://www.catacombe*.roma.it.

Johnson, E., M. Johnson, and M. Johnson Williams. 1993. "The Salafia Method: Alfredo Salafia's Embalming Produced Long Term Success, but How Did He Do It?" *The American Funeral Director*, May, 24–25, 64–68.
Johnstone, G. (producer). 2009. *Who Was Jesus?* [DVD].
Justin Martyr. 1995. "Apology I." In R. Barclay (ed.), *Early Christian Fathers*. Retrieved from http://www.ccel.org/search/fulltext/apology.
Kaufman, P. 1994. "Augustine, Martyrs, and Misery." *American Society of Church History*, 63(1), 1–14.
Kelley, D. 1972. "Martyrs, Myths, and the Massacre: The Background of St. Bartholomew." *The American Historical Review*, 77(5), 1323–1342.
Kim, Y. 1973. *Oriental Thought: An Introduction to the Philosophical and Religious Thought of Asia*. Lanham, MD: Littlefield, Adams Quality Paperbacks.
Konig, G. 2006. *Christianity Was Not Influenced by Paganism: A Review and Response to Claims That Christianity Was Influenced by Paganism and Other Religions*. "About Jesus." Retrieved from http://www.about-jesus.org/paganism.htm.
Lamy, L. 1981. *Egyptian Mysteries*. New York: Thames and Hudson.
Lange, K. 2009. "Lost 'Sleeping Beauty' Mummification Formula Found." *National Geographic*. Retrieved from http://news.nationalgeographic.com/news/2009/01/090126-sicily-mummy.html.
Lanzi, F., and G. Lanzi. 2007. *Come riconoscere i santi e i patroni nell'arte e nelle immagini popolari* [How to recognize saints and patrons in art and in popular images]. Rome: Jaca.
Lapple, A. 1990. *Inchiesta sui grandi miracoli della storia* [Investigation of the great historical miracles]. Casale Monferrato, Italy: Piemme.
Levine, N. 2004. *Dharma Punx*. New York: Harper Collins.
Locrius, T. n.d. *The Soul and the World*. Retrieved from http://www.completepythagoras.net/mainframeset.html.
Logan, A. 1997. "The Mystery of the Five Seals: Gnostic Initiation Reconsidered." *Vigiliae Christianae*, 51(2), 188–206.
Loomis, G. 1935. "Folklore of the Uncorrupted Body." *The Journal of American Folklore*, 48(190), 374–378.
Lucian of Samosata. 2009. *The Syrian Godess*. (Kindle Edition.) Santa Cruz, CA: Evinity.
Mangasarian, M. 2004. *The Truth About Jesus: Is He a Myth?* (Kindle Edition.) Public Domain Books.
Margnelli, M. 1988. *Gente di Dio* [People of God]. Sugarco Edizioni.
Martin, D. 1989. "Restructuring Teacher Education Programs for Higher-Order Thinking Skills." *Journal of Teacher Education*, 40(2), 2–8.
Massey, G. 2000. *The Historical Jesus and the Mythical Christ: Natural Genesis and Typology of Equinoctial Christolatry*. New York: Book Tree.
Matsumoto, A. 2002. *Nihon no Miira Butsu* [Japanese Buddhist mummies]. Tokyo: Rokkō Shuppan.
Maynard, T. 1950. *The Odyssey of Francis Xavier*. Westminster, MD: Newman Press.
Mazzacane, L. 1990. "Storie di corallari, di miracoli e di predoni nella Torre del Greco tra Settecento e Ottocento Source: La Ricerca Folklorica." *La cultura del mare*, 21, 75–83.
McGiffert, A. 1909. "Was Jesus or Paul the Founder of Christianity?" *The American Journal of Theology*, 13(1), 1–20.
_____. 1915. "Christianity and War: A Historical Sketch." *The American Journal of Theology*, 19(3), 323–345.
McGregor, A. 1985. *Padre Pio: His Early Years*. TX: OCSO.
McKinley, A. 2006. "The First Two Centuries of Saint Martin of Tours." *Early Medieval Europe*, 14(2), 173–200.
Meier, J. 1991. "The Testimonium: Evidence for Jesus Outside the Bible." *Catholic Biblical Quarterly*, 7, 20–25.
_____. 1992. "The Brothers and Sisters of Jesus in Ecumenical Perspective." *Catholic Biblical Quarterly*, 54, 1–28.
Meinardus, O. 1977. *Christian Egypt, Ancient and Modern*. Cairo: AUC Press.
Menzies, G. 2008. *1421: The Year China Discovered America*. New York: Harper Collins.
Miele, M. 1977. *La basilica di S. Domenico Maggiore in Napoli* [The basilica of S. Domenico Maggiore in Naples]. Naples: Laurenziana.
Miller, W. 1982. *Dorothy Day: A Biography*. New York: Harper & Row.
Minima, M. 1958. *Seraph Among Angels: The Life of St. Mary Magdalene de' Pazzi*. Chicago: The Carmelite Press.

Mojsov, B. 2005. *Osiris: Death and Afterlife of a God.* Malden, MA: Blackwell.
Moody, R. 2001. *Life After Death: The Investigation of a Phenomenon — Survival of Bodily Death.* New York: Harper Collins.
Morin, E. 1970. *L'homme et la mort* [Man and death]. Paris: Editions du Seuil.
Mosheim, J. 1842. *An Ecclesiastical History, Ancient and Modern, from the Birth of Christ to the Beginning of the Modern Century.* London: A. Miller.
Murdock, D., and S. Acharya. 2011. *Christ in Egypt: The Horus-Jesus Connection.* New York: Stellar House.
Newcomb, J. 1934. *Teresa Margaret of the Sacred Heart of Jesus (Anna Maria Redi).* New York: Benzinger Brothers.
Notovitch, N. 1894. *The Unknown Life of Jesus Christ: The Original Text of Nicolas Notovitch's 1887 Discovery.* (Translated by J. Connelly and L. Landsberg.) (Kindle Edition.) New York: Dillingham.
O'Connell, R. 1983. "The Emergence of Horus: An Analysis of Coffin Text Spell 148." *The Journal of Egyptian Archaeology,* 69, 66–87.
Olivato, R. 2009. *Sacrari, santi patroni e preghiere militari* [Memorials, patron saints and military prayers]. Rome: Edizioni Messaggero.
Orlandi, P. 1996. *I fenomeni fisici del misticismo* [The physical phenomena of mysticism]. Milan: Gribauldi.
Otto, R., and P. Almond. 1984. "Buddhism and Christianity: Compared and Contrasted." *Buddhist-Christian Studies,* 4, 87–101.
Paul, R., and L. Elder. 2009. "Critical Thinking: Ethical Reasoning and Fairminded Thinking, Part 1." *Journal of Developmental Education,* 33(1), 36–37.
Peck, W. 1998. "Mummies of Ancient Egypt." In A. Cockburn, E. Cockburn, and T. Reyman (eds.), *Mummies, Disease and Ancient Cultures* (pp. 15–37). Cambridge: Cambridge University Press.
Pedote, P. 2010. *La Chiesa del Peccato* [The Church of Sin]. Rome: Tazebao.
Peter, J. 1965. *Finding the Historical Jesus: A Statement of the Principles Involved.* New York: Harper & Row.
Pettinger, T. 2007. "Biography of Bernadette Soubirous." *Biography Online.* Retrieved from http://www.biographyonline.net/spiritual/bernadette-soubirious.html.
Plante, T. 2004. *Sin Against the Innocents: Sexual Abuse by Priests and the Role of the Catholic Church.* New York: Praeger.
Pringle, H. 2001. *The Mummy Congress: Science, Obsession, and the Everlasting Dead.* New York: Hyperion.
Quigley, C. 1998. *Modern Mummies: The Preservation of the Human Body in the Twentieth Century.* London: McFarland & Company.
Quispel, G. 1996. "The Original Doctrine of Valentinus the Gnostic." *Vigiliae Christianae,* 50(4), 327–352.
Raveri, M. 1992. *Il corpo e il paradiso: Le tentazioni estreme dell'ascesi* [The body and paradise: Extreme practices of ascetics]. Venice: Saggi Marsilio Editori.
Raymond of Capua. n.d. *Life of Saint Catherine of Siena.* New York: P. J. Kennedy & Sons.
Reade, W. 1861. *The Veil of Isis, or Mysteries of the Druids.* Retrieved from http://www.sacred-texts.com/pag/motd/motd.htm.
Rengers, C. 1986. *The Youngest Prophet: The Life of Jacinta Marto, Fatima Visionary.* New York: Alba House.
Riad, H. n.d. "Egyptian Influence on Daily Life in Ancient Alexandria." *Hellenistic Alexandria,* 29–39. Retrieved from http://www.utexas.edu/courses/citylife/readings/riad.pdf.
Ritzinger, J., and M. Bingenheimer. 2006. "Whole Body Relics in Chinese Buddhism: Previous Research and Historical Overview." *Indian International Journal of Buddhist Studies,* 7, 37–94.
Robertson, A. 1949. *Jesus: Myth or History?* London: Watts.
Robertson, J. 1911a. *The Jesus Problem.* London: Rationalist Press Association.
_____. 1911b. *Pagan Christs.* London: Rationalist Press Association.
Rodriguez, W. 1997. "Decomposition of Buried and Submerged Bodies." In William D. Haglund and Marcella H. Sorg (eds.), *Forensic Taphonomy.* Boca Raton, FL: CRC Press.
Ruffin, B. 1991. *Padre Pio: The True Story.* Huntingdon, IN: Our Sunday Visitor.
Sacred Destinations. 2005. *Ivolginsky Datsan Buddhist Temple.* Retrieved from http://www.sacred-destinations.com/russia/ivolginsky-datsan-buddhist-temple.htm.

Salotti, C. 1922. *La Beata Anna Maria Taigi: Madre di Famiglia* [The Beata Anna Maria Taigi: Mother of the Family]. Rome: Francesco Ferrari.
Sandars, N. (trans.). 1972. *The Epic of Gilgamesh.* (Kindle Edition). New York: Penguin.
Schaff, P. (trans.). 1890. *Eusebius Pamphilius: Church History, Life of Constantine, Oration in Praise of Constantine.* Edinburgh: T & T Clark.
Schobinger, J. 1991. "Sacrifices of the High Andes." *Natural History,* 4, 63–68.
Schoenbeck, S. 1993. "Exploring the Mystery of Near-Death Experiences." *The American Journal of Nursing,* 93(5): 42–46.
Segre, C. 1990. *Fuori del Mondo: I modelli nella follia e nelle immagini dell'aldilà* [Outside of the world: Models of lunacy and images of the hereafter]. Turin: Einaudi.
Serrano, M. 1972. *Serpent of Paradise: The Story of an Indian Pilgrimage.* New York: Harper Collins.
Shaff, P. 1953. *New Schaff-Herzog Encyclopedia of Religious Knowledge,* vol. 7. (Online Version.) Retrieved from http://www.ccel.org/ccel/schaff/encyc07.
Sharf, R. 1992. "The Idolization of Enlightenment: On the Mummification of Ch'an Masters in Medieval China." *History of Religion,* 32(1), 1–31.
_____. 1999. "On the Allure of Buddhist Relics." *Representations,* 66, 75–99.
Sharpe, S. 1863. *Egyptian Mythology and Egyptian Christianity.* Retrieved from http://www.sacred-texts.com/egy/emec/index.htm.
Shiba, R. 2003. *Kukai: The Universal.* New York: IBC.
Shortell, E. 1997. "Dismembering Saint Quentin: Gothic Architecture and the Display of Relics." *International Center of Medieval Art Stable,* 36(1), 32–47.
Sideri, M. 1999. *Santi con le stigmate* [Saints with stigmata]. Tavagnacco, Italy: Edizioni Segno.
Sitchen, Zecharia. 2010. *There Were Giants upon the Earth: Gods, Demigods, and Human Ancestry: The Evidence of Alien DNA.* Rochester, VT: Bear & Company.
Society of Jesus. n.d. *The Recognition of a Saint.* Retrieved from http://www.sjweb.info/jesuits/saintsProcess.cfm.
Sora, S. 2004. *The Lost Colony of the Templars.* Rochester, VT: Destiny.
Stark, R. 2001. "Reconceptualizing Religion, Magic and Science." *Review of Religious Research,* 43(2), 101–120.
Tepes, V. 1462. *Letter to Corvinus.* Retrieved from http://wanderingplaces.wordpress.com/category/historical-figures/.
Terribile, V., and C. Corraine. 1986. "Practiche imbalsamatorie in Europa [Embalming practices in Europe]." *Pathologica,* 18, 107–118.
Thomas, L. 1976. *Anthropologie de la Mort* [Anthropology of Death]. Paris: Payot.
Thomas, N. 1920. "What Is the KA?" *The Journal of Egyptian Archaeology,* 6(4), 265–273.
Travagnin, S. 2006. "Shi Cihang: The First Case of a Mummified Buddhist in Taiwan." *Kervan: Rivista Internazionale di Studi Afroasiatici,* 3, 77–100.
Vago, M. 2007. *Piccole storie di grandi santi* [Short histories of great saints]. Rome: Edizioni Messaggero.
Vreeland, J. 1998. "Mummies of Peru." In A. Cockburn, E. Cockburn, and T. Reyman (eds.), *Mummies, Disease and Ancient Cultures* (pp. 154–189). Cambridge: Cambridge University Press.
Wagner, T. 2008. *The Global Achievement Gap.* New York: Basic Books.
Ward, M. 1925. *Life of Saint Madeleine Sophie: Foundress of the Society of the Sacred Heart of Jesus (1779–1865).* Roehampton, UK: Convent of the Sacred Heart.
Wax, M., and R. Wax. 1963. "The Notion of Magic." *Current Anthropology,* 4(5), 495–518.
Weigall, A. 2003. *The Paganism in Our Christianity.* Whitefish, MT: Kessinger.
Wells, G. 1971. *The Jesus of the Early Christians: A Study in Christian Origins.* London: Pemberton.
_____. 1975. *Did Jesus Exist?* London: Pemberton.
Werner, M. 1957. *The Formation of Christian Dogma.* New York: Harper.
Willingham, D. 2007. "Critical Thinking: Why Is It So Hard to Teach?" *American Educator,* Summer, 8–19.
Wills, G. 2001. *Papal Sin: Structures of Deceit.* New York: Image.
Wilson, I. 1984. *Jesus: The Evidence.* New York: Weidenfeld and Nicolson.
Wood, H. 1938. *Did Christ Really Live?* London: Student Christian Movement Press.
Woodward, K.L. 1996. *Making Saints: How the Catholic Church Determines Who Becomes a Saint, Who Doesn't, and Why.* New York: Simon and Schuster.

Yalman, N. 1962. "The Ascetic Buddhist Monks of Ceylon." *Ethnology*, 1(3), 315–328.
Yu, Y. 1987. "O Soul, Come Back! (A Study in the Changing Conceptions of the Soul and Afterlife in Pre-Buddhist China)." *Harvard Journal of Asiatic Studies*, 47(2), 363–395.
Zammit-Maempel, G. 1968. "The Evil-Eye and Protective Cattle Horns in Malta." *Folklore*, 79(1), 1–16.
Zeitlin, S. 1965. "The Ecumenical Council Vatican II and the Jews." *The Jewish Quarterly Review*, 56(2), 93–111.
Zimmerman, M. 1998. "Alaskan and Aleutian Mummies." In A. Cockburn, E. Cockburn, and T. Reyman (eds.), *Mummies, Disease and Ancient Cultures* (pp. 138–153). Cambridge: Cambridge University Press.

Index

ab 194
adipocere 12, 17, 109
adon 165
Adonis 165, 170, 173–174
Agliata, Don Bernardino 49
Agliata, Don Carlo 49
Agliata, Giuseppina 49
Agnes 41
Ahmed, Pasha 54–55
Akh 193
Akhu 193
Alaska 13
alcohol 51, 172
Alexander III 90
Alexandria 47, 183, 188–191, 198, 211
Alfonso I 59
Ammut 194
Anchieta, José 64
anchor as Christian symbol 40
angels 22, 46, 68–69, 80–81, 114, 160, 164, 217–219, 223
ankh 197, 206–208
Annunaki 148
Antherus 41
Anu 150
Anubis 176
Aphrodite 65
apocalypse 205; *see also* rapture
Apollo 65, 170–171, 173, 202–203
Aquinas, Thomas 96, 199
archangels 68–69, 80–81
archbishop 20, 54, 76, 112, 125
arcosolia 40
Ares 65
Arhat 159
arsenic 24, 33, 49, 51, 134
asannyasi 94
asceticism 23, 92–95, 108, 132, 224
Athena 65
Attis 160, 163, 165–166, 175
Augustine 46, 82, 99, 139, 154, 204, 220, 223
Augustus 182–183, 187
Aurelian 168
Aurelius 39, 189
autolysis 3, 12, 17, 29

Avellino, Andrea 124
Awliya' Allah 69, 162

Ba 25, 39, 97, 98, 192, 193–195
Baal 37, 173
Babylon 165, 170, 174
Bacchus 172; *see also* Dionysus
Bagnesi, Mary 122–123
Baiwe 173
Barat, Madeline Sophie 114
Barrow 13
Basilica of Cortona 3, 132
beata *see* beati
beati 1, 22, 28, 42, 64–65, 70, 91, 93, 109, 115–117, 120, 124, 129–130, 136, 227, 234, 238
beatus *see* beati
Bernadino of Siena 111–112
Bernardo da Corleone 129
Bernini 187
Bethlehem 153
Bible 1, 20–21, 93, 142–155, 161–163, 170–171, 177, 189, 199, 205, 207, 210, 215, 222, 229
Bibliotheca Sanctorum 100
bilocation 83, 171
Bobola, Andrea 107
Bodhisattva 67–69, 193
bog bodies 33
Bojaxhiu, Agnes Gonxha 73, 77
Bosco, John 125
Bosio, Antonio 42
Bradbury, Ray 16
Brahmans 156
Brindisi 54
Bruno, Giordano 222
Buddha 67, 157–160, 163, 193
Buddhism 9–11, 23, 26, 30, 34, 67–68, 95, 156–160, 167, 193
Bunyan, John 44
Busiris 174

Callixtus 41–42
Calvin, John 44
Capuchins 48–52, 55, 68, 92, 223
cappuccini see Capuchins
Cascata delle Marmone 57
caskets 1, 3, 10, 14, 16, 19–21, 23, 29–30, 38, 58, 61, 102, 111,
114, 123, 130, 194, 196, 198, 205, 215–216; three in one 1, 10, 19–20, 61, 114
catacombs 28, 39–58, 61, 96, 118, 203, 208, 223
Cathedral of Skulls 45
Catherine de Medici 32
Catherine of Genoa 114
Catherine of Siena 85–86, 133
Cecilia 41
Celestia, Michaelangelo 134
Cestius, Caius 181
Chapel of the Dead 53, 55–56
Chehrabad Salt Mine 15
cherubim 80
chi 98
Chinchorro 17–19
Chinese 9, 16–17, 24–26, 59, 96, 98
Christianity, contrasted with Buddhism 10–11, 67–68, 155–160
Christmas 153–154, 161
Christopher 80
Church of St. Ignacio of Loyola 46–47, 234
Church of Saint Mary 230
Church of St. Stephen 58–60
Church of the Immaculate Conception 51–52, 84
Church of the Nativity 153
Circus Maximus 182–183
Clare of Assisi 118
Clement VIII 61
Clement IX 61
Code of Canon Law 99
Coloman 111
Colombia 16
Columbus, Christopher 9
Comiso 55–56, 223
Commodus 168
Constantine 144, 146, 168, 190, 229–230
Constantinople 53
Constantius 168, 183
Coptic Christianity 188–191, 198
Cottone, Don Scipione 49
Council of Chalcedon 189–190
Council of Nicea 99, 189, 226, 230
Council of Trent 128, 145

critical thinking 9–11, 37–39
Crotona 170
crucifixion 78, 85, 87, 93, 143–145, 151, 207, 237, 238
cubicula 40
Cult of the Saints 63, 68, 79–80, 96, 99–100
Cyprian 46
Cyril VI 47

daimon 98; *see also* guardian angel
Dalai Lama 233
Damasus 41
Dante Alighieri 108
Dark Ages 168–169
Dashi Dorzho Itigilou 23
David 98, 153, 161–162, 164, 196
David, Gerard (artist) 162
decapitation 53
decomposition 3–4, 10–12, 15–17, 30, 107, 117, 157, 225, 227
Dedu 174
Delphi 170
deluge *see* flood stories
Demeter 65, 170
Dhu l' Shara 174
diabolical mimicry 168, 209
Diodorus Siculus 174, 176
Dionysus 65, 142, 160, 170–175, 207
Dionysus the Areopagite 80
Divine Comedy 108
dominions 80
Domitian 183, 186
Domitilla 41
Dorothy Day 74–77
dove as Christian symbol 40
Drexel, Katherine 89
Dumuzi 174

Ea 148
Egypt 14, 21; beliefs about the nature of the soul 25
el-Fatih 53–54
embalmment 3–4, 10, 13–14, 17–23, 29, 30, 38–39, 49–51, 59, 61, 65, 102, 107–109, 111–112, 114, 117, 128, 131–135, 137, 141, 165, 196–197, 205, 215–216, 222, 227–228, 233, 238–239
Enlil 148–150
Epic of Gilgamesh 2, 148–149
Eratosthenes 169
Escrivá de Balaguer, Josemaria 73–74
Eshmun 174
Eunapius of Sardis 99
Eusebius 41, 146
Eutichian 41
evil-eye 100
Expositions of the Orthodox Faith 101

Fabian 41
Fatima, Portugal 22
Ferdinando d'Avalos 61

Ferentillo 17, 57–60, 236
Ferrente I 59
Ferrente II 59
Ferron, Marie Rose Alma 86
Fioretti 84–85
Firmatura, Don Carlo 49
Firmicus, Julius 144
fish as Christian sign 40
flood stories 49, 148–150, 183
formae 41
formalin 51
Foxe, John 44
Francis de Geronimo 122
Francis of Assisi 84
Francis of Naples 124
Fulcheri, Ezio 4, 109, 115, 118, 132–133, 136
fungus 13, 17, 58, 102, 107

Gabriel, Archangel 164
Gabrielli, Nazzareno 136
Gaius 41
Galileo 221
Galuzzi, Castora 125
Germaine de Pibrac 122
gilding 10
Giovanni IV 59
Girlani of Mantova, Arcangela 117
glycerin 51, 114, 233
Goretti, Maria 126
Grottarossa Mummy 141–142
Guanajuato 16
guardian angel 98, 192

Hades 65, 217
haku 24
Hall of Judgment 176
Heb Sed Festival 199
Heliopolis 182
Hephaestus 65
Hera 65, 172
Herod 21, 143, 153, 170, 173–174, 196, 203
Herodotus 21, 170, 173–174, 196, 203
Hestia 65
Hill of Martyrs 46, 55
Hill of Minerva 53, 55
Himmis 156
Hinduism 11, 67, 237
Holy Trinity 67, 155, 165, 199–204, 210, 230
Horus 142, 160, 163–165, 167, 170, 174–175, 178, 199–203, 207, 210–212
Hu 173
hun 24–25

Ib 25, 194
Ikhu 193
Immaculate Conception 161–166; *see also* Virgin Birth
Immanuel 164
Inca 13
incorruptibility 13, 17, 22

Innocent III 44
Innocent X 187
Innocent XI 124
Inquisition 44–45
Ishtar 150–165
Issa 164
Ivolginsky Datsan 23

James of the Marches 123
Jerome 61
Joachim 234
John of Damascus 101
John of the Cross 94–95, 103, 122
John Paul I 20
John Paul II 41, 48, 55, 74, 76, 93
John the Baptist 144, 155, 164
John XXIII 117
Joseph of Arimathea 215
Josephat 4–5, 113
Josephus, Flavius 155
Juan de Yepes *see* John of the Cross
Judaism 11, 69, 78
Julian Calendar 153
Jupiter 65, 229
Justin Martyr 168, 229

Ka 25, 39, 97, 98, 192, 193–195
Kambho Lama *see* Dashi Dorzho Itigilou
Kashmir 156
Kha 192
Khaibit 25, 193
Khat 192, 195
Khent 175
Khu 25, 193
ki 98
kon 24
Koran 164
Krishna 160, 163, 224
Krst 178, 203

Laboure, Catherine 114
lactic acid 12
Lama 23, 233
Lambertini, Egano 125
Lenin, Vladimir 233
Leonardo da Vinci 151
loculi 40
Lombardo, Rosalia 50–51, 134
London 17, 157, 175
Lucian 165
Lucifer 81 *see also* Satan
Lucius 41
Lutgarde of Tonges 85

Maat 194
Magdalen de' Pazz, Mary 122–123, 135
magic 30–31, 43, 78–79, 85, 99–101, 112, 194, 197, 204–206, 212
Mahayana Buddhism 67
mal'occhio see evil-eye
manganese pigment 18

Index

Mao Zedong 233
Margaret of Cortona 3–4, 109, 132–133
Mark 47
Marto, Jacinto 22–23
martyr 26, 28, 39–48, 55, 63, 69, 78–80, 89, 91, 93–94, 96–97, 99, 107, 118, 120, 126–128, 136, 146–147, 153, 165, 168, 216–217, 223, 229; *see also* Hill of Martyrs
martyrdom 114, 120; *see also* martyr
Mazzarello, Maria 125
Medusa 97
Merici, Angela 111–112
Michael the Archangel 80, 85, 219
Michaelmas 85
Mehmet II 53–54
Metapontum 171
Mihr 167; *see also* Mithra
Miltiades 41
miracle 79–83, 87–91, 95, 101–102, 112, 118, 123–124, 135, 143, 170,-171, 205, 224
miter 45, 61, 201, 212
Mithra 150, 154, 160–161, 167–169, 171–173
Mithraism 167–168; *see also* Mithra
Mitra *see* Mithra
Montevecchia 181
mortification 92–93
Mosheim 108
Mother Teresa *see* Bojaxhiu, Agnes Gonxha
mummy: drug 32–33; used as paint 33–34
Museo de las Mumias *see* Guanajuato
Mysteries, Inner and Outer 169–170, 172, 176–177

Nana 165
Naples 19, 28, 59, 62, 115, 122–125, 128, 134, 173, 227
Napoleonic Edict of Saint-Cloud 57
natron 141
natrum 21, 196; *see also* natron
Nazareth 43, 68, 78, 146, 151–153, 216
Nergal 148
Neri, Philip 118
Nicholas IV 61
Nicodemus 215
nihil obstat 90
Ninurta 148
Nisir 149
Nissa 174
Noah 67, 149–150
Nolli, Gianfranco 137
Notovich, Nicholas 156, 176
Nuzzi, Oreste 19

obelisks 182–187, 198, 230
Ochotenko, Sergei 20
Odin 148–149, 173
Odor of Sanctity 3–4, 86, 91, 95, 99, 109, 112–113, 122, 130, 133–134
L'Odore della Santità see Odor of Sanctity
Opus Dei 73–74
Orcagna, Andrea 108
Ordinary Process 89–90
Orthodox 20–22, 44, 91, 101, 113
Osiris 68, 160, 163–165, 170–178, 181–183, 188, 194, 199–202, 210–211, 229–230
osmosis 19, 135, 205, 216
Otranto 45, 53–55
Ottoman 45, 53–55
Otzal Alps 39

Padre Pio 83, 86, 90, 92–94, 171
pagan 96–97, 101, 143, 145, 147, 151, 154, 161, 167–169, 177, 229
Palermo 48–51, 115, 129, 134, 146, 200–201, 223
Pantheon 187, 200
Paul VI 20, 47
Persia 44
Persius 97
Peru 17–19
Phoenician Mysteries 170
Piazza del Popolo 182
Piazza di Porta Maggiore 88
Piazza Navona 186, 207
Piazza San Giovanni 184
Pietro della Madre di Dio 118, 120
Pius V 61
Pius VI 183
Pius VII 211
Pius X 19
Pius XII 19, 135
Plutarch 25, 98, 171, 173–174, 176
po 24–25
Polycamus 41
Pontianus 41
Pontius Pilate 143–144, 215
pope 1, 5, 19–20, 23, 29, 41, 44, 47–48, 54–55, 61, 64–65, 74, 76, 84, 90, 93, 108–109, 113–114, 117–119, 124, 133, 135, 156, 182–183, 187, 190, 197–202, 210–212, 233–235
Pope Alexander III *see* Alexander III
Pope Antherus *see* Antherus
Pope Clement VIII *see* Clement VIII
Pope Clement IX *see* Clement IX
Pope Cyril VI *see* Cyril VI
Pope Damasus *see* Damasus
Pope Eutichian *see* Eutichian
Pope Fabian *see* Fabian
Pope Innocent III *see* Innocent III

Pope Innocentius X *see* Innocent X
Pope John Paul I *see* John Paul I
Pope John Paul II *see* John Paul II
Pope John XXIII *see* John XXIII
Pope Lucius *see* Lucius
Pope Nicholas IV *see* Nicholas IV
Pope Paul VI *see* Paul VI
Pope Pius V *see* Pius V
Pope Pius VI *see* Pius VI
Pope Pius X *see* Pius X
Pope Pius XII *see* Pius XII
Pope Pontianus *see* Pontianus
Pope Sixtus II *see* Sixtus II
Pope Sixtus V *see* Sixtus V
Pope Urban VIII *see* Urban VIII
Poseidon 65
Posidonius 168
positio 73–74, 88, 90, 130
positiones 88
powers 80
Primaldi, Antonio 54–55
principalities 80
Priscilla 41
Psammetichus II 183
putrefaction 3
Pyramid of Cestius 181
Pythagoras 170–173

Qi see chi
Quirinius (census) 143
Quirinus 41
Qur'an *see* Koran

Ra 68, 163, 167, 176
Rameses II 182
Ranieri 119
rapture 125, 217–221
relics 20, 25–31, 226–228
Ren 25, 194
resurrection 25–26, 34, 52, 96–97, 161, 163, 165–167, 175–177, 187–188, 198, 204–209, 211–212, 220, 229, 237
rigor mortis 12
Rita of Cascia 85–86, 133
Romana, Francesca 116
rosary 29, 119, 205
Rossi, Paolo 68

Sacred Numbers 72, 177, 229
Sahu 25, 193
St. Agnes *see* Agnes
St. Andrea Bobola *see* Bobola, Andrea
St. Bernadette Soubirous *see* Soubirous, Bernadette
St. Bernadino of Siena *see* Bernadino of Siena
St. Callixtus *see* Callixtus
St. Catherine Laboure *see* Laboure, Catherine

St. Catherine of Genoa *see* Catherine of Genoa
St. Catherine of Siena *see* Catherine of Siena
St. Cecilia *see* Cecilia
St. Christopher *see* Christopher
St. Clare of Assisi *see* Clare of Assisi
St. Coloman *see* Coloman
St. Cyprian *see* Cyprian
St. Domitilla *see* Domitilla
St. Eusebius *see* Eusebius
St. Francis de Geronimo *see* Francis de Geronimo
St. Gaius *see* Gaius
St. Germaine de Pibrac *see* Germaine de Pibrac
St. Jerome *see* Jerome
St. John Bosco *see* Bosco, John
St. John of Damascus *see* John of Damascus
St. John of the Cross *see* John of the Cross
St. Josephat *see* Josephat
St. Margaret of Cortona *see* Margaret of Cortona
St. Mark *see* Mark
St. Michael the Archangel *see* Michael the Archangel
St. Miltiades *see* Miltiades
St. Peter's Cathedral 19–20, 54, 89, 93, 117, 124, 135, 166–167, 183, 185, 211
St. Philip Neri *see* Neri, Philip
St. Priscilla *see* Priscilla
St. Ranieri *see* Ranieri
St. Rita of Cascia *see* Rita of Cascia
St. Sebastian *see* Sebastian
St. Stephen *see* Stephen
St. Tarcisius *see* Tarcisius
St. Teresa Margaret of the Sacred Heart *see* Teresa Margaret of the Sacred Heart
St. Teresa of Avila *see* Teresa of Avila
St. Victoria *see* Victoria
St. Zephyrinus *see* Zephyrinus
Sakkara 174
Salafia, Dr. Alfredo 51, 134
salicylic acid 51
Salvifici Doloris 93
San Bernardo, Columbia 16
Sanderson, Sir John 32–33

San Domenico Maggiore 62
San Giovanni Rotondo 83
San Giuseppe dei Teatini 200
Sanhedrin 43, 155
Santa Maria della Grazia 55
Santa Maria della Scala 118–119
Santa Maria Maggiore 61, 183
saponification 12, 17, 109
Satan 69, 80, 144, 168, 176, 203; *see also* Lucifer
Sebastian 41–42
Sekhem 25, 194
self-mummification 22–24, 94
Semele 172
seraph 85
seraphim 80
Serapis 183, 188–189
Servant of God 76, 89
Set 176, 203
Seth 176–177, 202; *see also* Set
Seton, Mother Elizabeth Bayley 89
sheitan 176
Shi Cihang 27–28
Shinto 66–67
Shugendo 94
Siberia 23
Signoracci brothers 20
Silvestro of Gubbio 49
Sisters of Loreto 73
Sixtus II 41
Sixtus V 61, 182–183
Socrates 9
Soubirous, Bernadette 29–31
soul 4, 10, 24–26, 34, 39, 46, 54, 59, 93, 97–102, 167–168, 170, 175, 177, 192–194, 199, 204, 211, 223–225, 235, 238–239; multiple aspects 24–26, 39, 97–102, 223–225
Spanish Steps (Rome) 231
Spindler, Konrad 39
Stephen 43; *see also* Church of St. Stephen
Stephen the Great of Moldavia 53
stigmata 82–90, 133, 224
Sumerians 2, 148–150, 162
Summa Theologica 96

Tacitus 143
Taigi, Anna Maria 116
Tammuz 165, 170–171, 174, 229
Tarcisius 28, 41

Tauromenium 171
Templar Knights 9
Teresa Margaret of the Sacred Heart 112, 129
Teresa of Avila 94, 114
Tertullian 168
Thothmes IV 183
thrones 80
Tiberius 143–144
Tinia 65
Tipografia Guerra 88
Trinitarian Faith 190
Tyndale, William 44
Typhon 176

Umbria 57
Umiliana dei Cerchi 234
The Unknown Life of Jesus Christ 156
Urban VIII 113
Urbanus VIII *see* Urban VIII
Urbini, Giovanni 47
Utnapishtim 148–149

Vaslui, Battle of 53
Vatican 20, 61, 68–69, 73–74, 82, 88–90, 93, 109, 113, 117, 130, 135–137, 156, 166–167, 183, 185, 199, 226
Vatican Council II 68, 73
Venus 141
Vici, Antonio 123
Victoria 136
Virgin Birth 145–146, 161–163, 188, 199–200, 212, 230; *see also* Immaculate Conception
Vishnu 67
Vlad Dracul *see* Vlad Tepes
Vlad Tepes 53–54
Vlad the Impaler *see* Vlad Tepes
volcanic soil 3, 12, 16

wax 3, 30
winter solstice 153, 178

Zechariah 164
Zephyrinus 41
Zeus 65, 172
zinc 30, 51
Ziusudra 148
Zoroastrians 154, 163, 167; *see also* Mithra